THE FORTUNE-TELLER'S WORKBOOK

THE
FORTUNE~TELLER'S
WORKBOOK

A Practical Introduction to the World of Divination

SASHA FENTON

THE AQUARIAN PRESS

First published 1988

British Library Cataloguing in Publication Data

Fenton, Sasha
The fortune-teller's workbook
1. Fortune-telling
I. Title
133.3'24'028   BF1861

ISBN 0–85030–678–7

The Aquarian Press is part of the Thorsons Publishing Group,
Wellingborough, Northamptonshire, NN8 2RQ, England

Printed and bound by Adlard and Son Limited, Dorking, Surrey, and Letchworth, Hertfordshire

3 5 7 9 10 8 6 4 2

This book is dedicated to Rose Davies
without whose loving-kindness
I couldn't have managed half as well.

Acknowledgements

With grateful thanks to all those who have contributed information to this book, especially Seldiy Bate, Nigel Bourne, Barbara Ellen Narbeth, Robin Lown, Gordon Smith, Fred Curtis, Nina Ashby, Douglas Ashby, Denise Russell, Simon Franklin and many others who have given me ideas.

For help with some of the illustrations, George Dale, Nigel Bourne and Helen Fenton.

Thanks to Stuart Fenton for help with my awful spelling and Linda Tulley for word-processing and being a willing guinea-pig.

To Tony Fenton, as always, for liaison, help and support.

Special thanks to Frank Anderson for taking on the awesome chore of proof-reading and being an equally willing guinea-pig.

Bibliography

These books were helpful in cross-checking information which had been given to me over the years by various people:

Everybody's Book of Fate and Fortune by Edward Lyndoe. Published by Odhams Press Limited (1936).

The Complete Gypsy Fortune Teller by Kevin Martin. Published by Mayflower Books.

The Complete Illustrated Book of Divination and Prophecy by Walter B Gibson and Litzka R Gibson.
Published by Souvenir Press (1973).

Develop your Psychic Skills by Enid Hoffman. Published by Para Research, Rockport, Massachusetts (1981).

Fortune Telling by Cards by Ida B Prangley. Published by the Dennis Wheatley Library of the Occult (1899).

The Book of Divination by Christine Smith. Published by Rider (1978).

The Seventy-Eight Degrees of Wisdom by Rachel Pollack. Published by the Aquarian Press Ltd (1983).

Contents

Introduction

Men and women have visited fortune-tellers of one kind or another since the dawn of time. Even the most sceptical person enjoys an occasional reading while many others visit their favourite Reader at least once a year. There are hundreds of different methods of fortune-telling which range from highly developed skills to methods which simply prod the divinator's psychic awareness. A professional psychic knows how to get the best from his spiritual guides because he has spent years studying and training in psychic development. A skilled astrologer, palmist, numerologist etc. is not really a fortune-teller at all but a combination of map-reader, mathematician and psycho-analyst. Not everyone, however, wants to devote his or her life to this kind of training, many people just want the fun and insight of being able to tell someone's fortune by a simple method of prediction. This book investigates a number of different methods, some simple, others complicated, as a means of introducing you to the mysteries of these ancient crafts.

My own skills run to astrology, palmistry, Tarot and playing cards. Like many other professional Readers, I have some knowledge of other methods but cannot possibly be skilled in all of them. I have drawn information for the divinations with which I am *not* so familiar from other professional Readers, and I hope that by doing this, rather than taking it all from other books, I will be able to bring these subjects to life and show the reality of working in these fields rather than simply explaining the theories behind the methods.

Where the information has come from other Readers, I have given them full acknowledgement for their contributions; where I *have* had to use books in order to cross-reference my information, I have given their names. It was a compendium much like this one which set me on the road to becoming a professional Reader, therefore, if this book hands on the torch of inspiration to *just one* person, I shall have come full circle and made all the work and effort worthwhile.

One final note: I have used a variety of terms such as Questioner, Enquirer, Querent, Reader, Sitter and Consultant in this book because all these terms are in common use. I have mainly used the masculine terms 'he' and 'him' in order to keep the text simple: fortune tellers and their clients are masculine, feminine, gay and straight, old and young, rich and poor, and from every country in the world.

1.

Numerology

This ancient method of divination is yet another one of those which can be taken on a superficial level or can be looked at very deeply. The details for this section were given to me by numerologist, **Fred Curtis,** who is also a good source of many other kinds of esoteric information. Numerology like astrology, will give a good deal of information about a person's character as well as being helpful in predicting the pattern of trends and tendencies for the future. It is fascinating to work out and look at in the context of one's lifestyle at any given period of time.

The Character of Name

Firstly the letters of the name must be translated into a number system as follows:

The Alphabet code

1	2	3	4	5	6	7	8	9
A	B	C	D	E	F	G	H	I
J	K	L	M	N	O	P	Q	R
S	T	U	V	W	X	Y	Z	

Count up the numbers in the whole name and then reduce the number to one digit. This will show the basic character of the person. The 'soul urge' or inner personality is shown by the vowels while the outermost personality, the one we show to the world outside, is contained in the consonants.

  Here is an example:
Full name

```
L I N D A   T U L L E Y
3 9 5 4 1   2 3 3 3 5 7
```

Total of numbers   =   45
Reduction: 4 + 5   =   9
Therefore Linda Tulley is a **9.**

Vowels

         L   I   N   D   A   T   U   L   L   E   Y
         9   1   3   5

Total of numbers   =   18
Reduction: 1 + 8   =   **9**

Consonants

         L   I   N   D   A   T   U   L   L   E   Y
         5   4   2   3   3   3   7

Total of numbers   =   27
Reduction: 2 + 7   =   **9**

Linda Tulley therefore has much the same feelings inside as those which she shows to the world. Her inner desires and her day-to-day requirements are the same. She is an uncomplicated lady; in the words of the Tina Turner song, 'What you see is what you get'. She has reached a comfortable stage in her evolution.

Here is an example of someone far more complex:

Full name

         F   R   A   N   K   A   N   D   E   R   S   O   N
         6   9   1   5   2   1   5   4   5   9   1   6   5

Total of numbers   =   59
Reduction: 5 + 9   =   14
Reduction: 1 + 4   =   **5**

Vowels

         F   R   A   N   K   A   N   D   E   R   S   O   N
              1   1   5   6

Total of numbers   =   13
Reduction: 1 + 3   =   **4**

Consonants

         F   R   A   N   K   A   N   D   E   R   S   O   N
         6   9   5   2   5   4   9   1   5

Total of numbers   =   46
Reduction: 4 + 6   =   10
Reduction: 1 + 0   =   **1**

Frank projects an outward appearance of confidence and competence due to his consonant (**1**) while being basically a Mercurial type of person with many interests, a need to communicate, plus a strong sexual nature (**5**). Inside himself he is reaching for security, a logical routine and method to his life and a reliable inner world of stable relationships which make some kind of realistic sense to him (**4**).

Of course there is more to it than that. Each letter has a value according to its position in the alphabet. An 'A' for instance being more important than an **E** or an **O.** The birth date is also interesting as it is said to show the 'life lesson' for that person.

Example One

Linda Tulley   17–7–1946

Reduction: 1 + 7 + 7 + 1 + 9 + 4 + 6   =   35
Reduction: 3 + 5   =   **8**

Therefore Linda's life lesson is to cope with a structured and organized lifestyle which doesn't leave a lot of time for personal freedom and pleasure. Poor Linda. Well, Linda is here at the moment doing my word-processing for me and she doesn't look too bad on it, but she agrees that the needs of her family do tend to structure her life and prevent her from getting out doing her own thing at times.

Example Two

Frank Anderson   27–3–1935
Reduction: 2 + 7 + 3 + 1 + 9 + 3 + 5   =   30
Reduction: 3 + 0   =   **3**

Frank's life lesson is to have the courage to grow and develop in a creative manner, also to cope with success and material gain. Not bad, eh! However, Frank's soul urge being a highly structured rather idealistic and security minded **4** makes this hard for him. He needs fun, humour and to be able to own and enjoy things of value without feeling guilty. He will also have to accept that he is strongly psychic with a gift for prophecy.

The Characteristics of each Number:
An Explanation by Fred Curtis

Number One
This is the first number in the series from 1 to 9, therefore it suggests the

beginning of something. The number one relates to the self, it is a mental number and refers to the conscious, rational, reasoning mind. Any achievement has to be preceded by an idea and this number represents that idea, the thought which can be translated into action. Number 1 stands alone, it is bold, powerful and dominant it is a positive number which radiates a force for potential. It is the driving force which transforms energy into matter. It has strongly masculine qualities and like the Magician in the Tarot it is pioneering, the first in line, dominant, original and independent. The following is a list of positive and negative keywords attributed to the number 1 character.

Positive	*Negative*
Will-power	Over-dominant
Individualistic	Egotistical
Leadership	A 'know-it-all'
Inventive	Selfish
Pioneering	All talk—no action
Dominant	Introversion
Originality	Weak-willed
Creative ideas	Domineering
Self-determination	Bossy
Proud	Inertia
Courageous	Boastful
Strength	Too much pride
Executive ability	Lacking originality
Planner	Aggression
Imaginative	Wilful
Independent	Cynical
Idealistic	Impulsive
Drive, Force	Single-minded
Knowledge	Possessive
Strong opinions	Indecisive
Masculinity	Confidence can evaporate
Decisive	
Confident	

Number Two
This is the first of the feminine numbers and it implies duality. It also represents the womb-like quality of nurturing a seed which was planted by the number 1 energy. It represents a drive for harmony and balance, a need for a Yin to go with the masculinity of Yang. It is passive, intuitive, receptive and emotional.

Positive	*Negative*
Mediation	Indecisive
Arbitration	Tactlessness
Visionary	Undignified
Passive	Extroversion
Receptivity	Clumsy, careless
Peace	Over-emotional
Harmony	Non-feeling
Balance	Agitation
Intuition	Reticent
Wisdom	Extremist
The go-between	Depression
Rhythm and timing	Fussy
Spiritual influence	Over-conscientious
Tact	Loss of time
Diplomacy	Too much detail
Charm	Alone
Grace	Strife, discord
Poise	Self-centred
Dignified	Adaptability
Sensitivity	Over-tolerant
Calm	Worrisome
Persuasion	Moody
Association	Touchy
Consideration	Easily upset
Agreement	
Modesty	
Sincerity	
Inspiration	
Emotion	
Artistic feeling	
Punctuality	

Number Three
This is a creative number, it represents creative enterprise and is a growth factor. The seed which was planted in the number 1 year nurtured in the number 2 year now shows signs of growth. It represents all that is active and fertile, the springtime of life. It is similar to the Empress in the Tarot and therefore suggests that material benefits will come from a fruitful harvest.

Positive	Negative
Growth	Unfinished undertakings
Fertility	Talkative
Self-expression	Gossip
Joy	Busybody
Happiness	Moody
Optimism	Cynical
Creativity	Unimaginative
Humour	Argumentative
Abundance	Critical of others
Luck	Scattered energies
Birth	Contrary
Prophetic impressions	Shyness
Gifts	Reservedness
Health	Timidity
Imagination	Fearful
Success	Stagnation
Literary ability	Fads and fancies
Articulation	Inarticulation
Gifts of words and speech	Pessimistic
Writing	Killjoy
Love and pleasure	Sad
Bubbly	Sly
Carefree nature	Deceitful
	Exaggeration
	Extravagance
	Lack of direction
	Unforgiving
	Self advertisment
	Conceit
	Snobbishness

Number Four

This signifies the earth, the physical and the material world. It is the number of form and relates to the Emperor in the Tarot. Number 4 represents sense and reason, implying control over the energies which are at our command. It is the foundation on which we can build for the future. This represents balance, stability and security, also restrictions and limitations. Logical thinking and systematic work belong to the number 4.

Positive	*Negative*
System	Impractical
Order	Unstable
Practicality	Disciplinarian
Law and order	Untidy
Restriction	Lack of application
Stability	Fussy about details
Security	Lack of concentration
Logic and reason	Lazy
Building	Weak
Commonsense	Unreliable
Down-to-earth	Legal dealings
Methodical	Soft-hearted
Routine	Lacking in method
Finances	Unimaginative
Material success	Worry
Work	Habitual
Application	Serious-minded
Detail	Destructive
Concentration	Obstinate
Strong	Tenacious
Firm	Determined
Reliable	Stubborn
Matter-of-fact	Careless
Change	Too set in ways
Transformation	
Constructive	

Number Five

The number 5 shows the need to break out of the enclosed structure which is signified in the number 4. This vibration breeds activity, hates routine and restriction and becomes very nervous and restless if held down. It hates to see its freedom threatened because it needs a wide area to move and express itself with drive and boundless energy. Representing activity, the number 5 seeks constant change and variety, also the scope to put into action the fruits of physical experience. This vibration requires social contact, education, ideas and communication with other people.

Positive	*Negative*
Energetic	Nervous

Resourceful
Drive
Independence
Freedom loving
Change
Variety
Versatile
Adaptable
Loves to travel
Brighter than average
Learns quickly and easily
Needs excitement
Mental agility
Breadth of contact
Idealistic
Drives others
Seeks knowledge
Thrifty
Curiosity
Adventurous
Progressive
Sexual attraction

Dislike of routine
Hates restriction
Many irons in fire
Unfinished undertakings
Enjoys applause
Self appraisal
Drives too hard
Demanding of others
Impulsive
Over-cautious
Destructive
Pessimistic
Unreliable
Confidence trickster
Avoids responsibility
Restless

Number Six
This relates to our feelings and emotions as well as to our homes and families. This is where as a child we experienced parental love and where we, as parents in our turn, give love and care to families of our own. Here we exercise responsibility for others and provide for those around us by supplying food, warmth, love and security. Number 6 relates to all which is beautiful and harmonious in giving, caring, and of looking after the health of others.

Positive

Love
Peace
Harmony
Beauty
Love of home
Domesticity
Artistic
Unselfishness

Negative

Duty
Sympathy
Others' troubles
Self-righteous
Obstinacy
Outspokenness
Family ties
Slowness in decision

Caring
Responsibility
Adjustment
Creativity
Food
Nutrition
Health
Emotions
Feelings
Love of nature
Love of children/animals
Idealistic
Service
Entertainer
Conservative views
Seeks improvement

Self-sacrifice
Stubbornness
Complaint
Falling for flattery
Jealousy
Interference

Number Seven
This number represents two ideas which are linked. The first is the need for rest and relaxation, time off to think things out or just to let one's thoughts drift around aimlessly. After a while, the thoughts will take shape and something useful will emerge. The other idea is of occult and spiritual significance as it encompasses the kind of reflection, analysis and inward journeys which lead to enlightenment of both a practical and a spiritual nature. In essence, this is a meditative number.

Positive

Investigation
Research
Calculation
Analysis
Observation
Reflection
Contemplation
Specialist
Detection
Discovery
Invention
Discrimination
Thinker
Dignity

Negative

Shrewdness
Hidden motives
Too much pride
Reservedness
Misunderstanding
Silence
Sarcasm
Suspicion
Over-analytical
Cynical
Repression
Unreasonableness
Lacking self-expression
Over-positive

Pride
Perfection
Intelligence
Love of solitude

Argumentative
Temper
Independence
Hidden thoughts
Lacks generosity

Number Eight

This suggests material success but also spiritual attainment. There has to be progress in both areas and a balance maintained between the two in order for the energy to be found for success and achievement. This is a Karmic number as it shows that what one sows, one must reap. It relates to the Strength card in the Tarot pack and clearly indicates mastery over the physical world, an acceptance of responsibility, and an ability to rule by divine standards.

Positive	*Negative*
Drive	Drives too hard
Authority	Needs balance
Executive ability	Repressed feelings
Material success	Obsessive with money
Leadership	Weak
Responsibility	Non-acceptance of responsibility
Power	Striving to attain
Business acumen	Overaction
Larger organizations	Tension
Thinks big	Ambition
Recognition	Love of display
Financial rewards	Demanding recognition
Karma	Money difficulties
Perseverance	Lacks true humanitarianism
Organization	Impatience with others
Good judgement	Forcefulness
Energetic	Few illusions
Discriminating	Too much energy
Authority	
Supervision	
Strength	
Capability	
Working for a cause	
Character analysis	

Number Nine

This incorporates all the previous numbers and is the number of the universe. It signifies the last evolution, the completion of human experience and suggests true love of the highest order, the love of humanity. It implies that we may never reach perfection while inside the physical body. This number is similar to the Hermit in the Tarot pack which shows clearly that a certain point in human evolution has been reached—however, there are always higher levels to reach for. Only by listening to the inner voice and working by divine standards can we hope to succeed. In this case the soul may be old, there may have been many incarnations before but there is always something more to learn.

Positive

Perfection
Love
Compassion
Ideality
Impressionability
Charitable ways
Brotherhood of mankind
Impersonality
Forgiveness
Leader in philanthropic
  endeavour
Artist
Writer
Religionist
Has big opportunity in life
Capacity for living by divine
  standards
Money attraction
Leader in art or good works
Dramatic talent

Negative

Too much love of self
Jack of all trades
Personal interests
Impulsive action
Takes no blame
Changeable in love affairs
Possessiveness
Demanding approval and
  appreciation
Moods and depression
Failure to use talent for good of
  the world
Dissipation of higher forces
Carelessness in financial affairs
Seeking an easy time or approval
Wrong habits
Unforgiving

Personal Year Vibration

If you wish to find out what kind of year you are having or are going to have, add the day and the month of your birthdate to the current year. An explanation of all the numbers follows these examples.

Linda   17–7–1988
$1 + 7 + 7 + 1 + 9 + 8 + 8$ $= 41$
Reduction $4 + 1$ $=$ **5**

Therefore Linda's current year is number **5.**

In addition to looking at the year as a whole, it is possible to break it down into three four-month blocks:
a) The first-four month block is made up from the person's age plus the current year.
b) The second is made up from the 'life lesson' plus the current year.
c) The third is made up from the 'soul urge' number plus the current year.

Therefore:

Linda *age 42* (July to October 1988)
$1988 + 42$ $= 2030$
Reduction: $2 + 0 + 3 + 0$ $=$ 5

The first period (July to October) is therefore a **5.**

Linda *'life lesson' No. 8* (November to February 1989)
(Reminder: the 'life lesson' is found by adding up the Subject's date of birth; in Linda's case this was 17 July 1946.

$1988 + 8$ $= 1996$
Reduction: $1 + 9 + 9 + 6$ $=$ 25
Reduction: $2 + 5$ $=$ 7

The second period (November to February) is therefore a **7.**

Linda *'soul urge' No. 9* (March to June 1989)
(Reminder: the 'soul urge' is found by adding up the numbers contained in the vowels in the name; in Linda's case $I=9$ $A=1$ $U=3$ $E=5$)

$1988 + 9$ $= 1997$
Reduction: $1 + 9 + 9 + 7$ $=$ 26
Reduction: $2 + 6$ $=$ 8

The third period (March to June) is therefore an **8.**

Personal Year (or partial year) Vibrations

(This section is taken from Fred's numerology literature and is, therefore, in his own words.)

The name that you were given at birth and the day you were born cannot change. You may change your name through marriage or through choice, but the God-given talents and the 'life lesson' numbers cannot change. A change of name will have an influence for better or worse. Each year we will be influenced by a temporary vibration which must be recognized in order to achieve the maximum benefit from that vibration. The influence starts to take effect from a few weeks before to a few weeks after your birthday, and will last for the whole year until your next birthday.

Number One

You are starting a new nine-year cycle in your life. What you do this year will determine the pattern of events for the next nine years; therefore it is most important that you get your affairs into some sort of perspective.

The keywords for this first year in the cycle are *new beginnings, initiative, decisions and individuality.*

You may feel quite alone during this year, even if surrounded by family and friends. You will find yourself wondering how you are going to make it on your own. You will have to centre your energies and your will upon yourself and decide how you are going to operate your life during the next nine years. Decisions will need to be made at this time which will determine your course for several years to come.

You will feel strange surges of energy and determination, recognizing that you must do things for yourself. This may be because others are not able to help or because you are driven to take your life into your own hands. Defeat is not a word that you will want to accept now. Even if you are convinced that your own instincts are accurate, you should still try to listen to sensible advice from others. This is the time to put yourself first and to put your own plans into action.

Your view of life will change and any lingering timidity will vanish now. You will discover new methods of working and new ways of looking at old problems, shedding them and going forward in a new direction. An important person may come into your life now who will act as an inspiration, a guide and a teacher. Be discriminating in your choice of friends now because alliances which are formed at this time are likely to last. This is the time to stand up for what you believe in, to be independent, self-motivated and self-reliant.

Number Two

You are in the second year of your current nine-year cycle. Last year demanded that you stand on your own two feet and decide positively what you need to do in your life to guarantee success, happiness and fulfilment.

The keywords for this second year are *co-operation, partnerships, creativity, peace, harmony* and *peaceful co-existence.*

You will need to work in harmony with others and therefore, you will have to be aware of their requirements as well as your own. You may have to take a slightly passive role and to be diplomatic when handling other people. You may be called upon to judge situations on behalf of others and to settle disputes. Partnership matters will become important but there will be personal creativity as well; some people have useful flashes of inspiration under this vibration.

The number 2 implies duality. It is the force between two pairs of opposites. It is the point of balance. Do not make any major decisions during this period. The positive seeds that were sown last year during your number 1 cycle are now sprouting beneath the surface. If things seem uncertain, unstable or fluctuating at the moment, it is only because you are being asked to remain passive while nature takes its course. Love affairs may be unstable now due to hidden elements and underlying problems; however if each becomes attuned to the needs of the other there will be a feeling of deep satisfaction. You may find some kind of deception around you, secret energies which are working against you, therefore at least be honest with yourself and have faith in your own ideals. In your quieter moments, relax, study, and tune into your own intuition.

Number Three
You are now in the third year of your current nine-year cycle. Last year demanded that you take a somewhat passive role, and wait for the seeds which were planted in your number 1 cycle to take root.

The keywords for this year are *activity, expansion, travel, creativity* and *self-expression.*

You may feel to urge to travel, either within your own country or overseas, certainly there will be a need to move freely and explore. Take the opportunity to do so as it will prove to be a mind-broadening experience. New faces and new horizons will enable you to assess yourself in a different light.

This is a year of activity and social events and you will find yourself the centre of attention. This new exposure will make you take a fresh look at yourself and possibly change your image and appearance. It is important that you look and feel good because a good appearance as well as an air of confidence will impress those with whom you come into contact now. This could be an unusually lucky period in your life. You may find some reward from entering competitions, bingo, or sweepstakes. Business opportunities are also possible now.

There may be a new baby in your circle now, there will certainly be new and far more creative projects to get your teeth into at this time. Be sure that the enthusiasm, optimism and expansion does not lead towards extravagance, wastefulness and loss. Over-indulgence could lead to weight gain. The domestic scene could prove troublesome, possibly because you will be busy elsewhere. If you scatter your energies too much, you will lose some of their effectiveness.

If you drift along, expecting results without the expenditure of effort, this could be a wasted and unhappy year, but if you make a real effort to express and carry out some of these ideas in a constructive way, this could be one of the happiest years of your life. However, you must try not to allow the behaviour of others to get you down.

Number Four

You are now in the fourth year of your current nine-year cycle. Last year there was much activity and expansion. It should have been a very creative and fertile year if you made the positive effort to co-operate with the forces that were at play within your life.

The keywords for this year are *work, law and order, budgeting, foundations, sex,* and *regeneration* or *recycling* in some way.

This is the time to concentrate on work on the material plane. You have such a need to organize your life that you may begin by cleaning out the attic, the cellar, cupboards, desks, drawers and the garage. There is a very strong desire to build a firm secure foundation in your life that seems to drive you to clean up your environment and to put it in order. Once your subconscious notices that order is what is required it will drive you to set things right in all areas of your life.

Everything pertaining to money and possessions will become important now, it will be necessary for you to make your life secure and stable. You will need to budget carefully now especially if you decide to spend out on specific goods or services at this time. Land, property, building and renovations are highlighted by this vibration, so you could find yourself involved in extra expense in this area of your life. Take care of your money and it will take care of you. Your body is your home as well, so the extravagances and excesses of the previous 3 cycle will make you want to get out the jogging suit, attend a yoga class or a slimming club. As all physical senses become heightened, your current sexual relationships should also become rewarding and physically stimulating. You are aware of sensations now which are often muted under the other cycles. For males, this vibration could bring fatherhood.

The 4 vibration relates also to law and order. It is also a doorway to wordly success and acquisition of material possessions. You can become stubborn, tenacious and over-sensitive. Make sure that you do not allow yourself to become dominated by wordly possessions, or become a prisoner to the desires of the material world. Enjoy them, own them, but do not let them own you. You will need to pay attention to your own health and finances and also those of your family.

Number Five

You are now in the fifth year of your current nine-year cycle. Last year there was much emphasis on the material, earthly side of your life. It showed a need to ensure that your life was built upon a firm secure basis and that it was not dominated by the desires and pleasures of the material world.

The keywords for this year are *communication, decisions, change, experience* and *sexual magnetism*.

There is so much activity in your life at the moment that you are finding it hard to keep up the pace. You are totally involved with attending meetings, running errands, answering letters and the telephone, making arrangements and attending parties and social functions. Suddenly everyone needs you, and you feel as if you are on a merry-go-round.

This is a period of communication. Gaining experience is your most important activity now, and change will be the end result. You will need to look closely at your life now in order to choose the right direction, and if you are dissatisfied with your current situation, then this is the time to do something about it. New doors will open for you and you will begin to find solutions to your problems.

Under this 5 vibration, you are sexually magnetic. The opposite sex suddenly 'discovers' you; your diary will be filled and you will become the life and soul of any party and you will be surrounded by admirers.

This activity will include travel and you will have to make sure that you don't deplete either your petrol tank or your energy reserves. Your nervous system is highly active now so you should avoid alcohol and drugs; you will also need to be on guard against accidents because you are now in top gear. Try not to waste your energies in superficial activities and relationships, and resist temptations that will plague you during this period.

This year should also see a time for freedom from routine—there will be some rather agreeable unexpected events. Without change there is no growth, but to 'live' does not mean to sow wild oats; rather it suggests that you aim for a definite goal while being flexible and resourceful enough to cope with the unexpected. You may feel some resentment towards those who attempt to hold you down. Resentment wastes emotional energy and gets you nowhere, so try to avoid it. The welter of changes, new contacts and new opportunities may confuse you, but accept them all in the spirit of progress and advancement. Live up to the 'push' that life is exerting on you.

Number Six

You are now in the sixth year of your current nine-year cycle. Last year was a whirlwind year for you. You had many experiences and made lots of new friends; you also had to cope with major changes in your routine. Last year was a turning point in your life due to the fact that you were half through your current cycle of experiences.

The keywords for this year are *duty, responsibility, love, home and family, justice and beauty,* and *emotional influences.*

During a 6 period, the emphasis is usually on the home and family. There may be changes in the home, there will be new people entering the family and others leaving home. Responsibilities at home will increase.

The number 6 vibration rules marriage but, as it also involves balance, it may negatively also rule divorce. During the restlessness of the previous 5 year, you may have experimented with new relationships and may now feel that you are ready to cope with a settled relationship and establish your own home. You will be seeking a balance at the very roots of your being, manifesting in your home, your relationships and yourself.

Beauty will become important, both in relation to your own personal appearance and your surroundings. You might, therefore, decorate your home or take more care with your appearance. You are so tuned to the requirements for balance that others may come to you for help in settling their differences. You effectively become a Father/Mother Confessor during this period. Some legal decisions may be forthcoming which will restore balance and harmony.

If balance is not restored, separations will occur, differences may become irreconcilable. Try to settle arguments or problems with a sense of fairness. Try to show understanding for your loved ones during this period. This is your duty year for unselfish love, charity, truth and justice; you will not obtain satisfactory results in any other way.

Number Seven

You are now in the seventh year of your current nine-year cycle. Last year there were responsibilities and duty within the home and towards loved ones. It was a time to preserve harmony and balance in both your own life and in the lives of others. The past two years may have seemed somewhat hectic but now will be the time to rest.

The keywords for this year are *rest, physical completion, perfection, health* and *analysis.*

This is a period of retreat. You may feel more tired than usual and not wish to socialize. You need to be alone, to think, to meditate, reflect and retreat within yourself. It is a good time for holidays or weekends away by the sea or in the country, or just being alone at home. The accent is on rest. God rested on the seventh day and admired His handiwork. Outer activities and interests will become less pressing whilst activity is transferred to the inner realms of the mind. You will be doing a lot of necessary thinking now and your previous experiences will be mentally reviewed.

Try to set material worries aside and do not try too hard to accomplish goals. If you strive too hard at this point of your life, you could make yourself ill. Take a course of study, metaphysical studies would appeal to you as you are in a particularly receptive frame of mind just now. You could experience interesting dreams, visions and psychic experiences. You have spent much energy during the past few years getting your body, mind, home and emotions into some form of perspective, now it is time to study your inner, spiritual nature.

Number Eight

You are now in the eighth year of your current nine-year cycle. Last year saw the need to rest and to consider the spiritual side of your life. It was a time to stop and to consider present conditions and to look towards perfecting your future.

The keywords for this year are *Karma, responsibility, strength, business, service, sex, balance* and *harmony.*

Under the 8 vibration truth is clearly defined and Karma reigns. The law of 'cause and effect' is completed, and you will receive exactly what you deserve. For some, there will be a job advancement, higher salaries, public recognition, honours, awards and legacies. For others, material loss, financial hardships, unemployment, and sometimes bankruptcy. The emphasis will be on the more serious aspects of finance and security.

Pressures and responsibilities at work will begin to mount and you may feel the strain of the extra work load. This itself may come about as a result of a promotion. Additional money will be available, so your bank balance should look healthier. Since this is a year of Karmic balance (reaping what has been sown), you could even win a lottery or receive an inheritance. The negative reaction could be the loss of a job and the ensuing financial burdens. At any rate, pressure and responsibility become key issues.

Intense sexual relationships are needed now. The 8 vibration links with the sign of Scorpio and it represents a union of equality and balance. Sex is one outlet for this need. It is also a spiritual vibration, the relationship must be spiritually fulfilled as well in the meeting of mind and body, heaven and earth. Under this vibration your sexual relationships could well become 'heaven on earth' especially if both you and your partner feel a sense of responsibility for the other's happiness.

Negatively, the loss of material possessions and resources are possible. You could become so dominated by the desires and pleasures of the material world that you could launch into a power drive that crushes all who get in the way. Don't be blind to the suffering of others or resort to displays of cruelty due to your own feelings of helplessness. You could suffer personal limitation or spiritual freedom. A keen sense of balance between the material and spiritual worlds will be required.

Number Nine

You are now in the last year of your current nine-year cycle. The wheel of fortune has turned a full circle and you are almost back to the beginning again, ready for the wheel to make yet another revolution. If you have been operating your life in harmony with the universal energies, you will have gained much experience and knowledge over the past nine years. If your life has been out of balance then you may have experienced loss, heartache, and upheaval. Now is the time to get back into the right path with new values, greater understanding, stronger mental attitudes and spiritual awareness.

The keywords for this year are *endings, transition, charity, friendships* and *wisdom*.

It is time to let go of outworn values, to give up those associations which have no place in your life or future. People may leave your life. You may have to change jobs or relocate, and things that you are attached to may have to be given up. The status quo is upset.

This can be an emotionally trying experience if change and transition are difficult for you. You may feel like crying, and you will need to retreat from life and to reflect. You will have to come into contact with your inner self. However, when endings occur, it is because there is something new just around the corner. When one door closes, another opens. Try to be aware of this and try to accept any changes because ultimately, they will be for your own good. Use some of your energies in charitable deeds. You have gathered much from the past nine years and, in this final phase, you should give back to the universe part of what you have gained.

You should not work alone now but rather with others for the common good. Be sympathetic, compassionate, understanding and loving to all those you encounter in this cycle. Old friendships become especially meaningful and heart-warming, and beautiful new relationships can develop. Many of your goals will have been accomplished now.

Negatively, some people become over-emotional during the nine vibration year. They refuse to listen to reason or even try to understand. They seem to cling to those things that they can no longer have and thereby prolong a transitional period that should pass quickly and painlessly. Don't look back at past insecurities; look to the future; you cannot change the past, but you will have the chance soon to mould the future.

2.

Flower Reading

Gordon Smith, who is Chairman of the British Astrological and Psychic Society, gave me the information for this section of the book. Gordon is a psychic medium, Psy-card Reader and Dakini-card Reader. He has been involved with the world of spirituality for many years and is respected for his knowledge. He is an excellent healer and a very acute telepathic receiver.

The Method

Flower reading is an unusual form of divination which I hadn't come across until Gordon demonstrated it for me. It requires a good measure of spiritual development and a keen perception. The flower should be chosen by the Enquirer and brought to the Reader for interpretation. The flower should be left to rest in a vase or on a piece of tissue until the Reader is ready to begin. The Reader then picks up the flower and reads it from the bottom of the stem up to the top of the bloom. The bottom of the stem represents the Enquirer's childhood while the bloom represents the future. The following list shows how to interpret the various parts of the flower:

- A roughly torn stem indicates a difficult childhood. A smoothly and carefully cut one suggests an easy start in life.

- Smooth sections of stalk indicate smooth patches in life whereas rough, torn or discoloured patches denote times of trouble. Discolorations will also suggest problems with a relationship.

- New branches suggest 'new beginnings' and a division of stems denotes a choice of routes forward in life.

- Buds which come to nothing suggest losses or situations which have never really worked out. A new shoot or a group of leaves at the appropriate age could also indicate children. Strong leaves represent living children while weak ones which fizzle out denote miscarriages or even losses in infancy.

- Illness may be shown by a weak patch such as a thinning or twisting of the stalk.

- The bloom shows whether the Enquirer is going to achieve his current ambitions. Obviously a bud indicates desires which have yet to be achieved, whereas an open flower would show success and achievement of goals, whatever those goals may be.

- Friends and relations are represented by leaves, therefore one must look at the leaves to see what condition they are in so as to judge how these friends and relatives will affect the Enquirer.

- Career matters which are just beginning would be highlighted by a bud; when in top gear, by a bloom; or when coming to an end, by a dying bunch of petals.

- Anything which is curling up, dying, etc., suggests that some part of the Enquirer's life is wending its way to an end.

- Thorns are really knotty problems.

As you can see, this kind of reading is very open to interpretation by the individual Reader but added to any natural psychic ability, it works surprisingly well. Certainly the sample reading which Gordon gave me was very successful; he picked up a number of facts about my past which he could never otherwise have known. He also correctly identified a couple of major decisions and career matters which were actually on my mind at the time of the reading, and he was able to advise me in a most useful manner.

Gordon told me that an important offer would come to me from overseas when the flower was in full bloom. Over the succeeding days, the bud opened, the flower bloomed and then began to die. I threw it out with a shrug of my shoulders. A few days later I received an important offer from Australia. The letter had actually been posted on the day when the flower was in full bloom!

3.

The Oracle of Napoleon

The original material for this section came from a book called 'Everybody's Book of Fate and Fortune' which was written and compiled by **Edward Lyndoe.** This book was published in 1936 by Odhams Press Ltd. Odhams has since been taken over by Reed International Ltd who have given me their kind permission to make use of this information.

The Oracle

This version of the oracle was translated from French by a Miss Stacey, secretary of the famous pre-war occultist Edward Lyndoe. I have modernized the instructions but left the interpretations in their original form as provided by Edward Lyndoe and Miss Stacey.

While I was working on this book some very ancient and interesting books on the occult came into my hands. One of them had a shortened form of the oracle in it and some information as to its history. Apparently, it turned up in Leipzig after the defeat of Bonaparte's armies there. It was in his Cabinet of Curiosities, which had been left behind in the confusion after the battle. The text, which was written in German, had been translated from a hieroglyphic scroll discovered in an Egyptian tomb in 1801 during Napoleon's expedition there. It is likely that the Lyndoe version here comes from an intermediate French translation.

The Method

1. The Enquirer is asked to make five rows of dots on a page. He mustn't think beforehand about the number of dots he will use, *the number of dots in each row must be arrived at purely by chance.* However each line *must* contain at least eleven dots. I shall now use the oracle myself in order to provide an example:

First row:	. . . .	= 15 dots
Second row:	. . . .	= 12 dots
Third row:	. . . .	= 16 dots
Fourth row:	. . . .	= 13 dots
Fifth row:	. . . .	= 14 dots

2. I now note whether the rows are oddly or evenly numbered and translate the result into a kind of binary system of dots:

15 dots:	odd number	=	**one**
12 dots:	even number	=	**two**
16 dots:	even number	=	**two**
13 dots:	odd number	=	**one**
14 dots:	even number	=	**two**

3. I turn to page 38 to choose a question which I would like answered. My choice on this occasion is question 9: *SHALL I BENEFIT FROM THIS FRIENDSHIP?*

4. I turn to the key on page 39 and look at the series of dots which are lined up along the top of the page to find the shape which matches my own. I then trace downwards from the dot shape key to row number 9.

5. Ths shape which matches mine is in column 21. I trace downwards to row 9, where I find the letter **c**. I then turn to oracle **c** on page 54.

6. Then I look for answer 21 (corresponding to the shape which I made) down the side of the column. In this case the answer is: *FRIENDSHIP IN THIS CASE AVAILS LITTLE.*

I tried this out for myself in all seriousness and really gave some thought to my question beforehand. As it happened, I had recently been offered a rather dubious friendship which had worried me a little. The Oracle has answered my question quite definitely.

My first feelings while I was teaching myself how to use this Oracle was that it seems terribly cumbersome. Would an intuitive chap such as Bonaparte really have used such a method? However as I became more used to it, I found that I was speeding up with each try. This is a cypher, a code book; just the kind of thing which might appeal to a military-minded person. It is not based on religion or faith, nor on the subjective interpretations of a clairvoyant; it seems closer in its feeling to the intuitive science of numerology. The Oracle doesn't appear to give half-answers, there are no ambivalent replies.

If there is a question, the oracle will answer it by stating a bald fact, *yes, this course of action will work,* or *no it won't.* There could be something in it after all.

The List of Questions

1. Shall I succeed in this endeavour?
2. Will it benefit me financially?
3. Shall I encounter difficulties?
4. What losses shall I sustain?
5. Shall I make money this month?
6. Shall I be promoted?
7. Is this speculation likely to succeed?
8. Shall I marry this person?
9. Shall I benefit by this friendship?
10. Shall I have children?
11. Shall I take this journey?
12. Is my friend faithful to me?
13. Will my family prosper?
14. Will these plans mature successfully?
15. Shall I make this change?
16. Will this new venture be wise?
17. Shall I be happy in this matter?
18. Will a change produce financial benefit?
19. Will there be more settlement if I do this thing?
20. Shall I prosper from this sport?
21. How will women friends influence this matter?
22. Shall I undertake this pleasure?
23. Will I be wise to write this letter?
24. Shall I win?
25. Shall I seek advancement now?
26. Will marriage bring me happiness?
27. Can I safely undertake this thing?
28. Am I opposed in this matter?
29. Is this partnership wise?
30. Shall I hold my present gains?
31. Shall I become better known and liked?
32. What chance of success have I?

The Key

Q \ Fig.	1	2	3	4	5	6	7	8	9	10	11	12	13	14	15	16	17	18	19	20	21	22	23	24	25	26	27	28	29	30	31	32
1	A	B	C	D	E	F	G	H	I	J	K	L	M	N	O	P	Q	R	S	T	U	V	W	X	Y	Z	a	b	c	d	e	f
2	B	C	D	E	F	G	H	I	J	K	L	M	N	O	P	Q	R	S	T	U	V	W	X	Y	Z	a	b	c	d	e	f	A
3	C	D	E	F	G	H	I	J	K	L	M	N	O	P	Q	R	S	T	U	V	W	X	Y	Z	a	b	c	d	e	f	A	B
4	D	E	F	G	H	I	J	K	L	M	N	O	P	Q	R	S	T	U	V	W	X	Y	Z	a	b	c	d	e	f	A	B	C
5	E	F	G	H	I	J	K	L	M	N	O	P	Q	R	S	T	U	V	W	X	Y	Z	a	b	c	d	e	f	A	B	C	D
6	F	G	H	I	J	K	L	M	N	O	P	Q	R	S	T	U	V	W	X	Y	Z	a	b	c	d	e	f	A	B	C	D	E
7	G	H	I	J	K	L	M	N	O	P	Q	R	S	T	U	V	W	X	Y	Z	a	b	c	d	e	f	A	B	C	D	E	F
8	H	I	J	K	L	M	N	O	P	Q	R	S	T	U	V	W	X	Y	Z	a	b	c	d	e	f	A	B	C	D	E	F	G
9	I	J	K	L	M	N	O	P	Q	R	S	T	U	V	W	X	Y	Z	a	b	c	d	e	f	A	B	C	D	E	F	G	H
10	J	K	L	M	N	O	P	Q	R	S	T	U	V	W	X	Y	Z	a	b	c	d	e	f	A	B	C	D	E	F	G	H	I
11	K	L	M	N	O	P	Q	R	S	T	U	V	W	X	Y	Z	a	b	c	d	e	f	A	B	C	D	E	F	G	H	I	J
12	L	M	N	O	P	Q	R	S	T	U	V	W	X	Y	Z	a	b	c	d	e	f	A	B	C	D	E	F	G	H	I	J	K
13	M	N	O	P	Q	R	S	T	U	V	W	X	Y	Z	a	b	c	d	e	f	A	B	C	D	E	F	G	H	I	J	K	L
14	N	O	P	Q	R	S	T	U	V	W	X	Y	Z	a	b	c	d	e	f	A	B	C	D	E	F	G	H	I	J	K	L	M
15	O	P	Q	R	S	T	U	V	W	X	Y	Z	a	b	c	d	e	f	A	B	C	D	E	F	G	H	I	J	K	L	M	N
16	P	Q	R	S	T	U	V	W	X	Y	Z	a	b	c	d	e	f	A	B	C	D	E	F	G	H	I	J	K	L	M	N	O
17	Q	R	S	T	U	V	W	X	Y	Z	a	b	c	d	e	f	A	B	C	D	E	F	G	H	I	J	K	L	M	N	O	P
18	R	S	T	U	V	W	X	Y	Z	a	b	c	d	e	f	A	B	C	D	E	F	G	H	I	J	K	L	M	N	O	P	Q
19	S	T	U	V	W	X	Y	Z	a	b	c	d	e	f	A	B	C	D	E	F	G	H	I	J	K	L	M	N	O	P	Q	R
20	T	U	V	W	X	Y	Z	a	b	c	d	e	f	A	B	C	D	E	F	G	H	I	J	K	L	M	N	O	P	Q	R	S
21	U	V	W	X	Y	Z	a	b	c	d	e	f	A	B	C	D	E	F	G	H	I	J	K	L	M	N	O	P	Q	R	S	T
22	V	W	X	Y	Z	a	b	c	d	e	f	A	B	C	D	E	F	G	H	I	J	K	L	M	N	O	P	Q	R	S	T	U
23	W	X	Y	Z	a	b	c	d	e	f	A	B	C	D	E	F	G	H	I	J	K	L	M	N	O	P	Q	R	S	T	U	V
24	X	Y	Z	a	b	c	d	e	f	A	B	C	D	E	F	G	H	I	J	K	L	M	N	O	P	Q	R	S	T	U	V	W
25	Y	Z	a	b	c	d	e	f	A	B	C	D	E	F	G	H	I	J	K	L	M	N	O	P	Q	R	S	T	U	V	W	X
26	Z	a	b	c	d	e	f	A	B	C	D	E	F	G	H	I	J	K	L	M	N	O	P	Q	R	S	T	U	V	W	X	Y
27	a	b	c	d	e	f	A	B	C	D	E	F	G	H	I	J	K	L	M	N	O	P	Q	R	S	T	U	V	W	X	Y	Z
28	b	c	d	e	f	A	B	C	D	E	F	G	H	I	J	K	L	M	N	O	P	Q	R	S	T	U	V	W	X	Y	Z	a
29	c	d	e	f	A	B	C	D	E	F	G	H	I	J	K	L	M	N	O	P	Q	R	S	T	U	V	W	X	Y	Z	a	b
30	d	e	f	A	B	C	D	E	F	G	H	I	J	K	L	M	N	O	P	Q	R	S	T	U	V	W	X	Y	Z	a	b	c
31	e	f	A	B	C	D	E	F	G	H	I	J	K	L	M	N	O	P	Q	R	S	T	U	V	W	X	Y	Z	a	b	c	d
32	f	A	B	C	D	E	F	G	H	I	J	K	L	M	N	O	P	Q	R	S	T	U	V	W	X	Y	Z	a	b	c	d	e

Figure		A	Figure		B
1	⠿	Yes, strong possibilities.	1	⠿	A little perhaps.
2	⠿	Every possible chance.	2	⠿	Little chance of success.
3	⠿	If you use your capabilities.	3	⠿	Not a great deal yet.
4	⠿	They remain in your possession.	4	⠿	To a certain extent.
5	⠿	It opens up some good chances.	5	⠿	To a large extent, yes.
6	⠿	Definitely, not.	6	⠿	Neither wise or unwise.
7	⠿	It is quite safe.	7	⠿	To a mild extent.
8	⠿	More than you now enjoy.	8	⠿	Only if you exercise caution.
9	⠿	Advancement would reward you.	9	⠿	Some, perhaps.
10	⠿	It is very likely.	10	⠿	It is scarcely worth the attempt.
11	⠿	You should write it at once.	11	⠿	Not a great deal for hope.
12	⠿	Do so, by all means.	12	⠿	Write, if you feel so inclined.
13	⠿	Fairly well.	13	⠿	It scarcely matters either way.
14	⠿	You cannot fail to do so.	14	⠿	Only moderately well.
15	⠿	Some sound settlement is possible.	15	⠿	You are mistaken about this matter.
16	⠿	Very likely it will.	16	⠿	An unsettled atmosphere.
17	⠿	Very happy.	17	⠿	It is possible, but unlikely.
18	⠿	There would be good possibilities.	18	⠿	Not too happy.
19	⠿	Do so, by all means.	19	⠿	Few opportunities in this direction.
20	⠿	The Fates consent.	20	⠿	The outcome is doubtful.
21	⠿	They have every possibility.	21	⠿	It is just possible.
22	⠿	His integrity cannot be doubted.	22	⠿	With much effort.
23	⠿	If you do, it will be fruitful.	23	⠿	It is just possible—some doubt.
24	⠿	Children are a possibility.	24	⠿	There is little point in doing so.
25	⠿	Your friends bring you good fortune.	25	⠿	Not much chance of having any.
26	⠿	If so, happiness seems probable.	26	⠿	Friendship, in this instance avails little.
27	⠿	It stands a good chance.	27	⠿	Your chances are not good.
28	⠿	It appears very likely.	28	⠿	Doubtful.
29	⠿	A strong probability.	29	⠿	Not much chance.
30	⠿	None.	30	⠿	Little possibility.
31	⠿	Not much possibility, if any.	31	⠿	Not much gain possible.
32	⠿	Yes, most certainly.	32	⠿	Not many, if any.

Figure		C		Figure		D
1		Yes.		1		Some loss and some gain.
2		Yes.		2		Chances are about even.
3		Yes.		3		Fair chances.
4		Enormous chances.		4		Your chances are about equal.
5		Better known and liked.		5		About an even chance.
6		Most assuredly.		6		No reason why not.
7		Very sound in all respects.		7		Certainly, if you are prudent now.
8		Violently so.		8		If you have imagination.
9		The dangers are few.		9		Opposition is fairly strong.
10		Much more than you suppose.		10		Some dangers, but you will rise above them.
11		The promotion awaits you.		11		Some joy and some sorrow.
12		You will do very well.		12		A rival runs you close.
13		You will do well to do so.		13		No tangible gain if you do.
14		You should do so.		14		There can be no harm if you do.
15		Very well indeed.		15		Some doubt about this.
16		You will have some good opportunities to do so.		16		Their influence will be good.
17		All will go well.		17		There are some good chances.
18		There will be much benefit.		18		Little actual stability.
19		You will rejoice.		19		Fair prospects of gain.
20		Very wise indeed.		20		Laughter and tears will come.
21		You will do well to do this thing.		21		Fair possibilities are attached.
22		Certainly, they will.		22		It will turn out neither well nor ill.
23		Most decidedly.		23		Only if you are very persistent.
24		A faithful friend in all ways.		24		They stand a good chance.
25		By all means, do so.		25		Sometimes.
26		You will have several.		26		The chances, if you do, are equal.
27		You will benefit greatly.		27		Yes, but with some misgiving.
28		Yes.		28		Your friend brings some gain and some loss.
29		Yes.		29		Fair chance of marriage.
30		Yes.		30		Quite good possibilities.
31		Yes.		31		Fairly good chances.
32		Losses unlikely.		32		Some will be made.

Figure		**E**	Figure		**F**
1	⋮	Good fortune in this matter.	1	⋮	The circumstances are favourable.
2	⋮	Losses are not possible.	2	⋮	Favourable opportunities will arise.
3	⋮	Fortune will dispel them.	3	⋮	Chances too favourable for losses.
4	⋮	You are promised good fortune.	4	⋮	Favourable chances of success.
5	⋮	Splendid good fortune is promised.	5	⋮	Favourable prospects of it.
6	⋮	Tremendous opportunities greet you.	6	⋮	The prospects are favourable.
7	⋮	Fame of a kind is certain.	7	⋮	All goes well for you.
8	⋮	There is no doubt of it.	8	⋮	You will be one of the favoured few.
9	⋮	Undoubtedly for your gain.	9	⋮	No real reason why not.
10	⋮	You win all along the line.	10	⋮	It is a good and useful combination.
11	⋮	Of course—it is quite safe.	11	⋮	Yes, but not strongly.
12	⋮	Happiness in great quantity.	12	⋮	No doubt about it.
13	⋮	A big and surprising leap is before you.	13	⋮	Pleasant possibilities.
14	⋮	A great victory.	14	⋮	This is a good time.
15	⋮	Amazingly good results if you do so.	15	⋮	Some excellent possibilities of winning.
16	⋮	Do—you will not regret it.	16	⋮	This is a good time.
17	⋮	They will help it to success.	17	⋮	Moderately only.
18	⋮	You profit immensely.	18	⋮	Only in a small measure, but for good.
19	⋮	The whole affair tends to bring you happiness.	19	⋮	There is some profit.
20	⋮	Much gain will be made.	20	⋮	Some good results will follow.
21	⋮	Happy, because it is fortunate.	21	⋮	You will receive favourable treatment.
22	⋮	You will be successful if you do venture.	22	⋮	Reasonably happy.
23	⋮	Great success is promised if you do.	23	⋮	There will be a good result.
24	⋮	The outcome will be surprisingly good.	24	⋮	All will go well, if you are prudent.
25	⋮	There is tremendous good fortune ahead.	25	⋮	Very good possibilities.
26	⋮	Your friend is full of good faith.	26	⋮	They are well-conditioned to do so.
27	⋮	Good fortune will follow this journey.	27	⋮	You are blessed in this person.
28	⋮	You will, and they will bring you good fortune.	28	⋮	You should go—it favours you.
29	⋮	You are fortunate in your friend.	29	⋮	Everything favours your desires.
30	⋮	Great good fortune attends the matter.	30	⋮	This person is favourably disposed.
31	⋮	First-rate chances of much success.	31	⋮	A favourable opportunity is coming.
32	⋮	Excellent possibilities.	32	⋮	Favourable opportunities will arise.

Figure		**G**	Figure		**H**
1		No.	1		You will change your mind.
2		No.	2		The matter is affected by changes.
3		No.	3		Changes are foreshadowed.
4		Much loss.	4		Prospects very changeable.
5		No.	5		Circumstances very changeable.
6		No.	6		Some, but more good-fortune than bad.
7		No.	7		Many ups and downs in the matter.
8		Not any.	8		Prospects are very changeable.
9		Exceedingly unlikely, alas!	9		Plenty when your mind is fixed.
10		They are likely to be lost.	10		By fits and starts.
11		One of the unwisest propositions.	11		A friend involves alteration.
12		In such a measure as to make it unwise.	12		The fortune is not sufficiently stable.
13		Resist the temptation to act in this way.	13		At times only.
14		There is only unhappiness in store.	14		A change in your plans will intervene.
15		Your efforts will not be successful.	15		Marriage brings a change for the better.
16		Failure is inevitable.	16		Only if your mind is fixed upon it.
17		You should not write it.	17		Conditions change in your favour.
18		Leave this thing alone.	18		It has uncertain possibilities.
19		Adversely.	19		Yes, but you will not be satisfied.
20		Not at the present time.	20		The influence will ebb and flow.
21		Grave unsettlement will result.	21		Variable results will be seen.
22		In this you make no gain at all.	22		Yes, but only for a time.
23		Unhappy, unfortunately.	23		Make the change by all means and see!
24		Nothing more foolish could be imagined.	24		A moody atmosphere.
25		To make it would be unwise.	25		Too many ups and downs here.
26		They would be best abandoned.	26		You will not make it, anyway.
27		Little chance of your hope being realized.	27		They need alteration.
28		There is an element of treachery.	28		They could if they were more stable.
29		Do not undertake this journey.	29		He is too fickle to trust.
30		The answer is 'No.'	30		Conditions will change; think again.
31		There will be ill-fortune from it.	31		Your present mood will change in this respect.
32		No.	32		The friend in question is changeable.

Figure		I	Figure		J
1		You dare not trust too far.	1		Children are a possibility.
2		Marriage would be too much of a speculation.	2		Your friends bring you good-fortune.
3		Yes.	3		If so, happiness seems probable.
4		Chances are good, but may be lost.	4		It stands a good chance.
5		Speculation is your best opportunity.	5		It appears very likely.
6		Good prospects of avoiding losses.	6		A strong probability.
7		Results purely speculative.	7		None.
8		Doubtful, but good opportunities.	8		Not much possibility, if any.
9		The results are purely speculative.	9		Yes, most certainly.
10		A moderately good one.	10		Yes, strong possibilities.
11		It is doubtful.	11		Every possible chance.
12		You will use them to multiply them.	12		If you use your capabilities.
13		It is a gamble, but you win.	13		They remain in your possession.
14		By a friend in all probability.	14		It opens up some good chances.
15		There are too many risks.	15		Denfinitely, not.
16		Some rare joys are in the project.	16		It is quite safe.
17		Everything is in your own hands.	17		More than you now enjoy.
18		Go in boldly and you will win.	18		Advancement would reward you.
19		Think carefully beforehand, then.	19		It is very likely.
20		No gain either way.	20		You should write it at once.
21		They will make the issue uncertain.	21		Do so by all means.
22		Your best chance is in a gamble.	22		Fairly well.
23		Perhaps, but not for long.	23		You cannot fail to do so.
24		Rather a risky undertaking.	24		Some sound settlement is possible.
25		It is doubtful.	25		Very likely it will.
26		Only if you care for uncertainty.	26		Very happy.
27		The results are highly speculative.	27		There would be good possibilities.
28		You need to devote more thought to them.	28		Do so by all means.
29		It is entirely in the lap of the gods.	29		The Fates consent.
30		Too much toying with deceit.	30		They have every possibility.
31		Unlikely you will go.	31		His integrity cannot be doubted.
32		Few, if any.	32		If you do, it will be fruitful.

Figure		K	Figure		L
1		There is little point in doing so.	1		A faithful friend in all ways.
2		Not much chance of having any.	2		By all means do so.
3		Friendship, in this instance, avails little.	3		You will have several.
4		Your chances are not good.	4		You will benefit greatly.
5		Doubtful.	5		Yes.
6		Not much chance.	6		Yes.
7		Little possibility.	7		Yes.
8		Not much gain possible.	8		Yes.
9		Not many, if any.	9		Losses unlikely.
10		A little, perhaps.	10		Yes.
11		Little chance of success.	11		Yes.
12		Not a great deal yet.	12		Yes.
13		To a certain extent.	13		Enormous chances.
14		To a large extent, yes.	14		Better known and liked.
15		Neither wise nor unwise.	15		Most assuredly.
16		To a mild extent.	16		Very sound in all respects.
17		Only if you exercise caution.	17		Violently so.
18		Some, perhaps.	18		The dangers are few.
19		It is scarcely worth the attempt.	19		Much more than you suppose.
20		Not a great deal of hope.	20		The promotion awaits you.
21		Write if you feel so inclined.	21		You will do very well.
22		It scarcely matters either way.	22		You will do well to do so.
23		Only moderately well.	23		You should do so.
24		You are mistaken about this matter.	24		Very well indeed.
25		An unsettled atmosphere.	25		You will have some good opportunities to do so.
26		It is possible, but unlikely.	26		All will go well.
27		Not too happy.	27		There will be much benefit.
28		Few opportunities in this direction.	28		You will rejoice.
29		The outcome is doubtful.	29		Very wise indeed.
30		It is just possible.	30		You will do well to do this thing.
31		With much effort.	31		Certainly, they will.
32		It is just possible—some doubt.	32		Most decidedly.

Figure		**M**	Figure		**N**
1		They stand a good chance.	1		The outcome will be surprisingly good.
2		Sometimes.	2		There is tremendous good fortune ahead.
3		The chances if you do are equal.	3		Your friend is full of good faith.
4		Yes, but with some misgiving.	4		Good fortune will follow this journey.
5		Your friend brings some gain and some loss.	5		You will, and they will bring good fortune.
6		Fair chance of marriage.	6		You are fortunate in your friend.
7		Quite good possibilities.	7		Great good fortune attends the matter.
8		Fairly good chances.	8		First-rate chances of much success.
9		Some will be made.	9		Excellent possibilities.
10		Some loss and some gain.	10		Good fortune in this matter.
11		Chances are about even.	11		Losses are not possible.
12		Fair chances.	12		Fortune will dispel them.
13		Your chances are about equal.	13		You are promised good fortune.
14		About an even chance.	14		Splendid good fortune is promised.
15		No reason why not.	15		Tremendous opportunities greet you.
16		Certainly, if you are prudent.	16		Fame of a kind is certain.
17		If you have imagination.	17		There is no doubt of it.
18		Opposition is fairly strong.	18		Undoubtedly for your gain.
19		Some dangers, but you will rise above them.	19		You win all along the line.
20		Some joy and some sorrow.	20		Of course—it is quite safe.
21		A rival runs you close.	21		Happiness in great quantity.
22		No tangible gain if you do.	22		A big and surprising leap is before you.
23		There can be no harm done.	23		A great victory.
24		Some doubt about this.	24		Amazingly good results if you do so.
25		Their influence will be good.	25		Do—you will not regret it.
26		There are some good chances.	26		They will help it to success.
27		Little actual stability.	27		You profit immensely.
28		Fair prospects of gain.	28		The whole affair tends to bring you happiness.
29		Laughter and tears will come.	29		Much gain will be made.
30		Fair possibilities are attached.	30		Happy, because it is fortunate.
31		It will turn out neither well nor ill.	31		You will be successful if you do venture.
32		Only if you are very persistent.	32		Great success is promised if you do.

Figure		O	Figure		P
1		All will go well, if you are prudent.	1		Nothing more foolish could be imagined.
2		Very good possibilities.	2		To make it would be unwise.
3		They are well-conditioned to do so.	3		They would be best abandoned.
4		You are blessed in this person.	4		Little chance of your hope being realized.
5		You should go—it favours you.	5		There is an element of treachery.
6		Everything favours your desires.	6		Do not undertake the journey.
7		This person is favourably disposed.	7		The answer is 'No.'
8		A favourable opportunity is coming.	8		There will be ill-fortune from it.
9		Favourable opportunities will arise.	9		No.
10		The circumstances are favourable.	10		No.
11		Favourable opportunities will arise.	11		No.
12		Chances too favourable for losses.	12		No.
13		Favourable chances of success.	13		Much loss.
14		Favourable prospects of it.	14		No.
15		The prospects are favourable.	15		No.
16		All goes well for you.	16		No.
17		You will be one of the favoured few.	17		Not any.
18		No real reason why not.	18		Exceedingly unlikely, alas!.
19		It is a good and useful combination.	19		They are likely to be lost.
20		Yes, but not strongly.	20		One of the unwisest propositions.
21		No doubt about it.	21		In such a measure as to make it unwise.
22		Pleasant possibilities.	22		Resist the temptation to act in this way.
23		This is a good time.	23		There is only unhappiness in store.
24		Some excellent possibility of winning.	24		Your efforts will not be successful.
25		This is a good time.	25		Failure is inevitable.
26		Moderately only.	26		You should not write it.
27		Only in a small measure, but for good.	27		Leave this thing alone.
28		There is some profit.	28		Adversely.
29		Some good results will follow.	29		Not at the present time.
30		You will receive favourable treatment.	30		Grave unsettlement will result.
31		Reasonably happy.	31		In this you make no gain at all.
32		There will be a good result.	32		Unhappy, unfortunately.

Figure	Q	Figure	R
1	A moody atmosphere.	1	Rather a risky undertaking.
2	Too many ups and downs here.	2	It is doubtful.
3	You will not make it, anyway.	3	Only if you care for uncertainty.
4	They need alteration.	4	The results are highly speculative.
5	They could, if they were more stable.	5	You need to devote more thought to them.
6	He is too fickle to trust.	6	It is entirely in the lap of the gods.
7	Conditions will change; think again.	7	Too much toying with deceit.
8	You present mood will change in this respect.	8	Unlikely you will go.
9	The friend in question is changeable.	9	Few, if any.
10	You will change your mind.	10	You dare not trust too far.
11	The matter is affected by changes.	11	Marriage would be too much of a speculation.
12	Changes are foreshadowed.	12	Yes.
13	Prospects very changeable.	13	Chances are good, but may be lost.
14	Circumstances very changeable.	14	Speculation is your best opportunity.
15	Some, but more good-fortune than bad.	15	Good prospects of avoiding losses.
16	Many ups and downs in this matter.	16	Results purely speculative.
17	Prospects are very changeable.	17	Doubtful, but good opportunities.
18	Plenty, when your mind is fixed.	18	The results are purely speculative.
19	By fits and starts.	19	A moderately good one.
20	A friend involves alteration.	20	It is doubtful.
21	The fortune is not sufficiently stable.	21	You will use them to multiply them.
22	At times only.	22	It is a gamble, but you win.
23	A change in your plans will intervene.	23	By a friend, in all probability.
24	Marriage brings a change for the better.	24	There are too many risks.
25	Only if your mind is fixed upon it.	25	Some rare joys in the project.
26	Conditions change in your favour.	26	Everything is in your own hands.
27	It has uncertain possibilities.	27	Go in boldly and you will.
28	Yes, but you will not be satisfied.	28	Think carefully beforehand, then.
29	Their influence will ebb and flow.	29	No gain either way.
30	Variable results will be seen.	30	They will make the issue uncertain.
31	Yes, but only for a time.	31	Your best chance is in a gamble.
32	Make the change, by all means, and see!	32	Perhaps, but not for long.

Figure		S	Figure		T
1		Some sound settlement is possible.	1		You are mistaken about this matter.
2		Very likely it will.	2		An unsettled atmosphere.
3		Very happy.	3		It is possible, but unlikely.
4		There would be good possibilities.	4		Not too happy.
5		Do so by all means.	5		Few opportunities in this direction.
6		The Fates consent.	6		The outcome is doubtful.
7		They have every possibility.	7		It is just possible.
8		His integrity cannot be doubted.	8		With much effort.
9		If you do, it will be fruitful.	9		It is just possible—some doubt.
10		Children are a possibility.	10		There is little point in doing so.
11		Your friends bring you good fortune.	11		Not much chance of having any.
12		If so, happiness seems probable.	12		Friendship, in this instance, avails little.
13		It stands a good chance.	13		Your chances are not good.
14		It appears very likely.	14		Doubtful.
15		A strong probability.	15		Not much chance.
16		None.	16		Little possibility.
17		Not much possibility, if any.	17		Not much gain possible.
18		Yes, most certainly.	18		Not many, if any.
19		Yes, strong possibilities.	19		A little, perhaps.
20		Every possible chance.	20		Little chance of success.
21		If you use your capabilities.	21		Not a great deal yet.
22		They remain in your possession.	22		To a certain extent.
23		It opens up some good chances.	23		To a large extent, yes.
24		Definitely not.	24		Neither wise or unwise.
25		It is quite safe.	25		To a mild extent.
26		More than you now enjoy.	26		Only if you exercise caution.
27		Advancement would reward you.	27		Some, perhaps.
28		It is very likely.	28		It is scarcely worth the attempt.
29		You should write it at once.	29		Not a great deal of hope.
30		Do so by all means.	30		Write, if you feel so inclined.
31		Fairly well.	31		It scarecely matters either way.
32		You cannot fail to do so.	32		Only moderately well.

Figure		U	Figure		V
1	⋮	Very well indeed.	1	⋮	Some doubt about this.
2	⋮	You will have some good opportunities to do so.	2	⋮	Their influence will be good.
3	⋮	All will go well.	3	⋮	There are some good chances.
4	⋮	There will be much benefit.	4	⋮	Little actual stability.
5	⋮	You will rejoice.	5	⋮	Fair prospects of gain.
6	⋮	Very wise indeed.	6	⋮	Laughter and tears will come.
7	⋮	You will do well to do this thing.	7	⋮	Fair possibilities are attached.
8	⋮	Certainly, they will.	8	⋮	It will turn out neither well nor ill.
9	⋮	Most decidedly.	9	⋮	Only if you are very persistent.
10	⋮	A faithful friend in all ways.	10	⋮	They stand a good chance.
11	⋮	By all means do so.	11	⋮	Sometimes.
12	⋮	You will have several.	12	⋮	The chances, if you do, are equal.
13	⋮	You will benefit greatly.	13	⋮	Yes, but with some misgiving.
14	⋮	Yes.	14	⋮	Your friend brings some gain and some loss.
15	⋮	Yes.	15	⋮	Fair chance of marriage.
16	⋮	Yes.	16	⋮	Quite good possibilities.
17	⋮	Yes.	17	⋮	Fairly good chances.
18	⋮	Losses unlikely.	18	⋮	Some will be made.
19	⋮	Yes.	19	⋮	Some loss and some gain.
20	⋮	Yes.	20	⋮	Chances are about even.
21	⋮	Yes.	21	⋮	Fair chances.
22	⋮	Enormous chances.	22	⋮	Your chances are about equal.
23	⋮	Better known and liked.	23	⋮	About an even chance.
24	⋮	Most assuredly.	24	⋮	No reason why not.
25	⋮	Very sound in all respects.	25	⋮	Certainly, if you are prudent now.
26	⋮	Violently so.	26	⋮	If you have imagination.
27	⋮	The dangers are few.	27	⋮	Opposition is fairly strong.
28	⋮	Much more than you suppose.	28	⋮	Some dangers, but you will rise above them.
29	⋮	The promotion awaits you.	29	⋮	Some joy and some sorrow.
30	⋮	You will do very well.	30	⋮	A rival runs you close.
31	⋮	You will do well to do so.	31	⋮	No tangible gain if you do.
32	⋮	You should do so.	32	⋮	There can be no harm done.

Figure	**W**	Figure	**X**
1	Amazingly good results, if you do so.	1	Some excellent possibility of winning.
2	Do—you will not regret it.	2	This is a good time.
3	They will help it to success.	3	Moderately only.
4	You profit immensely.	4	Only in a small measure, but for good.
5	The whole affair tends to bring you happiness.	5	There is some profit.
6	Much gain will be made.	6	Some good results will follow.
7	Happy, because it is fortunate.	7	You will receive favourable treatment.
8	You will be successful, if you do venture.	8	Reasonably happy.
9	Great success is promised, if you do.	9	There will be a good result.
10	The outcome will be surprisingly good.	10	All will go well, if you are prudent.
11	There is tremendous good-fortune ahead.	11	Very good possibilities.
12	Your friend is full of good faith.	12	They are well-conditioned to do so.
13	Good fortune will follow this journey.	13	You are blessed in this person.
14	You will, and they will bring good fortune.	14	You should go—it favours you.
15	You are fortunate in your friend.	15	Everything favours your desires.
16	Great good fortune attends the matter.	16	This person is favourably disposed.
17	First-rate chances of much success.	17	A favourable opportunity is coming.
18	Excellent possibilities.	18	Favourable opportunities will arise.
19	Good fortune in this matter.	19	The circumstances are favourable.
20	Losses are not possible.	20	Favourable opportunites will arise.
21	Fortune will dispel them.	21	Chances too favourable for losses.
22	You are promised a good fortune.	22	Favourable chances of success.
23	Splendid good fortune is promised.	23	Favourable propects of it.
24	Tremendous opportunities greet you.	24	The prospects are favourable.
25	Fame of a kind is certain.	25	All goes well for you.
26	There is no doubt of it.	26	You will be one of the favoured few.
27	Undoubtedly for your gain.	27	No real reason why not.
28	You win all along the line.	28	It is a good and useful combination.
29	Of course—it is quite safe.	29	Yes, but not strongly.
30	Happiness in great quantity.	30	No doubt about it.
31	A big and surprising leap is before you.	31	Pleasant possibilities.
32	A great victory.	32	This is a good time.

Figure	Y	Figure	Z
1	Your efforts will not be successful.	1	Marriage brings a change for the better.
2	Failure is inevitable.	2	Only if your mind is fixed on it.
3	You should not write it.	3	Conditions change in your favour.
4	Leave this thing alone.	4	It has uncertain possibilities.
5	Adversely.	5	Yes, but you will not be satisfied.
6	Not at the present time.	6	Their influence will ebb and flow.
7	Grave unsettlement will result.	7	Variable results will be seen.
8	In this you make no gain at all.	8	Yes, but only for a time.
9	Unhappy, unfortunately.	9	Make the change, by all means, and see!
10	Nothing more foolish could be imagined.	10	A moody atmosphere.
11	To make it would be unwise.	11	Too many ups and downs here.
12	They would be best abandoned.	12	You will not make it, anyway.
13	Little chance of your hope being realized.	13	They need alteration.
14	There is an element of treachery.	14	They could, if they were more stable.
15	Do not undertake the journey.	15	He is too fickle to trust.
16	The answer is 'No'.	16	Conditions will change; think again.
17	There will be ill-fortune from it.	17	Your present mood will change in this respect.
18	No.	18	The friend in question is changeable.
19	No.	19	You will change your mind.
20	No.	20	The matter is affected by changes.
21	No.	21	Changes are foreshadowed.
22	Much loss.	22	Prospects very changeable.
23	No.	23	Circumstances very changeable.
24	No.	24	Some, but more good fortune than bad.
25	No.	25	Many ups and downs in the matter.
26	Not any.	26	Prospects are very changeable.
27	Exceedingly unlikely, alas!	27	Plenty, when your mind is fixed.
28	They are likely to be lost.	28	By fits and starts.
29	One of the unwisest propositions.	29	A friend involves alteration.
30	In such a measure as to make it unwise.	30	The fortune is not sufficiently stable.
31	Resist the temptation to act in this way.	31	At times only.
32	There is only unhappiness in store.	32	A change in your plans will intervene.

Figure		a	Figure		b
1		There are too many risks.	1		Definitely, not.
2		Some rare joys are in the project.	2		It is quite safe.
3		Everything is in your own hands.	3		More than you now enjoy.
4		Go in boldly and you will.	4		Advancement will reward you.
5		Think carefully beforehand, then.	5		It is very likely.
6		No gain either way.	6		You should write it at once.
7		They will make the issue uncertain.	7		Do so by all means.
8		Your best chance is in a gamble.	8		Fairly well.
9		Perhaps, but not for long.	9		You cannot fail to do so.
10		Rather a risky undertaking.	10		Some sound settlement is possible.
11		It is doubtful.	11		Very likely it will.
12		Only if you care for uncertainty.	12		Very happy.
13		The results are highly speculative.	13		There would be good possibilities.
14		You need to devote more thought to them.	14		Do so, by all means.
15		It is entirely in the lap of the gods.	15		The Fates consent.
16		Too much toying with deceit.	16		They have every possibility.
17		Unlikely you will go.	17		His integrity cannot be doubted.
18		Few if any.	18		If you do, it will be fruitful.
19		You dare not trust too far.	19		Children are a possibility.
20		Marriage would be too much of a speculation.	20		Your friends bring you good fortune.
21		Yes.	21		If so, happiness seems probable.
22		Chances are good, but may be lost.	22		It stands a good chance.
23		Speculation is your best opportunity.	23		It appears very likely.
24		Good prospects of avoiding losses.	24		A strong probability.
25		Results purely speculative.	25		None.
26		Doubtful, but good opportunities.	26		Not much possibility, if any.
27		The results are purely speculative.	27		Yes most certainly.
28		A moderately good one.	28		Yes, strong possibilities.
29		It is doubtful.	29		Every possible chance.
30		You will use them to multiply them.	30		If you use your capabilities.
31		It is a gamble, but you win.	31		They remain in your possession.
32		By a friend, in all probability.	32		It opens up some good chances.

Figure		c	Figure		d
1		Neither wise nor unwise.	1		Most assuredly.
2		To a mild extent.	2		Very sound in all repects.
3		Only if you exercise caution.	3		Violently so.
4		Some, perhaps.	4		The dangers are few.
5		It is scarcely worth the attempt.	5		Much more than you suppose.
6		Not a great deal of hope.	6		The promotion awaits you.
7		Write, if you feel so inclined.	7		You will do very well.
8		It scarcely matters either way.	8		You will do well to do so.
9		Only moderately well.	9		You should do so.
10		You are mistaken about this matter.	10		Their inflence will be good.
11		An unsettled atmosphere.	11		You will have some good opportunities to do so.
12		It is possible, but unlikely.	12		All will go well.
13		Not too happy.	13		There will be much benefit.
14		Few opportunities in this direction.	14		You will rejoice.
15		The outcome is doubtful.	15		Very wise indeed.
16		It is just possible.	16		You will do well to do this thing.
17		With much effort.	17		Certainly, they will.
18		It is just possible—some doubt.	18		Most decidedly.
19		There is little point in doing so.	19		A faithful friend in all ways.
20		Not much chance of having any.	20		By all means, do so.
21		Friendship, in this instance, avails little.	21		You will have several.
22		Your chances are not good.	22		You will benefit greatly.
23		Doubtful.	23		Yes.
24		Not much chance.	24		Yes.
25		Little possibility.	25		Yes.
26		Not much gain possible.	26		Yes.
27		Not many, if any.	27		Losses unlikely.
28		A little, perhaps.	28		Yes.
29		Little chance of success.	29		Yes.
30		Not a great deal yet.	30		Yes.
31		To a certain extent.	31		Enormous chances.
32		To a large extent, yes.	32		Better known and liked.

Figure		e	Figure		f
1		No reason why not.	1		Tremendous opportunities greet you.
2		Certainly, if you are prudent now.	2		Fame of a kind is certain.
3		If you have imagination.	3		There is no doubt of it.
4		Opposition is fairly strong.	4		Undoubtedly of your gain.
5		Some dangers, but you will rise above them.	5		You win all along the line.
6		Some joy and some sorrow.	6		Of course—it is quite safe.
7		A rival runs you close.	7		Happiness in great quantity.
8		No tangible gain if you do.	8		A big and surprising leap before you.
9		There can be no harm done.	9		A great victory.
10		Some doubt about this.	10		Amazingly good results if you do so.
11		Their influence will be good.	11		Do—you will not regret it.
12		There are some good chances.	12		They will help it to success.
13		Little actual stability.	13		You profit immensely.
14		Fair prospects of gain.	14		The whole affair tends to bring you happiness.
15		Laughter and tears will come.	15		Much gain will be made.
16		Fair possibilities are attached.	16		Happy, it is fortunate.
17		It will turn out neither well nor ill.	17		You will be successful, if you do venture.
18		Only if you are very persistent.	18		Great success is promised if you do.
19		They stand a good chance.	19		The outcome will be surprisingly good.
20		Sometimes.	20		There is tremendous good fortune ahead.
21		The chances, if you do, are equal.	21		Your friend is full of good faith.
22		Yes, but with some misgiving.	22		Good fortune will follow this journey.
23		Your friend brings some gain and some loss.	23		You will, and they will bring you good fortune.
24		Fair chance of marriage.	24		You are fortunate in your friend.
25		Quite good possibilities.	25		Great good fortune attends the matter.
26		Fairly good chances.	26		First-rate chances of much success.
27		Some will be made.	27		Excellent possibilities.
28		Some loss and some gain.	28		Good fortune in this matter.
29		Chances are about even.	29		Losses are not possible.
30		Fair chances.	30		Fortune will dispel them.
31		Your chances are about equal.	31		You are promised good fortune.
32		About an even chance.	32		Splendid good fortune is promised.

4.

The Crystal Ball

When a client visits an astrologer or card Reader, he may not understand the process by which the Reader obtains his information but he can at least *see* it. When he visits a clairvoyant, there is nothing to see, but when he visits a crystal Reader, his eyes tell him that there is a solid glass ball with nothing inside it, but judging by what he is being given by the Reader, it's obvious that *there must be something!* What is crystal reading? How is it done? Can anyone do it? I put these questions to a couple of crystal reading friends of mine and I am now pleased to be able to pass on to you the information which they gave me.

Robin Lown

Robin is a palmist, Tarot Reader and crystal Reader. He is also a consultant for the British Astrological and Psychic Society. He comes from a family of people who have an intelligent interest in the philosophy of Karmic and psychic thought. This is what he had to tell me about crystal ball reading.

Setting the Scene
'If you want to buy a crystal ball, visit a psychic festival or a shop specializing in these things and have a look at their crystals. Weigh the ones you like in your hand and see which you feel drawn to; even the shape and size is important here. Never buy any item of this nature by mail order, because you must try it to see if it feels right. Most professionals seem to have their crystals *given* to them or bought for them, they don't seem to buy them for themselves. Make sure the crystal is clean, then 'psychically' clean it by using meditative techniques. Finally, charge it up.
  'I charged up my crystal by holding it in my hands within my aura, telling the spirit world that I wanted to use it in order to give help, service and truth to those who needed it. I meditated on it as being part of myself, re-affirming myself as a seeker of truth. Even now when reading my crystal, my motives have to be clear; I must have the desire

to be of service and help the Enquirer because any other feelings will disrupt the reading and I have to start again. Most people respect the crystal for what it is—they ask before picking it up. I have noticed that only crass materialists, the totally unaware, attempt to pick it up without asking permission, and I'm afraid that I get quite shirty with them if that happens.'

How do I read?

'I use palmistry first in order to create a link, then I give the Enquirer the crystal to hold. I tell them that it is not necessary for them to think of anything special. I ask for it back, then place it on a stand on a black silk cloth and tune in slowly. I use it as a form of psychometry and I don't think I actually *see* anything in the crystal itself. Rather, I see images which are projected from my head in a kind of psychic ventriloquism and a projection of what is in my mind. Firstly, I see scenes, people, situations and then I begin to feel impressions of feelings and emotions. This is definitely allied to psychometry, clairvoyance, clairaudience, clairsentience.'

I asked Robin whether crystal reading had ever lead him to mediumistic experiences where he was definitely in contact with dead friends or relatives of the Enquirer. He said that this had happened and that he had felt himself on occasion being 'taken over' by one of these in order that they could express themselves through him.

'At this point, I obviously don't know whether these are images of the present, the past or the future, so I ask inwardly; I ask my guiding spirit, silently, inside my head. I literally ask 'is this the past?' and wait for a 'yes' or 'no' feeling. If it turns out to be the past, I ask to be shown what relevance this might have to the present and this will bring another image to me. By now, I will be aware that my Chakras* are open and that both the crystal and the Enquirer are within my auric bubble. I then start to tell the Enquirer what I am getting and as he or she begins to connect with what I am saying, the images and impressions speed up and become more definite, more certain and then it becomes much easier. Sometimes an Enquirer can 'block' me, either because they are sceptical or for some other reason. Then I see or feel only a shaft of light as if it were coming down a tunnel, at which point I give up and resort to the palm or the cards which are less subject to psychic disturbance.'

I asked Robin how long he would spend on a reading like this and he said that it depended upon the rapport with the Enquirer and the amount of information which came through. He told me that he always finished a reading by giving a summary of the main points as he saw

---

* Seven centres in the body which 'open' to allow psychic energy to flow in and out.

them. He also kept a pencil and a pad of paper nearby so that he could sketch an item if he wanted to; and as Robin is artistic, sketching comes easily to him. He also told me that he tended to see certain particular symbols as his centres were opening up, one of them being the figure-of-eight symbol for infinity (∞) which appears over the Magician's head in the Tarot pack and the other being the caduceus (the winged staff of Mercury which signifies enlightenment, healing abilities and magical powers).

Barbara Ellen

Barbara is a full-time professional clairvoyant and medium. She is also a consultant for the British Astrological and Psychic Society. Barbara has had many years of experience, she is highly trained and very skilled and knowledgeable. She is, in my opinion, the very best, the absolute tops. Although Barbara is not primarily a crystal reader—she tells me that she finds pure clairvoyance quicker and easier—she can use a crystal very well when asked. This is what she had to tell me:

Preparing a new crystal ball
'It is far better to *acquire* a crystal than to buy a new one; mine was given to me years ago by another Reader. Wherever your crystal has come from, the first thing you must do is to immerse it for 12 hours in salt water. Some Readers use a solution of vinegar and water. Wash the crystal under *running* water, ideally from some natural source, such as a waterfull or a stream. If you haven't access to a natural source, then try to make something that will collect fresh rain water and allow it to overflow in some way. Polish the crystal with a chamois leather and leave it in sunlight for at least four hours. After that, don't ever allow anyone else to touch or even look into your crystal.

Training and preparation
'Some Readers spin the crystal with a finger while they are tuning themselves in; many work from mental impressions, but I try to use the crystal itself as it should be used.
    'Place the crystal on a small plinth covered by a black cloth. Ideally the cloth should be silk because this is a completely natural product; many Readers prefer to use velvet because it has a denser texture. Partially cover or surround the crystal with another cloth, which should be made of silk. If you wish, you can darken the room slightly and put on a dim light. Some Readers use a red light, as this is known to draw the spirit world close. Practice sessions should always be carried out the same time of the day and never late at night, as somehow this helps our guides to work better. Cup the ball in the cloth and hold it up close to your forehead; that is close to, but not touching, the third eye. While training, you must

keep the crystal within your aura. This means keeping it wrapped in its silk or velvet on a table next to you while you sleep, read, watch television, etc.

'Never read on a full stomach or if you are upset or angry. Do some yoga breathing each time before you start training or reading. To do this, you breath in from the stomach for a count of four, hold the breath for a count of two, and let it out for a count of four. Do this exercise four times. Relax, get yourself into a peaceful state of mind, and then go ahead.

'If you begin to see symbols during this time, note them down. You might be aware of certain symbols which are personal to you; a black cat, for instance, or a white rabbit etc. Keep a note of what these mean and build up a vocabulary of signs and symbols.

'The crystal should begin to cloud and it is important that when this happens you stay calm and not get excited or the vision will disappear. Red or orange 'smoke' is a warning of danger, blue or green is all right. Objects which are coloured red or orange are another thing altogether, only red 'smoke' warns you to be on the alert. The visions will go out of focus and then come back sharply into focus but you will have to wait for this to happen; sometimes as long as five minutes. This training period will last for about eight days but you must persevere with it until the ability comes. When an image comes, wait for the message to go with it. This message will come into your mind through the help of your spiritual guides. Sometimes the objects will come first and the clouds later because every Reader works slightly different. Be sure to ask your spiritual guides to help you.

'When I see images moving in the crystal I know that, *for me*, the ones which come in from the left represents events which are coming to the Enquirer while those on or travelling towards the right represent those which are passing away from him.

'As soon as you feel that you are making a link with your crystal, either with mental pictures or actually *seeing* milky-type smoke or pictures within the ball itself, find yourself some patient sitters to act as guinea-pigs. Try to find people about whom you know nothing. Ask your Enquirers to cup their hands around the ball without actually touching it and to remain in that position for approximately two minutes. Then take the crystal back from the Enquirer and then both relax. Shade the crystal from the light and begin giving out whatever comes. As soon as your sitter can acknowledge that you are getting something meaningful through, it will come through even more quickly. Any sort of feedback will help. Be sure to keep notes so that you can assess your progress and make any adjustments in your thinking.'

A sample reading

At this point the fun really began, because Barbara went on to give *me* a reading. I hadn't expected this so it was an unaccustomed treat. The first thing she saw was an aeroplane. This was not surprising as I travel a lot and was due to take a trip to New York two weeks from the time of the reading. She then saw my son, Stuart, delightedly waving a document of some kind. Stuart was about to take the final examinations for the Ordinary National Diploma in computer and business studies. He had worked hard and done well. My reading of his horoscope confirmed that he would pass these examinations and go on to College for a further course. Various other disjointed images came and then Barbara told me that she could see my husband with a bad back and pain down his left leg. My husband, Tony, had been doing a lot of lifting at work at that time, his back is bad at the best of times and was particularly painful just then. The pain did, in fact, run down his left leg. Barbara also mentioned that my daughter, Helen, needed new glasses. As it happened, Helen had just had some new specs made so this didn't make much sense at the time. A few days later, Helen told me that there was something wrong with her specs and she subsequently had replacement lenses made for them!

From that point onwards, the reading flowed in a more logical sequence. Most of it made sense and the bits which didn't seem to fit at the moment fell into place in due course. Some of the things Barbara was seeing had been told to me by other clairvoyants, although they were so far into the future that I couldn't envisage them happening at that time. One more thing which Barbara told me which cheered me considerably was that after writing several more books on this kind of subject I would change my style of writing completely and make a name for myself in a different way.

This was *exactly* what I hope to do but I know that a few more years will have to pass before I can put those ideas into action.

5.

Predictive Astrology

Fortune-telling by astrology is not easy, but if it is done properly, it is the most accurate and detailed method which can be used. There is the world of difference beween the kind of forecast which newspapers use and a properly constructed and sensitively interpreted horoscope compiled by a skilled astrologer.

The Simplest Method: The Techniques of Newspaper Astrology

Newspapers and magazines work on the only method which is possible when dealing with large numbers of people who don't know what their rising signs are. This method is called 'Sun Sign Astrology' or 'Solar House Astrology' because the sign in which the Sun appears at birth is treated as the first (Solar) house. The following illustrations show the Solar house arrangements for people born under the signs of Taurus and Aquarius. (The signs of the zodiac are always arranged in an *anticlockwise direction* around the chart.)

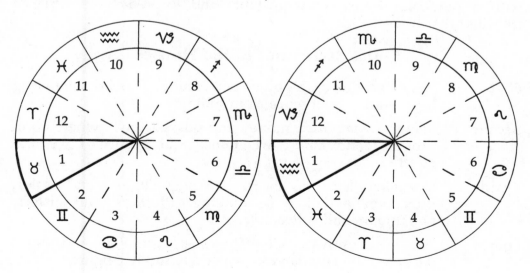

The signs of the zodiac are always written in the same order, with Aries being the first sign and Pisces the last.

♈	Aries
♉	Taurus
♊	Gemini
♋	Cancer
♌	Leo
♍	Virgo
♎	Libra
♏	Scorpio
♐	Sagittarius
♑	Capricorn
♒	Aquarius
♓	Pisces

Interpretation

Having got this far, you now need two specific bits of information which will allow you to interpret the chart predictively. The first is an explanation of the houses and the second is an explanation of the planets. As the planets travel through the various signs of the zodiac they will *activate* the houses which they pass through. This activity or energizing of each house will be done in a different way by different planets. For instance, Venus would cast a rosy glow on any house it passed through while Uranus would make the areas of life associated with a particular house very unstable and unpredictable while it transited that house.

Quick Reference to the Houses

First *The self:* the ego, the outer personality. Transits here bring fresh starts, emergence from hiding.

Second *Values and priorities:* money and possessions, ownership of property and land. Art, music and beauty. Love and affection.

Third *Communications:* local travel, negotiations and sales. Education and logical thinking. Brothers and sisters, neighbours and colleagues.

Fourth *The home:* private life. The past, tradition and one's background. The parents, especially mother figures.

Fifth   *Creative matters:* personal projects. Fun, holidays, sport and romance. Children.

Sixth   *Work and health:* duties to employers, employees, or anyone else. Health, healing, good food, and nutrition. Clothing. Colleagues.

Seventh   *Partnerships:* both business and romantic. Harmony, sometimes discord. Close relationships, close friends, and open enemies. Art, music and beauty.

Eighth   *Commitment and serious matters:* joint finances. Intense feelings. Surgery or involvement with the police. Beginnings and endings, birth and death. Also sex. Close relationships of all kinds which require commitment.

Ninth   *Expansion of horizons:* education, travel, philosophy and religion. The law, publishing. Escape, freedom, the great outdoors, large animals, second marriages, in-laws.

Tenth   *Aims and ambitions:* Status and position in life and career. Large organizations, authority figures. The church. Elderly relatives, parents, especially father figures.

Eleventh   *Group activities:* clubs, societies, hobbies, interests. Friends and acquaintances. New ideas and theories. Hopes and wishes, ideals.

Twelfth   *The inner self:* dreams, illusions and disillusion. Hidden emotions, deep thought of a spiritual kind. Love, service and sacrifice for others. Health, healing and mysticism. Self-undoing or inner strength.

Quick Reference to the Planets

The Sun   *Changes for the better:* emphasis of each house as it passes through. Events related to children. Creativity.

The Moon   *Emotions:* the home, property and premises. Parents, especially mother figures. Female matters.

Mercury   *Correspondence:* business, local travel, neighbours and relatives.

Venus   *Affection:* beauty, social life, partnerships with women.

Mars   *Activity:* energy, strength, fast movement. Accidents, partnerships with men.

Jupiter   *Expansion of one's horizons:* legal, educational and financial matters. Opportunity.

Saturn   *Limitations:* lessons of life. Parents. Career and ambitions.

Uranus   *Unexpected events:* tension and change. Novel ideas, education. Hopes and wishes.

Neptune   *Illusions and dreams:* disappointments and inspirations. Music and art. Mysticism. Charity and caring for others, being cared for.

Pluto   *Slow transformation:* the law and the police. Beginnings and endings. Birth, death, sex. Committed relationships and partnerships. Hidden matters. Mass movements and the state of the public mind.

The Hard Stuff: How the Professionals Do It

This will mean little to complete beginners but will be helpful to those of you who have some astrological knowledge.

Before he can work out future trends for a client, an astrologer has to make three sets of calculations. Firstly, he has to construct an accurate birth chart which plots the position of the eight planets of the solar system including the Sun and Moon (but excluding the Earth itself); he then has to find the Ascendant. The next step is to count forward a day for each year of his client's life and repeat the whole process for the new date. He then compares this progressed chart against the natal chart. Finally he compares the figures in his book of tables which correspond to the positions of the planets in the heavens at the actual time of the reading against both the preceding charts. Many professional astrologers use computers which take the drudgery out of the calculating part of the job, but the interpretation itself involves quite a lot of work.

The rising sign

All birth charts are divided into twelve segments called houses. There are various methods of house division in use but the simplest, and probably most popular, is the equal house system in which the chart is divided into twelve equal segments. The correct starting point of this house division is called the *Ascendant*.

The Ascendant is the point on the face of the earth where day meets night. The sign of the zodiac which is passing across the Ascendant at the time of birth is called the *rising sign*. To find your own Ascendant, either consult an astrologer or send off for one of the computerized chart calculations which you will find advertised in any magazine specializing in astrology and the occult. However, here is a rough and ready method of finding an Ascendant.

The speedy do-it-yourself Ascendant finder

Place your Sun in the house segment which corresponds to your time of birth and then place the Sun sign on the cusp (the point where one sign or house joins the next) which is between your time of birth and the next one along; then place the signs of the zodiac around the cusps in an *anticlockwise* direction and in the correct order.

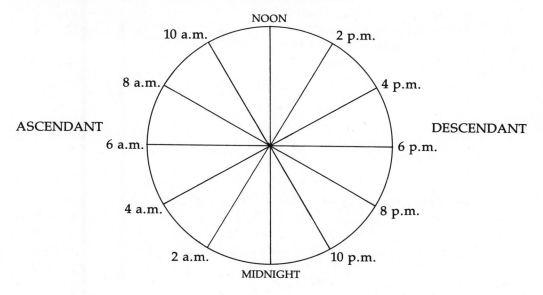

In this example, the Subject has the Sun in Leo. She was born just before midnight and therefore, her Ascendant is Gemini:

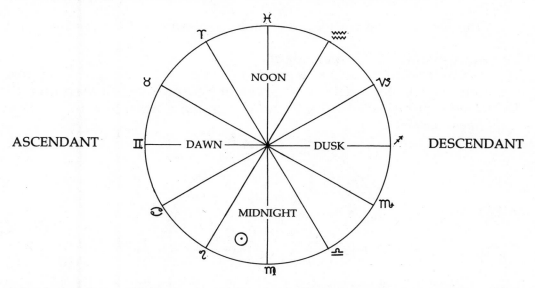

NB: Remember to deduct one hour when British Summer Time applies. (Extra calculations will be required for births outside Great Britain.)

The Sun and the Ascendant
It is worth noting that in the case of a dawn birth, the Sun and Ascendant are in the same place which means that they are in *conjuction*

with one another. A dusk birth puts the Sun and Ascendant in *opposition* to each other while a noon or midnight birth puts the Sun in a *square* aspect to the Ascendant. A noon birth means that the Sun is at the top of the cart, in *conjunction* with the mid-heaven while a midnight birth puts the Sun at the bottom of the chart, in *opposition* to the mid-heaven but in *conjunction* with the nadir:

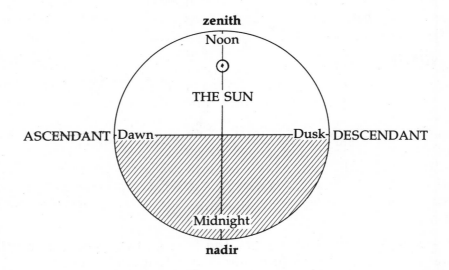

The position of the Sun for a noon birth—Sun square to the Ascendant

The exact degree of the Ascendant

The example shown below is a chart which is being prepared for someone who is born with 25 degrees of Scorpio as their Ascendant. The houses are divided up into equal segments, therefore this is the *equal house system:*

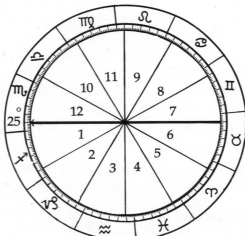

The Astrological Houses in Detail

First house

This shows how the subject appears to others, how he presents himself and his normal manner of expressing himself. In other words, it shows the outermost personality. It also represents childhood experiences of all kinds; these are also shown by other houses but the *impact* of events which occurred or, more especially, the emotions which were experienced in childhood and in youth are definitely reflected here in the first house. Our early experiences tend to modify our natural modes of behaviour towards others. To give a very simple example, has your childhood resulted in your behaving in a cautious or an open manner when dealing with people you meet for the first time? This kind of modification to behaviour is shown by this most crucial of houses.

From the point of view of predictive astrology, the first house represents a fresh start, the beginning of anything new or even a newly-optimistic and outward-looking attitude. Therefore any planet which transits this house will set off a new way of life in some form or another. This kind of transit would be doubly important because it is the most personal of all the houses.

Second house

This house concerned money, possessions and anything of value, also investments, the ability to earn money, one's own financial situation. Personal and moral values can show up here as well as the need for personal fulfilment and, to some extent, partners and relationships, especially where money and goods are involved. Also matters related to property, farming, building, gardening and the land. Artistic and musical abilities or interests, if any.

Third house

The local environment, matters under negotiation and, in some cases, papers to be signed. Messages, phone calls, correspondence of both a business and private nature. Local journeys, methods of transport. Brothers and sisters, neighbours, colleagues, sometimes nephews, nieces and friends. Business matters related to buying and selling. Education, training and re-training, foreign languages. Some sports and games. The way one thinks.

Fourth house

The home, property and premises of all kinds. Small businesses. Domestic life, roots, and background; the basis from which one grows into adulthood. The mother or any other person of either sex who nurtured the subject while he was young. The beginning and ending of life, also how one is viewed after death. Attitude towards family commitments. Security. Female goods and products. The public.

Fifth house

Children, young people and their education, even pregnancy. Fun, holidays, leisure pursuits of all kinds. Games of chance, sports, dancing, singing, writing, entertainments, and any aspirations to glamour or show-business. Creativity and personal projects, even a business of one's own, as long as it offers the possibility of making a personal statement. Also publication, politics, and social life—especially if it is influential. Traditional and religious attitudes. Most of all, this house involves lovers and love affairs.

Sixth house

Duties and day-to-day service to others, usually related to work but includes those taking place in the home. Employers and employees, superiors and subordinates. Health, doctors, hospitals and hygiene—this could apply to health problems encountered by the subject himself or by those who are close to him. Clothes and how they are worn. Details and analytical methods, meticulous work, analytical thinking and even changes in one's way of thinking. Aunts and uncles. Nutrition, healthy cooking.

Seventh house

Open partnerships and relationships, husband, wife, live-in lover. Open enemies. The giving and receiving of co-operation. Colleagues at work and business partners. Work in a glamorous or attractive field. Creative and artistic endeavours which are pursued in partnership or a small group. Attraction to places, things and people, therefore to some extent even sexual attitudes and exploration.

Eighth house

Beginnings and endings. Birth and death. Sexual matters. Money which involves other people, e.g. spouse's income, mortgages, taxes, wills, legacies, banking and insurance. Above all, the partner's assets or lack of them. Shared feelings, feedback of other people's feelings (especially if they are intense). Crime and investigations and the police. Surgeons and surgery, also some illnesses. Hidden assets, secrets. Coal mining, gold mining, etc. A sense of commitment to anything or anyone. The things the subject really needs from other people. The ability to regenerate or recycle anything. Also the occult, the hidden world of the spirit.

Ninth house

Expansion of one's horizons, e.g. travel, higher education, new environments. Foreigners, foreign goods and foreign dealings. Legal matters, important legal documents and court cases. Religious and mystical matters, including the philosophical and spiritual side of psychic matters. The church and the clergy. Sports and games which are taken fairly seriously. Outdoor pursuits. Gambling (especially on horses). Interest in, or work with, large animals. Need for personal freedom. Teaching and learning of a high standard, also ethics and some aspects of public and political opinion. In-laws and grandchildren.

Tenth house

Aims and aspirations, one's goal in life, professional reputation and standing in the community. This may represent one's career, but also political ambitions, creative aspirations and future success—or lack of it. The ego and its chances of being satisfied. The employer if the subject works for a large organization. Authority figures of all kinds, including governmental and public authorities. Achievements, fame and personal promotion. The organization of the church or any large organization. The parents, especially father or father figures. Status, one's standing in the world. Responsibilities and visible commitments. Self-promotion.

Eleventh house

Social life, friends and capacity for friendship, clubs and societies. Detached relationships but also love received, even the affection of friends. Intellectual pursuits and hobbies. Hopes, wishes, desires, and goals and the chances of achieving them. Conversation, learning for pleasure. Teaching and learning of all kinds, instruction at work, political or philosophical training of a specialized kind. Money from one's job, especially if there has been training involved. Eccentricities, unexpected changes and circumstances. Step-children and adopted children.

Twelfth house

One's inner thoughts and feelings, secrets and secret worries. Suffering, sorrows, limitations, frustration and handicaps. This house can show whether the subject is his own worst enemy. It also shows inner resources and inner weaknesses or anything which is too painful to face up to. Hidden talents, hidden thoughts, hidden love, hidden angers. Inhibitions, restraints, secret enemies, hidden danger. Any association with hospitals, mental institutions, prisons and other places of confinement, even exile. Any tendency to escapism or things that we seek to hide from others. The subconscious mind, plus Karmic or spiritual debts. Self-sacrifice, love and help freely given (and possibly received). Also public charity and kindness given and received. Inspiration and insights. Illusions, meditations and day-dreams. Hidden friends and enemies. Here is where one could reach the stars or mess up one's life completely.

The Planets

Astrologers use eight planets of the solar system as well as the Sun and the Moon but excluding the Earth. It is worth noting that the Sun and Moon also are usually referred to as 'planets' in order to keep things simple.

The Sun

The Sun takes a year to circle the zodiac; it is therefore easy to plot its path. Any astrological magazine will show the dates when the Sun changes from one sign to the next. The Sun throws a friendly light onto each sign as it passes by. It only causes problems when it is opposite (180°) or square (90°) to a major planet on one's birth chart, and then only for a few days. It emphasizes each house as it travels through it but it especially emphasizes the fifth house. The Sun is associated with children and creative pursuits, fun, holidays and romance. Also pride and ambition, leadership and honour.

The Moon

The Moon takes only four weeks to complete a transit of the zodiac; its travels are therefore not much use in the simplest forms of predictive work, although it is most useful in a properly progressed chart. Eclipses of the Moon however, which occur every few months, *do* have an impact and each new and full Moon has an effect, especially if it happens to be touching a 'sore spot' on one's chart at the time.

The Moon is concerned with the inner emotions, one's reactions, responses and habitual behaviour. It represents older females, mothers or mother figures in one's life, also the home, small businesses, security, and the care of those who need us. It is associated with the sea, even one's attachment to a pet animal. Because the moon is so concerned with emotion, a full Moon can make a sensitive person quite excitable while an eclipse can bring an underlying problem to a full rolling boil! The Moon is especially powerful when new, full or eclipsed in the fourth house.

Mercury

Mercury moves quickly but any good astrological magazine will give its position each month. Mercury is concerned with communications, transport, neighbourhood matters, phone calls, telex messages and letters. It is associated with documents, business negotiations — especially sales, education and conversation. It is interesting to note that healing and magic are under the spell of Mercury. In Roman mythology Mercury was also the god of thieves! The relationships with which this planet is concerned are those of brothers, sisters, neighbours and colleagues.

Mercury is especially powerful when in the third and sixth houses. When it turns to retrograde motion, all forms of communication tend to become disrupted. (Retrograde motion comes about because all the planets, including Earth, orbit the Sun. There are times when the relative positions of the Earth and one or more of the other planets make the planets in question *appear* to be travelling backwards for a while. This *apparent* backward motion is similar to the apparent backward motion of a slow-moving train when seen from a fast-moving train.)

Venus

Venus moves very quickly, therefore it would be best to consult either an astrologer's ephemeris or a good astrological magazine in order to find its current position. Venus is concerned with values, priorities and the way one chooses to live. It rules one's possessions, personal money, goods, land, gardens (including flowers) and one's property. It is most concerned with close partnerships of all kinds such as marriage, long-term live-in arrangements and business partners. It is associated with romance, attraction and affection. On a woman's chart Venus represents women in general, but on a man's chart it signifies a special woman in his life. Venus also rules the realms of art, music, beauty, refinement and culture.

Venus brings charm, beauty, fun and enjoyable social events to all it touches, together with romance and joy. When the transits are difficult or Venus is in retrograde motion, life may be dull and money can be rather hard to come by. Venus is at its most powerful when transiting the second and seventh houses.

Mars

Mars is associated with action and assertion, aggression and achievement. Mars was the Roman god of war. Mars represents drive and energy and it energizes each house it touches. Under the influence of Mars, one can have silly (or not so silly) accidents, lose one's temper or find the energy to make something happen. Mars rules the armed forces, engineering and racing cars — in fact the kind of activities which are traditionally masculine in character. It can represent a young man on a chart and is often the special man in a woman's life.

When Mars turns to retrograde motion, it is hard to get on with things, as life seems to slow down for a while. It is at its most forceful when transiting the first and eighth houses.

Jupiter

Jupiter takes $12\frac{1}{2}$ years to travel around the Sun, therefore it spends approximately a year in each sign of the zodiac which makes it an interesting planet to use for predictions.

Jupiter is associated with a number of apparently unrelated matters. These are higher education, the law, religion, philosophy and long-distance travel. Actually the idea behind all these matters is one of *expansion* and of pushing back boundaries as far as they can go. By travel, we expand our geographical horizons; by higher education, we expand our mental horizons; and similarly by the study of religion, philosophy, mediumship, etc., we expand our spiritual horizons. The law is a system of boundaries which has been imposed by man to limit man's own actions.

Ancient astrology books tell us that Jupiter, the great *benefic*, brings money, luck and opportunity; however, while it is true that Jupiter does bring change for the better, the process may be painful. On the whole, Jupiter is more likely to affect work and finance than love and sex. However, the legal aspect of marriage and divorce can sometimes be brought to a head by a Jupiter transit. Often Jupiter will work to create a situation which becomes so uncomfortable that the subject is *forced* to make a change, but that change will inevitably broaden the subject's horizons and make him do more with his life, thereby giving him the opportunity to earn more money.

Jupiter is most effective when transiting the ninth and the twelfth houses. When travelling in retrograde motion, legal, foreign, educational, travel and financial matters will be delayed.

Saturn

Saturn takes about two years to travel through each sign, therefore its effects are very noticable. This plant represents restrictive influences. It makes the Subject learn through experience and sometimes the lessons are quite tough. The key words for this planet are *difficult circumstances* and these can range from a rather hard and somewhat boring phase to real suffering and hardship. If the subject is sufficiently philosophical in outlook, he can use difficult Saturnian phases in which to develop awareness, patience, sympathy and understanding.

The other side of Saturn brings amibition, achievement and a rise in the subject's status, even honour and renown; however, before this can be gained, the subject will have to put in several months of hard work. Saturn is most comfortable when travelling through the tenth and eleventh houses. When Saturn turns retrograde, matters related to one's aims and aspirations may be held up. The transits of Saturn are particularly depressing when it is travelling backwards and forwards across, opposite (180°) or square (90°) to a major planet somewhere on the subject's birthchart.

Uranus

This planet spends about seven years in each sign and its effect is to galvanize into action the activities of the house it is transiting. Uranus has an unpredictable effect on all it touches and it may destroy some part of the subject's life in order to make him take a fresh look and begin to rebuild. Sometimes the changes are enjoyable; moving house would be a good example, but this still involves considerable re-organization and some inevitable change in lifestyle. Uranus can also introduce the subject to novel ideas and modern technology in the form of computers and other electronic gadgetry. Uranus is most effective when transiting the eleventh house. Its retrograde motion can last for months and have a very important effect on any planet which it aspects while doing so.

Neptune

This planet spends about 11 years in each sign and its work is therefore subtle and slow to take effect. Neptune has a softening effect on all it touches and can if one is not careful cause an apparent softening of the brain! This planet is associated with dreams and illusion, the creative sort of illusion expressed in both art and photography. The illusions might be the kind which befuddle the mind such as drink, drugs, strange ailments or emotional over-sensitivity. This weird planet can alter one's outlook by subtle means by providing the subject with inspiration on the one hand, or disillusion on the other. A Neptune transit can bring a change of consciousness and a depth of awareness, which may lead the subject to abandon all his previous beliefs and walk slowly and thoughtfully away from a way of life which he has followed for years. In exceptional cases, a subject could abandon a materialistic way of life altogether in favour of something which is spiritually or artistically satisfying.

Neptune is most at home when transiting the twelfth house. It's retrograde motion is slow moving but it can have profound effects on any planets it aspects while doing so.

Pluto

This planet has an eccentric orbit which means that it can spend from 13 to 33 years in any one sign, therefore its influence is generational. It will certainly have a profound effect on any planet which it aspects on its way round the birthchart but this effect is so slow that it has to be looked at in terms of years rather than weeks or months.

Pluto is associated with one's inner feelings, particularly those which are usually kept hidden from others. It is also concerned with commitment of one kind or another; for instance, commitment to a career, a relationship or even living in a particular place. Pluto's influence can make one increasingly dissatisfied with one's current way of living. The process of reviewing one's life and making necessary changes is rather slow under the influence of Pluto but it appears to be strangely inevitable, as if the hand of Fate were ruling one rather than the application of free will.

This planet is also associated with birth and death, beginnings and endings and major changes in lifestyle. It has some bearing on the finances of other people who are close to the subject. Pluto is supposed to be most effective when transiting the eighth house but it moves so slowly that this must be looked at in the light of whole segments of one's life rather than as a weekly or monthly guide. Because of the slowness of its journey, retrograde motion is only really important when transiting a 'sore spot' on the chart, in which case it will bring profound changes in lifestyle.

Synthesis

Now let us try to put it all together. Here are two examples:

1. Pluto through the ninth house

Pluto has the slowest orbit of all the planets which means that it will remain several years in any one house. During the time that Pluto spends in the ninth house, the subject could expect to review many aspects of his life and to make some long-term changes. He will review his religious and philosophical outlook and could change his beliefs completely. There will definitely be some kind of inward journey and a dramatic growth of spiritual and psychic awareness.

There will be an interest in higher education which may lead the subject either to educate himself or to become involved in the world of education. He may feel a need to reform educational, political or legal matters in his locality; this urge could attract him to public work of some kind. There will be an interest in travel and the subject could actually go to live in another country. This transit often brings involvement with foreigners, foreign goods and the export market in some way.

The subject may become involved with the law (even the *wrong* side of the law) under this transit. Suspect occult practices are another possibility, but whatever he becomes interested in, he must try to avoid becoming so obsessed by fanatical ideas that he drives his friends and family away from him.

2. A Subject who has Aquarius rising and Mercury transiting his tenth house

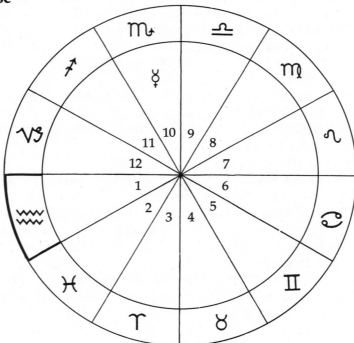

In this case the tenth house is ruled by the sign of Scorpio. With Mercury transiting this house, the Subject will be going through a particularly busy time when he will be furthering his career and concentrating on the outward aspects of his life, his authority and his status in the world. We can also see in this case that his career is coloured by a Scorpio influence. This suggests that, even without any planets transiting this house, his work would be particularly important to him. His job would probably involve supplying some kind of absolute necessity to the public. He could work in the fields of medicine, the police or some other kind of essential service. Other possibilities might be engineering, the money market, weaponry, even the slaughter of animals, and also the mining industry. There is an obsessive air about the sign of Scorpio, and this would lead our subject to be very determined in respect of his aims and ambitions. Therefore, a Mercury transit through this particular house and sign would be very significant.

The transit of Mercury in a case like this would tell us that the Subject will be travelling more than usual and contacting a number of people in connection with his work. It is possible that colleagues, neighbours and even relatives could become involved in his outer world for a while at this time. He will have to organize his mind and his paperwork, deal with documents and technicalities. Another possibility is that he could have to change his usual travel arrangements, even to the point of buying a new vehicle in connection with his work.

Table of the Movements of the Outer Planets

The slower-moving planets are the ones which have the most impact on one's life. The faster-moving inner planets of Venus, Mercury, and especially the Moon, move very quickly and, therefore, cannot be included in this short guide. Because of their speed of movement, they don't have the same kind of effect on one's life. The Moon, for instance, travels round the zodiac once every 28 days. Any good astrological magazine will show the positions of these planets in any month and it is often possible to buy a magazine at the beginning of the year which will show all the planetary movements for the year ahead. If you need more information, your local astrologer will be pleased to advise you.

THE PLANET **THE SIGN**

Pluto

Jan 1988 to Jan 1995	Scorpio
Feb 1995 to Apr 1995	Sagittarius
May 1995 to Nov 1995	Scorpio
Dec 1995 to end 2000	Sagittarius

Neptune

Jan 1988 to Mar 1998	Capricorn
Apr 1998 to Jul 1998	Aquarius
Aug 1998 to Jan 1999	Capricorn
Feb 1999 to end 2000	Aquarius

THE PLANET	THE SIGN

Uranus

Jan 1988 to Feb 1988	Sagittarius
Mar 1988 to Jun 1988	Capricorn
Jul 1988 to Nov 1988	Sagittarius
Dec 1988 to Mar 1995	Capricorn
Apr 1995 to Jun 1995	Aquarius
Jul 1995 to Jan 1996	Capricorn
Feb 1996 to end 2000	Aquarius

Saturn

Jan 1988 to Feb 1988	Sagittarius
Mar 1988 to Jun 1988	Capricorn
Jul 1988 to Nov 1988	Sagittarius
Dec 1988 to Jan 1991	Capricorn
Feb 1991 to May 1993	Aquarius
Jun 1993 to Jul 1993	Pisces
Aug 1993 to Jan 1994	Aquarius
Feb 1994 to Apr 1996	Pisces
May 1996 to Jun 1998	Aries
Jul 1998 to Oct 1998	Taurus
Nov 1998 to Mar 1999	Aries
Apr 1999 to Aug 2000	Taurus
Sep 2000 to Oct 2000	Gemini
Nov 2000 to end 2000	Taurus

Jupiter

Jan 1988 to Mar 1988	Aries
Apr 1988 to Jul 1988	Taurus
Aug 1988 to Dec 1988	Gemini
Jan 1989 to Mar 1989	Taurus
Apr 1989 to Jul 1989	Gemini
Aug 1989 to Aug 1990	Cancer
Sep 1990 to Sep 1991	Leo
Oct 1991 to Oct 1992	Virgo
Nov 1992 to Nov 1993	Libra
Dec 1993 to Dec 1994	Scorpio
Jan 1995 to Dec 1995	Sagittarius
Jan 1996 to Jan 1997	Capricorn
Feb 1987 to Feb 1998	Aquarius
Mar 1998 to Feb 1999	Pisces
Apr 1999 to Jun 1999	Aries
Jul 1999 to Oct 1999	Taurus
Dec 1999 to Feb 2000	Aries
Mar 2000 to Jun 2000	Taurus
Jul 2000 to end 2000	Gemini

Mars

	Jan	Feb	Mar	Apr	May	Jun	Jul	Aug	Sep	Oct	Nov	Dec
1988	Sc	Sg	Cp	Cp	Aq	Pi	Pi	Ar	Ar	Ar	Pi	Ar
1989	Ar	Ta	Ta	Ge	Ca	Ca	Le	Le	Vi	Li	Li	Sc
1990	Sg	Cp	Cp	Aq	Pi	Ar	Ar	Ta	Ge	Ge	Ge	Ge
1991	Ta	Ge	Ge	Ca	Ca	Le	Le	Vi	Li	Li	Sc	Sg
1992	Sg	Cp	Aq	Pi	Pi	Ar	Ta	Ge	Ge	Ca	Ca	Ca
1993	Ca	Ca	Ca	Ca	Le	Le	Vi	Vi	Li	Sc	Sc	Sg
1994	Cp	Aq	Aq	Pi	Ar	Ta	Ta	Ge	Ca	Ca	Le	Le
1995	Vi	Le	Le	Le	Le	Vi	Vi	Li	Li	Sc	Sg	Cp
1996	Cp	Aq	Pi	Ar	Ta	Ta	Ge	Ca	Ca	Le	Vi	Vi
1997	Vi	Li	Li	Vi	Vi	Li	Li	Sc	Sg	Sg	Sg	Cp
1998	Aq	Pi	Pi	Ar	Ta	Ge	Ge	Ca	Le	Le	Vi	Li
1999	Li	Sc	Sc	Sc	Sc	Li	Li	Sc	Sg	Sg	Cp	Aq
2000	Aq	Pi	Ar	Ta	Ta	Ge	Ca	Le	Le	Vi	Vi	Li

6.

Dice

Geomancy Method

This is rather like the system used in the Oracle of Napoleon shown in chapter 3. This is how it works:

1 The Reader gives the Querent a list of questions. The Querent selects the question which he would like answered.

2 The dice are thrown and the sum of the numbers on the two dice are noted down.

3 A sheaf of lists is taken out of the file (there are eleven of these separate lists in the file).

4 The list which has the same number as the sum of numbers on the dice is scrutinized.

5 The number which corresponds to the chosen question is found on the answer list and the answer read out to the Querent.

Colour Code Method

This method is fairly recent in origin. Several sets of different coloured dice are used and the combinations of dice and colours are used to give the answers.

The Simplest Method

This is the oldest method of reading dice. Two dice are thrown and the meaning of the sum of their numbers can be looked up on a list. I have set out a reasonably comprehensive list below but the list in the domino section, Chapter 13, can also be used when the Reader fancies a change.

Layout
The dice can merely be thrown onto a table and the list of interpretations

read off. It is helpful to prepare a piece of paper divided into sections something like the drawing shown below. A more comprehensive drawing can be obtained by using the astrological houses which are either drawn out on a circular background or a series of twelve blocks. (The houses are fully explained in the chapter on Predictive Astrology.)

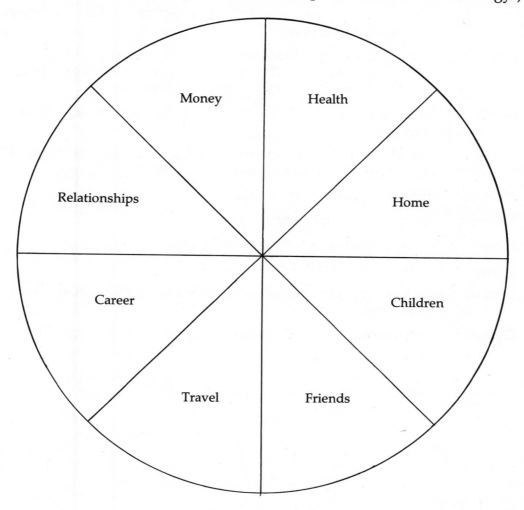

Suggestions for dice divination categories

The list of meanings

Two   A partnership—this could be business or personal; it will need working at but it should be successful.

Three   Joy, celebration, a wish fulfilled; good news.

Four   Security, putting down roots, rest and recuperation.

Five   Trouble and strife, arguments, losses and illnesses.

Six	Change—either back to a past situation or onwards to a different lifestyle.
Seven	Forward movement in events, end of muddle, slow growth.
Eight	Worry, stress, maybe a new job or a new environment.
Nine	Good family life, comfort, satisfaction, safety, money coming to the Querent.
Ten	Great success in all things, money, love and health. If the other omens are bad, this throw can reverse itself and bring the total loss of success, money, love, health, etc.
Eleven	News coming, small events which might lead to larger ones later on.
Twelve	Travel, visitors from overseas perhaps; a new vehicle or a new means of transport is also likely.
Thirteen	Help from an influential woman.
Fourteen	Help from an influential man.
Fifteen	A fresh start, something new begins.
Sixteen	A partnership will be successful.
Seventeen	Success in love affairs, but career matters will cause problems.
Eighteen	Promotion, money, happiness in love; all-round good luck.

7.

The I Ching

The I Ching is known as the 'Book of Changes' and it appears to date back at least 5,300 years. The Chinese use a variety of methods for I Ching divination, but the most popular method in use is by means of yarrow sticks which look a bit like spills or children's 'pick-up sticks'. Another method is to use special I Ching coins. These coins have the traditional hole in the middle so that they can be kept safely on a string around the neck or attached to a belt; they also have a combination of markings on them which look like the hexagrams shown here:

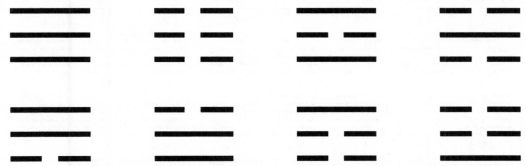

If you haven't the correct I Ching coins, ordinary coins will do but a few throws will have to be made in order to work out whether you have chosen the straight lines of Yang or the broken ones of Yin and in what order they are placed.

Ordinary Coins

The first thing to do is to think of a question which you would like answered. Then take three coins, shake them in your hands for a moment and then thrown them on to a table. If the majority of coins fall with their heads upwards, these would represent Yang, a solid line, but if they fall mainly with the tails upwards, you will have Yin, a broken line. Draw a picture of the line you have obtained from throwing the coins onto a piece of paper, this will be the bottom line of your hexagram. Throw once again and draw a picture of the resulting line above the first. Continue this process until you have drawn six lines and then look up the pattern which you have drawn to find the answer to your question.

Table of Modern I Ching

1	2	3	4	5	6	7	8

9	10	11	12	13	14	15	16

17	18	19	20	21	22	23	24

25	26	27	28	29	30	31	32

33	34	35	36	37	38	39	40

41	42	43	44	45	46	47	48

49	50	51	52	53	54	55	56

57	58	59	60	61	62	63	64

The Answers to the Hexagrams

When you have found the number of the hexagram, look it up in the list of answers. (This is, of course, a very abbreviated form of the I Ching. In addition to making a précis, I have also anglicized the answers in order to make them easy to understand. The I Ching, when seen in its complete form, is poetic and full of symbolism.)

1

Work hard to gain your objectives but don't overreach yourself.

2

To some extent, your future happiness is in the hands of others so don't rush in and grab at it for yourself.

3

Expect to reach your goals in a slow and steady manner. Other people will give you help and guidance.

4

Take advice and expect to learn slowly. Don't put on airs and graces but be ready to listen to the wisdom of others.

5

There is danger ahead. Don't plunge into anything, wait until times are better. When you *do* begin to make a move forward, there will be friends around who will help you.

6

Although you are probably in the right, this is not a good time to argue or to state your point. Accept criticism, even a lack of credit for work done just for the moment. Things will soon improve.

7

You will soon have to face some kind of battle but others will be there to help you. Whether you fight or retreat is for you to decide, but you will receive some kind of guidance.

8

Peace and harmony surround you now. Be sincere in all you do and expect to make some efforts on behalf of others, as well as for yourself.

9

Times may be hard for a while but with a sensible and economic approach you will achieve your aims and then you will appreciate all the more the good things when they arrive. Restraint, sincerity and regard for others will be needed.

10

Be firm, even with yourself. Tread the straight and narrow road. Don't hesitate or others will take advantage of you and you will lose your stride.

11

Share your happiness and good fortune with others who are less well off. This should be a time to get things done; to plant for the future or harvest from the past.

12

Move forward slowly and carefully; from small beginnings, you can make small growth but be careful to do this in a modest manner. Doors will soon open for you.

13

There is light at the end of the tunnel. You will soon be able to make better progress and pass from obscurity into a brighter and more successful future. Success will be yours but you should share the benefits of this with others in order to help them.

14

Work and study will go together. By learning or training, you will be in a better position to understand how to tackle the tasks ahead of you. Don't go overboard in trying to impress others, just grasp the basics and work at the job quietly.

15

Be modest—this will encourage others to help you rather than to stand in your way. You will need their help to grow and they will admire you for your progress as long as you don't push it down their throats.

16

You will need to advertise both yourself and your wares and to create an enthusiastic atmosphere. Avoid arrogance or self-satisfaction as this will put others off your ideas—don't fall for your own propaganda.

17

This is a time to drift with the current and to let others show you the way or take the initiative on your behalf. You will be in charge of your own affairs again soon enough.

18

You will have to put right something which is wrong, possibly apologize or sort out some kind of misunderstanding. Be scrupulously honest in all your dealings now—be *seen* to be in the right.

19

In the recent past it was right for you to assert yourself in order to get where you are now, but now is the time to be magnamimous. Be cautious and advance slowly forward. Be generous to others.

20

You will need to keep your eyes open in practical matters, and also to contemplate wider philosophical issues. Don't take things on trust—be penetrative and intuitive.

21

Be careful to stress any positive achievements which you have made, however small they may be. Don't let others stress the negative or unsuccessful aspects of your life. Don't let petty jealousy in others get you down.

22

Dress well and look successful in order to sell an idea to others or to give an appearance of success, but once you have accomplished your aim don't continue to live beyond your means. Contemplation and solitude will be necessary to bring equilibrium soon.

23

The odds are against you now. Some aspect of your life will be destroyed so that you can build afresh for the future. Guard against a situation where you are undermined from the inside by people who are close to you.

24

Attune yourself to nature and to the seasons and develop a sense of timing. A change of seasons will bring improvements and a renewal of energy. Be patient.

25

Don't rush in where angels fear to tread. Be honest and stay within your own limitations; heaven will guide you. Be unselfish and simple and don't let temporary setbacks upset you.

26

You will make great advances in your career, but probably not just yet. Work hard and progress slowly, for success in on the way to you.

30

Intellectual pursuits will go well. An intellectual and logical approach to life would be helpful now.

31

Don't envy those who seem to be cleverer or more successful than you are. Remember, the bigger they are, the harder they fall.

32

Stay put, persevere and allow things to take their course. Hastiness will bring problems. Don't insist on having things all your own way; a casual attitude would be far better. Wait, be yourself and you will get all that you want.

33

There are crafty people around you who will seek to take advantage. Watch out for traps and don't fall into them. However, you will have to use some guile yourself in order to slide out of any tricky situations.

34

If you have to use strong words, back them up with meaningful action otherwise no one will take you seriously and you will be seen as an empty blusterer.

35

Your situation is improving rapidly and your fortunes are on the up and up. Be honest in all your dealings and also be open so that jealous people will not be able to point fingers at you later.

36

When depression and hard times arrive, be cautious and restrained but don't allow yourself to be ground down by misery. Wait—things *will* improve. Just do what you have to do and refrain from moaning to others about your troubles.

37

Attend to your normal daily duties and make your present surroundings comfortable and your present situation happier. Deal with problems right away rather than trying to escape from them. The accent will be on family life where you will have to be fair but also tolerant.

38

Don't insist that you are right; be flexible and allow some leeway to others. Even if you *know* you are right, don't ram the fact down the throats of others.

39

If you have a problem, try to go around it rather than moan about it. Alternatively, you can go out on a limb to solve it. Get help from others and also help others where you can because one day you may be facing the same troubles which they now have.

40

An acute situation could come to a head now, after which you will at least know where you stand. Free yourself from unnecessary encumbrances so that you are in a position to move forward confidently.

41

When others have helped you to get on, don't keep all the proceeds to yourself. Redistribute some of the goodies so that everyone benefits.

42

Take the most of any opportunity which comes your way but realize that a good deal of your success will be due to luck rather than your own cleverness. It is worth bearing in mind that, at times like these, even an incompetent idiot can succeed.

43

Some form of insurance may be necessary now, as even the best placed of people can run into trouble. Don't allow evil to destroy the things which have been good up to now.

44

Don't be influenced by others, especially if they are stronger than you are. Calm persuasion will help you to influence other people both near and far.

45

You will be faced by opposition soon. Don't tackle this head-on or make yourself unpopular by opening your mouth too much. Go with the crowd or, if that is not possible, find one ally and stick to him.

46

Progress slowly and steadily now. Don't give up—just move steadily onwards and upwards.

47

There will be hard times soon. Don't run away from them but look within yourself and find the strength to cope with them. Adversity can sometimes be a good thing as it brings out abilities which you never realized you had. Have confidence—don't beat your head against the wall; stay calm and cope as well as you can with things.

48

Work will be monotonous but it has to be done. Share any benefits that you have accrued with others, but watch that they don't take the credit for your efforts or place difficulties in your way.

49

Your outer manner and presentation are going to improve and you will soon begin to look more impressive to others.

50

Whatever you are doing, take care to make sure your tools, equipment and vehicles are working properly. Don't worry about small mishaps but guard against major ones.

51

There will be stormy weather ahead. Don't panic, just wait until it passes and then reassess your situation.

52

Take things easily and progress slowly along your present path. Don't try to take on any unnecessary gambles or any more difficult jobs than you are already coping with.

53

Develop slowly. Your progress may be imperceptible to others but it is there nevertheless.

54

If you cannot get what you want, want what you can get. If you demand too much you could find yourself overburdened with responsibilities, whereas if you do well in what you are engaged upon right now, you will be appreciated all the more. More opportunity will shortly come your way.

55
You will be inwardly happy and troubles on the outside will not be able to harm you. They will pass away rapidly.

56
You may have to travel soon or have to sell yourself in some way to others, for instance by going out to get a new job. Look to your manner and your appearance and be careful with whom you associate at this time.

57
Be reasonable and your ideas will be accepted by others. Bend with the wind and go along with the majority opinion for the time being.

58
Inner contentment will be reflected outwardly to others and outer harmony will generate inner peace. In other words, a strong spiritual centre will be reflected back by others.

59
Don't be inflexible and allow your opinions to harden. On the other hand, don't allow them to dissolve into nothing either. Be reasonable.

60
You will need to be cautious and to accept certain limitations soon. Reserves of energy, goods or money will be needed while you sit out a difficult situation. When doors are once again open to you, you will be able to move forward through them. In the meantime, go by the rules—even if they are someone else's.

61
Watch out for warning signs; there will be stormy weather ahead.

62
Don't lose your way when storms arrive but make for a safe perch. Don't waste your energy or get in a flap needlessly.

63
You have gone through considerable troubles to get where you are now, so don't lose all that you have gained through stupidity. Try not to look backwards too much because your circumstances are changing so you will soon be able to be more optimistic. Work to consolidate what you have achieved so far in order to build for the future.

64
Move forward cautiously, keeping your eyes and ears open. Experience will count for much now. Wait for the right moment to make your move but, even then, do so with care and caution.

8.

Tarot Cards

The Origins of the Cards

Such evidence as there is about the origins of Tarot cards points to them being carried westwards by migrating gypsies who came from those areas which we now know as Pakistan, Afghanistan and northern India. The cards reached Italy and France by the fourteenth century and subsequently took on overtones of medieval and rennaisance court life. Tarot cards were originally used both for fortune-telling and for game playing, and even today a form of Tarot is still used in France, Italy and Spain as an alternative to conventional playing cards. The type of playing cards with which we are familiar today developed from the Minor Arcana of the Tarot, while the pieces which are used in the game of chess developed from figures which appear in both the Major and the Minor Arcana.

The composition of the Tarot deck
A pack of Tarot cards contains two sections called the Major and the Minor Arcana. The Minor Arcana of the Tarot has four suits which consist of Cups, Swords, Staves (also known as Wands or Rods) and Coins (also called Pentacles). These are similar to the Hearts, Spades, Clubs and Diamonds in a deck of playing cards. Each suit has an Ace, a set of numbered cards from two to ten, plus four court cards. Most Tarot decks have a King, Queen, Knight and Page although some decks have a King, Queen, Prince and Princess. The most obvious difference between Tarot and playing cards is the addition of twenty-two trump cards which are known as the Major Arcana. The only remnant of these trump cards which exists in ordinary playing cards is the Joker which is the equivalent of the Tarot Fool. Tarot decks are still used for game playing in southern Europe, and these are composed of the Minor Arcana only, with the addition of a Fool or Joker card. They are smaller in size and generally less pictorial than the usual Tarot deck.

For a reading using upright and reversed cards
The Questioner cuts the cards into three decks
and then chooses one of them.

The Reader turns the deck which the Questioner has chosen.

The end which was nearest to the Questioner must be placed nearest
to the Reader.

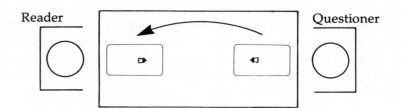

Ritual and procedure

Tarot cards which are to be used for divination should be kept safely, preferably in a special box. Some Tarot Readers keep the cards wrapped in a piece of silk as this is supposed to keep them safe from harmful influences. I don't use a silk scarf for my cards, but merely keep them in a cigar box. When you want to give a reading to your Questioner, ask him to shuffle the cards and cut them into three piles, preferably using his left hand. You can, if you wish, reverse the direction of one of the three piles of cards for him. Then ask him to put all the cards back into one pile in any order he likes. Take the cards from him, and as you do so, turn the end which was nearest to him so that it is now nearest to you. Now, you are ready to lay out the cards.

Spreads

There are many Tarot spreads; quite a number of these are demonstrated in my book *Tarot in Action*, which shows real life readings just as they happened. Some very spiritually-evolved Readers use spreads which have come to them during their meditations, while others use those which feel most comfortable to them. It is best to experiment a bit until something clicks into place for you.

Different levels of use and understanding

In this book, I am going to offer only a very brief sketch of each card. For futher information of the kind which would be suitable for a complete beginner please refer to my book *Fortune-Telling by Tarot Cards*. For those of you who are looking for something deeper and more meaningful than the bare bones of divination, I highly recommend a two-book set called the *Seventy-eight Degrees of Wisdom* by Rachel Pollack. Rachel's book brings a depth and spirituality to the cards which is helpful to even the most professional of Readers, whereas my own book is best suited to the total beginner who needs basic help and information.

Upright or reversed?

I have given both the upright and the reversed meanings in this book but many Readers prefer to use them in the upright position only whilst still bearing in mind their negative or reversed qualities.

When using both upright and reversed cards, you will notice that in most cases the reversal modifies the upright card a little, making splendid cards a little more ordinary while easing the effects of the really nasty ones. However, there are a few cards which are quite different in meaning when they are reversed.

The Minor Arcana

The court cards

The court cards are confusing to a beginner because they can represent either people or situations in a reading. Even when one reads the court cards exclusively as *people*, problems arise. How does one distinguish between one person and another? Some people associate the four suits with the Sun signs or rising signs of the zodiac (see chapter 5):

Cups   The *Water* signs of Cancer, Scorpio, and Pisces.

Staves   The *Fire* signs of Aries, Leo, and Sagittarius.

Swords   The *Air* signs of Gemini, Libra, and Aquarius.

Coins   The *Earth* signs of Taurus, Virgo, and Capricorn.

Some people associate the court cards of the four suits with a particular colour of hair or complexion:

Cups   Blonde

Staves   Light or dark brown hair

Swords   Very dark hair or alternatively, very blonde hair

Coins   Dark hair or grey hair

To be honest, I use a formula of my own making and even then, like all good Tarot Readers, I deviate from it! Sometimes I will use the idea of skin and hair colouring but at other times, I divide the cards into personality types, roughly as follows:

Cups   Kindly, emotional, sensual and rather greedy.

Staves   Good communicators, good company, but possibly inclined to tell lies or to be unreliable.

Swords   Decisive, outwardly cool, intellectual, well-qualified and apparently hard as nails, but often vulnerable underneath.

Coins   Practical, kindly, sensible, thoughtful, stick-in-the-mud and far too money-minded.

Please, please, do develop your own ideas. Remember the first rule of Tarot, 'if it *feels* right, it *is* right'.

The court cards as situations
It is rare for a King or a Queen to represent a situation. However, if a King or Queen card which doesn't seem to work out as a personality shows up in a reading, then it might be worth trying to assess the 'feel' of the card in terms of a situation.

Kings represent maturity and steady progress, dignity and achievement. Queens would represent much the same but with a feminine, supportive element added—this could suggest an advantageous alliance of some kind. Knights and Pages do often represent situations, the Knights suggesting movement and change in the life of the questioner while the Pages suggest the arrival of news and information. They also tend to herald the beginning or the ending of some circumstance. For a quick reference, think of the Cups for emotional matters, Staves for day-to-day matters, Swords for special action and Coins for the larger financial issues.

The suit of Cups

The suit of Cups is associated with romance, marriage and, to some extent, one's personal possessions. Cups also suggest warmth, friendship, happy working partnerships, and even the love of a pet. Educational and artistic matters are also associated with Cup cards.

The Ace of Cups
The beginning of love, affection, and friendship. A gift, perhaps a ring. Joyful news, possibly the birth of a child.
Reversed meaning
Friendship rather than passion, the possible ending of a romance.

Two of Cups
A successful relationship or a happy working partnership. Possibly some kind of reconciliation.
Reversed meaning
A parting, or the fizzling-out of a relationship which never really got off the ground.

Three of Cups
A wedding, either for the Questioner himself or in his family. Celebration, joy, childbirth, parties and fun.
Reversed meaning
Could herald a parting, divorce, or the failure of a romance to take off. There could still be parties and amusements, even flirtation and affairs, but not marriage.

Four of Cups
Dissatisfaction, because the Questioner may not appreciate what he already has, but is seeking something else. To some extent also a search for something new. The Questioner has friendship but he really wants love.
Reversed meaning
New friends and new experiences are on the way. Enlightenment and more satisfaction in life.

Five of Cups
Loss and sadness, but something is left from which the questioner can begin to re-build his life.
Reversed meaning
A sense of loss is passing; better times are ahead.

Six of Cups
Past skills and past associations will have meaning or will become useful again in the future. Family gatherings, probably with children around.
Reversed meaning
A time to look forward and put the past behind one. A pre-planned family celebration would not be too successful.

Seven of Cups
A period of muddle as there are so many options open that it is hard to choose. If money is a stumbling block to a romance, this difficulty will soon be overcome.
Reversed meaning
The end of a period of confusion.

Eight of Cups
The end of a miserable time, also turning one's back on trouble and moving slowly forward. A blonde woman may prove helpful.
Reversed meaning
A definite end to a bad time; fun and celebrations are ahead.

Nine of Cups
Satisfaction and possibly a touch of smugness. Possible marriage to a mature person.
Reversed meaning
Reasonable success and some satisfaction. If something hasn't worked out well, then the Questioner should try again, as it should come right soon.

Ten of Cups
The 'wish card' of love, joy, happiness and all prayers being answered. Happiness for the family; a birth is possible.
Reversed meaning
Happiness and contentment. Family life could be unsettled for a while. In extreme cases, this card could mean divorce (look at the surrounding cards for further evidence).

Page of Cups
A gentle, loving, and very sensitive youngster. A time to study and to reflect. Business matters will proceed slowly but surely.
Reversed meaning
Difficulties concerning a sensitive child. A time to grit one's teeth and get on with studies or work.

Knight of Cups
A kindly, good natured, youngish or immature type of man. Changes in relationships, love may be aproaching or departing. A lover or husband may travel soon.
Reversed meaning
Love is fading because someone cannot or will not commit himself.

Queen of Cups
A woman will bring love, comfort, and friendship to the Questioner. She is kind and generous, but also materialistic and lazy.
Reversed meaning
A woman may be disappointed in love or unable to express her feelings freely. She may be materialistic, jealous and greedy, or temporarily difficult due to feelings of hurt.

King of Cups
A kindly, emotional, man who cares for the Questioner. He has a complex character which makes him optimistic and exciting but possibly dogmatic and dictatorial. He is sensual, loving, fond of children and all the good things of life.
Reversed meaning
A caring and well-meaning man, who is either not interested in a relationship at this time or is not free to commit himself. Jealous and possessive or lazy and unreliable.

The suit of Staves
The suit of Staves (or Wands or Rods) is associated with negotiations which may be related to business matters, social or political clubs, neighbourhood events or family matters. Some Staves suggest overseas travel, while others imply local travel. Property dealings or home renovations are often indicated. Creativity, especially in the form of words is represented here, as are challenges, new processes and an air of optimism.

Ace of Staves
The birth of an idea, or even of a child. Exciting new opportunities of any kind.
Reversed meaning
New beginnings, but either delayed or with problems attached.

Two of Staves
A partnership or relationship which is based on joint interests and activities. Sometimes this card indicates a move of house. A proud man who has achieved much may be around the Questioner.
Reversed meaning
Delays in the sale of property. Partnership problems. A proud man may cause problems. Unexpected news may be on the way.

Three of Staves
New projects, a new job, good news coming. There could be travel in connection with work. Partnerships and relationships will go well in the future.
Reversed meaning
Wait and try again later because this is not a good time to get

anything new off the ground. Current difficulties will continue for a while longer.

Four of Staves
Security, especially where premises are concerned; a feeling of putting down roots. A house move soon, a holiday home is also possible.
Reversed meaning
Similar to above but delayed. Delays in the sale of any property or premises.

Five of Staves
A challenge or struggle, but the effort is worth it and may even be enjoyable. Courage will be needed. Travel plans may be delayed.
Reversed meaning
Delays, legal problems. Try again another time.

Six of Staves
Victory, achievement, problems overcome. Any delays will now end, negotiations and legal matters will be successful.
Reversed meaning
Other people will affect the Questioner adversely. Someone may win some kind of battle against the Questioner. Other adverse effects could come from other people's bad workmanship or delaying tactics. Leave things and try again another time.

Seven of Staves
Problems which can be tackled separately and overcome. These may include health, obstructive people or money, but they will pass soon.
Reversed meaning
Too many awkward problems now. The Questioner should sort out the worst of them and avoid taking on any more responsibilities for the time being. A potentially embarrassing situation to come.

Eight of Staves
Travel and a broadening of one's horizons. Friendship and even love could be on the way.
Reversed meaning
Cancelled plans. It would be better to stay on familiar ground. Public events, such as strike action, could affect the Questioner's actions soon. The Questioner might find himself feeling jealous of somebody; conversely, someone may be jealous and spiteful towards the Questioner himself.

Nine of Staves
The questioner is in a reasonably secure position but he must be alert. Most problems are behind him but prudence is still required.
Reversed meaning
Loss of status or position. Illness coming.

Ten of Staves
Burdens and responsibilities but the effort is worthwhile.
Reversed meaning
Onerous burdens can soon be put down. Responsibilities which the Questioner is pleased to be given, such as a promotion at work, could well be on the way now.

Page of Staves
A bright and rather restless child. A journey, visitors, letters and phone calls. Minor property matters will go smoothly now. Writing could become important in some way soon.
Reversed meaning
Problems regarding a child. Delays in negotiations or travels. Possibly sad news.

Knight of Staves
A friendly and intelligent young man. An interest in communications work of some kind or contacts with teachers. Visitors, house moves, correspondence and travel. A lively atmosphere.
Reversed meaning
A pleasant and intelligent young man will prove to be insincere. Setbacks with regard to property matters, negotiations and journeys.

Queen of Staves
A charming and clever woman, good companion, highly-sexed and a good business woman who has a definite mind of her own. She may lack confidence at times or be too quick to rush into things. A good friend.
Reversed meaning
This lady is either not in a position to do much for the Questioner or she is basically unreliable and untrustworthy.

King of Staves
An attractive man who has a nice smile, and good body. Amusing and interesting, a good communicator and teacher. Helpful in a working relationship but possibly slightly detached emotionally.
Reversed meaning
At worst, a cunning liar, a slippery customer. He could be well intentioned but not willing or able to put himself out for the Questioner. Great fun possibly, but no good for a deep relationship.

The suit of Swords
Sword cards indicate trouble and strife and problems which require action to be taken. Even if there are no problems as such, some kind of decisive action will be needed. Swords also suggest authority figures, people with special qualifications plus sadness, loss, betrayal and health problems. Courage will be needed when Sword Cards appear.

Ace of Swords
The beginning of a situation which will require concentration and effort. Deep feelings will be aroused either in the realms of theory or even due to physical passion. Power and justice are on the way soon.
Reversed meaning
Similar to above but milder and not so all-absorbing. Potential delays when putting new theories or business ideas into practice. Sudden health problems, may be on the way, injections and even operations are possible. The Questioner may over-react to some kind of situation.

Two of Swords
Stalemate, no change yet; possibly a reluctance to make change.
Reversed meaning
The end of stalemate; things will shortly begin to move. The Questioner will feel more like making changes now.

Three of Swords
Loss or heartache. Possible health problems, especially the heart, arteries and circulation system.
Reversed meaning
Heartache is passing away and the Questioner is learning to cope. Minor illness. Possibility of a funeral to attend.

Four of Swords
Rest and recuperation; recovery from illness or worries. Possibly a period of time spent in hospital, but with beneficial results.
Reversed meaning
Health may be continue to be worrying for a while yet. Otherwise, financial recovery.

Five of Swords
Quarrels, possibly violence, jealousy and partings. Someone may leave to go overseas. Jealousy and spite coming to the Questioner.
Reversed meaning
Similar to above but passing out of the Questioner's life. The Questioner may attend a funeral shortly.

Six of Swords
Travel over water; a journey may be a turning point. Visitors from overseas. A gradual improvement due to the Questioner moving on in some way.
Reversed meaning
Journeys will be delayed. Financial losses due to carelessness.

Seven of Swords
Legal or business advice. The Questioner may have to cut his losses and move on. In some circumstances this could indicate a robbery or fraud.

Reversed meaning
Advice coming soon, but beware of thieves.

Eight of Swords
The Questioner is temporarily tied down and cannot see how to change his circumstances.
Reversed meaning
Restrictions will lift soon. There may be accidents, disappointments. Someone close to the Questioner could be going into prison.

Nine of Swords
Illness, possibly miscarriage. Family problems, possibly a mother figure worrying about others in the family or causing others to worry about her.
Reversed meaning
Sleepless nights will soon come to an end. There could be unpleasant rumours and scandal soon.

Ten of Swords
Treachery and betrayal, a stab in the back. Loss, death, divorce—the ending of a situation.
Reversed meaning
Hard times will end soon. Minor disappointment. Someone may slander the Questioner. Bad times will pass away soon.

Page of Swords
An active, sporty, intelligent child. The Questioner must keep his eyes open, as there may soon be news of an opportunity or an unexpected problem around the corner. A contract or document to be signed. There may be some advice from someone who keeps his eyes open.
Reversed meaning
Problems regarding an aggressive or unsettled child. Arguments and even scandal; someone may be spying on the Questioner. Disappointments and delays regarding contracts or business documents.

Knight of Swords
A tough, brave, and very intelligent young man may help the Questioner. Sudden changes and decisions to be taken soon; things may move a little *too* quickly. New ideas and theories to be worked on.
Reversed meaning
An aggressive, destructive, or unstable man may be around the Questioner. Arguments or disputes are likely; quick decisions will have to be taken. Medical or legal matters will have to be faced soon.

Queen of Swords
A sharp, clever, highly-qualified woman who demands respect.

Professional help with clear, cool, unsentimental advice being offered.
Reversed meaning
This lady is sharp, unpleasant and possibly jealous of the Questioner. If this card does *not* represent a person, spite and jealousy could be on the way. Another possibility is that the Questioner could be pitting his wits against a professional adversary who may or may not be female.

King of Swords
Possibly a thin-faced, sharp-featured man. Whatever he looks like, he will be clever and well-qualified. Help could come from a doctor or lawyer who will help the Questioner through serious problems. Enlightenment, interesting theories and professional advice could come soon.
Reversed meaning
An aggressive man who wants to stir up trouble. Even if this person is not actually evil, he will not be able to help the Questioner just now. Also, a possible encounter with a professional adversary.

The suit of Coins
The suit of Coins is associated with money, goods, services, the organization of work and business. Status, possessions, land, property and larger financial issues are also indicated by the Coin cards.

Ace of Coins
Money coming; perhaps a win, bonus or increase in salary. Possibly a better job and a rise in status. Good news about money or a fresh start involving money.
Reversed meaning
Same as above but less important.

Two of Coins
Separation of resources; this may involve juggling with time or money, or borrowing from Peter to pay Paul. The financial workings of a divorce or some other kind of financial separation.
Reversed meaning
Similar to above but the problem may be passing now.

Three of Coins
Buying or renovating property and also successful use of skills and being encouraged at work. A good new start.
Reversed meaning
Similar to above, but delayed or beset with problems. There may be too much work for the Questioner to handle.

Four of Coins
Financial security is on the way but there may be too much emphasis on money in the Questioner's mind at this time. The outlook is good.

Reversed meaning
Delays in payment; a lack of security. Examination failures.

Five of Coins
Loss and loneliness and a feeling of being left out in the cold. Financial problems. Oddly enough, affairs and light-hearted romance will go well.
Reversed meaning
Loss and loneliness will end soon.

Six of Coins
Money will have to be paid out or shared out soon. This may be due to divorce or some other kind of parting. The Questioner may buy some expensive item but this should be worthwhile. Others may drain the Questioner or prey too much on his good nature.
Reversed meaning
Similar to above but any problems will pass soon. Could herald the end of a series of hire purchase payments.

Seven of Coins
Slow growth and steady achievement. Work which brings satisfaction rather than monetary gain.
Reversed meaning
A period of hard work will end soon. Frankly, it is not worth battling on now. Wait and try again later.

Eight of Coins
A new job or promotion. A new skill to be learned.
Reversed meaning
Problems at work; loss of job. An unwillingness to learn new methods.

Nine of Coins
Money and success is on the way. A good time to buy goods for the home. Home life will be good.
Reversed meaning
A project may be disappointing financially. Getting rid of old furniture, possibly to make way for something new.

Ten of Coins
Money, success, pleasure from personal achievement. Travel in connection with work. A good marriage and future life but money and business will be an integral part of this.
Reversed meaning
Some success coming, a gift, a prize or a pension is on the way.

Page of Coins
A steady businesslike youngster. Good news about money or travel. Promotion or success, especially for young people in the family.

Reversed meaning
Problems for a quiet child. Temporary shortage of money.

Knight of Coins
A cautious, youngish or rather immature man. News about business, money and similar matters. Travel in connection with work.
Reversed meaning
Problems regarding work, business, money or travel. A man may not be reliable financially.

Queen of Coins
A practical, businesslike woman. A skilled negotiator and good homemaker. She would be a loving companion to the man who could guarantee a good standard of living.
Reversed meaning
A tough and materialistic woman who will win any fight over money. She may just be down on her luck and fighting for her survival.

King of Coins
A sound, solid citizen, conservative and reliable — if rather boring. He is cautious and sensible with a need for security. A kindly family man with a responsible attitude, a good bargainer but with a slight tendency to meanness.
Reversed meaning
Possibly a hard-headed businessman who is not on the side of the Questioner or the type who looks steady but turns out to be a loser. Possibly mean, untrustworthy or possessive, or just temporarily down on his luck.

Quick Clues to the Minor Arcana

Aces   New beginnings.

2s   Partnership matters.

3s   New projects, joint enterprises, optimistic new beginnings.

4s   Stability, security, putting down roots. (The four of Cups shows dissatisfaction with what one has.)

5s   Loss, sadness, regret, looking backwards. The giving up of outworn attitudes in line with circumstances.

6s   Moving forward, either by travel, financial settlements, family matters or by taking up future challenges.

7s   Values and priorities to be worked out, a cautious move forward. Work, be patient, take care.

8s   Expansion of horizons. Changes in job, environment or attitude.

9s	Satisfaction and security, perhaps hanging on too tightly.
10s	Completion, happiness, achievement and emotional success. Joy, heart's desire, security; or total loss and rejection.
Pages	Children or information.
Knights	Young men (sometimes women too) and challenge, movement in one's affairs.
Queens	Mature women, satisfaction, feminine forms of achievement, comfort.
Kings	Mature men, assertion, achievement, worldly success, stability.

The Major Arcana

The Major Arcana can be read on its own but these cards are much easier to read in conjunction with the Minor Arcana cards. This is because the Major Arcana will show the emotional *impact* of a situation whereas the Minor Arcana fills in the mundane details and the background to the event. For instance, the Wheel of Fortune would suggest that changes were about to occur, but the surrounding cards would show whether those changes were in the area of the Questioner's job, home, health, partnerships, and so on.

It is a good idea to note the ratio of Major to Minor cards in a spread. There are twice as many Minor cards as Major cards in the deck, therefore an average spread should ideally have two Minor cards for every Major one. If the spread contains mostly Minor cards, the Questioner can expect the near future to be fairly ordinary and he will be in control of his life. If there are an unusually high number of Major cards, then change is in the air and the Questioner's life is more in the hands of fate than in his own hands.

The Fool
(A new chapter will soon begin)
This is both the first and the last card in the deck, therefore it suggests that as one door closes another opens. There will be changes and challenges which could take the Questioner anywhere. For those who have the courage to try something new, this will feel like a fresh breeze. The Fool is only foolish in that he is new to the circumstances and ignorant of the facts, but he is ready to learn and grow. Look at the position of the card for guidance and also look at the other nearby cards for further ideas.

Negative
Obviously any new situation needs careful consideration. The

Questioner should look before leaping because the new experiences could bring a few problems along with them. The worst aspect of this card is that the Questioner might become obsessed with something or with someone; he should strive to keep a sense of proportion about coming events.

The Magician
(A chance to shine)
This card shows that the Questioner has gained a certain amount of skill and experience which he is soon going to be required to put into action. This suggests that the new events involve the Questioner's career or status in life rather than emotional matters; however, nothing in Tarot is ever cut and dried. Once again, look around for clues elsewhere.

The Questioner will soon need to assess his abilities and make some decisions; he will need self-discipline and self-motivation. He will soon have to deal with other people, to promote himself and his ideas, with an appearance of confidence. He may need to impress others with his knowledge and ability. This is a wonderful card for anyone who is about to start a business or to launch a new concept with originality and flair. There will be a bold step forward implying faith in oneself and hope for the future. In some cases, this card shows the beginnings of psychic awareness or development; in others, an important person will be entering the life of the questioner.

Negative
The Questioner may miss an opportunity through fear, lack of faith in himself or a kind of clinging on to the familiarity of the past. Of course, over-confidence is an equally dangerous possibility. The Questioner will have to be on the look-out for trickery—things may not be all they seem when this card is reversed; it would be a good idea to check out any new schemes and to look behind other people's motives. Lastly, the time may not be quite right for action. Carefully consider any new ideas but wait until everything is clear and straightforward before plunging in.

The Priestess
(Intuition and knowledge, a cool head ruling a warm heart)
The Priestess stands for a mental approach, even when applied to a physical situation. The Questioner *must* apply intuition to any forthcoming decisions; he must listen to his inner voice and then bring his knowledge and experience to bear on the matter in hand. On another level, this card suggests education, because it often appears before the Questioner begins a course of training or, learns how to manage a new process or a new idea. The Questioner is not yet in possession of all the facts and will soon have to study, learn, or investigate for himself. He may have to wait until certain aspects of his life which he finds puzzling are completely revealed. If the card represents a person, this would be an

honest friend, a rather cool person whose advice would be sensible and worthwhile.

Negative

The reversed Priestess implies loss of control, hysterical outbursts and stupid careless remarks. The Questioner may find himself up against blind, stupid prejudice, but he must, in turn, be aware of behaving badly himself. Another warning carried in this card is to the woman who is being used and drained by her family. This would be the time to get out and about, attend to herself and let them all get on with it for a while. Finally, the reversal of this card sometimes suggests an improvement in the Questioner's sex life!

The Empress
(Fruitful achievement and loving comfort—the feminine force)
As a person, the Empress is a good homemaker and a loving companion. She is kind and helpful, if a little self-indulgent. As a situation, the Empress brings fruitful abundance in all things whether of loving kindness or solid achievement. Achievements will be rewarded, and these rewards will result in a better standard of living which will allow one to live in pleasant and comfortable surroundings. If any property dealings are involved, the new place would have a nice garden, and if the Questioner has been unsettled and unhappy, life will definitely improve. There is a feeling of good food, mellow wine and cheerful company about this card.

The Questioner may come into contact with a child shortly. In the case of a female Questioner, this card may indicate pregnancy. If marriage is in the air, the outlook for happiness is good. The practicality of this card makes it an unlikely prelude to mental or spiritual development, but it could provide the kind of relaxed atmosphere which would lead to such developments.

Negative

This is never a really unpleasant card even when reversed. However it can suggest greed, either due to an over-materialistic attitude on the part of the Questioner or of a woman around him. In some cases this can herald a vasectomy, sterilization, or some sort of problem regarding the Questioner's reproductive system. Finally, if there is to be a new home, it would not have much of a garden.

The Emperor
(Power and status—the masculine force)
This powerful card has practical and materialistic overtones. When it represents a person, then this might be the Questioner's boss, father or other strong masculine figure who will help and advise him. The Emperor would be a reliable and conscientious partner both at home or in business. Read as a situation, this gives the Questioner an

opportunity to gain power and status in his community and in his work. His reputation will grow and he could be offered a promotion. The Questioner's earnings will increase and he will reach his objectives by steady progress and by using his intelligence and reason.

Negative
This card is never really bad but it does suggest that someone around the Questioner is not all that he thinks he is. A man may be getting old or ill or may just be unreliable. The Questioner himself may not be as clever and successful as he would like. He could become too dependent or be too easily put off making the effort to work.

The Hierophant
(The straight and narrow path)
As a person, the Hierophant represents a kindly, spiritual man who would help and advise the Questioner. As a situation, this card carries an atmosphere of the ritual, belief and the kind of morality associated with the church. The Questioner is advised, in any future dealings, to behave in a correct and conventional manner, and to avoid anything illegal, underhand, immoral, or just plain wrong. The people who will be around the Questioner will probably be older, certainly wiser and also helpful. Bad influences are definitely to be avoided.

On other levels, a temporary situation may be made permanent; a growing relationship would be heading towards marriage—and a traditional one at that. The Questioner himself will act in a kindly and thoughtful manner towards others, and any periods of thoughtful introspection will lead to a greater spiritual awareness and a greater understanding of the laws of Karma. Finally, if the questioner has been waiting for something specific to happen, the appearance of this card tells him that it will do so soon.

Negative
There are three possible ideas here. The first is a warning to the Questioner not to be too kind and easy-going, or to let others get away with things which are not right. The second is not to expect anything to happen quickly, whilst the third is a warning not to coerce others into doing things that they really don't want to do.

The Lovers
(The choice between sacred and profane love)
The idea which is central to this card is of *choice*, traditionally the choice between a spouse and a lover. However, the choices which the Questioner will soon be making could involve any area of his life but whatever these maybe, they will inevitably affect the lives of others. The Lovers card may mean the beginning of a good relationship but can just as easily herald the beginning of a good business partnership. The Questioner will soon have pleasant people around him, and he

could soon spend some money on his appearance, his clothes or his surroundings.

Finally, true love may be on the way to the Questioner and he may soon meet someone new; alternatively, he could return to someone from whom he has been parted. Changes in relationships inevitably mean that choices will have to be made.

Negative
This could be a parting, the end of a relationship or the fizzling out of one which never really started. Frustration, sexual or otherwise, is another possibility; alternatively, the Questioner could fall in love with a totally inappropriate person. The idea here is of emotional pain due to the Questioner not being able to have the kind of relationship he wants.

The Chariot
(Movement, happenings and change)
This card suggests a period of hard but worthwhile effort *which may have already been made*. The Chariot is one of the few retroactive cards of the Tarot. The two horses represent conflicting interests which have to be drawn together, harnessed and used to good effect. A project will soon get off the ground so the Questioner will be busy, active and rushing about all over the place. Travel and transport will soon become important; perhaps the Questioner will learn to drive or begin to travel to and from work. He may renovate or renew his current car. Overseas travel is also possible soon.

Negative
There will be too much to do and unhelpful conflicting forces to deal with. Travel plans may not work out, and there may be a problem with a vehicle soon.

The Hermit
(A time for quiet introspection)
The Questioner will soon be doing some thinking and there could be serious decisions to be taken. He will probably take up some kind of study which could be philosophical and introspective in nature. This card suggests a period of patience and thoughtful retreat from the mainstream of life; this could include help and encouragement from an adviser or perhaps a teacher of some kind. There may be some loneliness but there will also be a kind of peace which will be followed by an enlightened move forward.

Negative
The Questioner may not enjoy this time of reflection. He may decline well-meaning offers of help; he could also refuse to grow up and take responsibility for himself. He may not enjoy his own company. There

is a fear of change and a lack of confidence with which to cope with it. It is possible that the Questioner will find it hard to keep his temper, he may also suffer from fits of unreasonable jealousy. Alternatively, he could find himself on the receiving end of someone else's jealousy or unreasonable behaviour. At worst, he could become bereaved, lost and lonely but even so, he should try to adjust and learn to live with a different life.

The Wheel of Fortune
(What goes up must come down)
This card lies at the very heart of the Tarot because it suggests the inevitability of change. The Wheel has no meaning of its own *except* for change. It tells us that nothing stays the same forever and everything, good and bad, passes in the end, even as human life itself passes. Being an optimist, I choose to interpret this card as change for the better, but for a clearer picture you must look at the surrounding cards to gauge which aspect of life is going to change and whether this will be for the better or not.

Negative
This card is the same whichever way one looks at it but if it is reversed the changes will be less important. This could imply that things are going to go against the Questioner for a while or that other people and outside circumstances are ruling his life for the time being.

Strength
(Patience, endurance, the gentle force)
On a straightforward level, if the Questioner or someone around him has been ill, recovery is on the way. If he has been down-hearted, he will soon feel more cheerful. On other levels, this card counsels patience, diplomacy and perseverance, especially when under pressure. There is an assurance that truth and light will triumph over jealous and spiteful behaviour. The Questioner will soon find himself in a stronger position and able to take the reins of his life with confidence. This card suggests an inner spiritual strength which helps the Questioner to cope with material matters.

Negative
If there is illness around, or if the questioner is unhappy, this will continue for a while longer. He may temporarily find himself in a weak position; he could be overtired and overworked for a while. This seems to imply a period of prolonged struggle which will require courage and an even temper.

The Hanged Man
(Suspension, sacrifice and initiation)
This is another of those cards which is at the heart of the Tarot. It

shows that, by going through some kind of loss or hardship, the Questioner gains both insight and understanding. The idea of *initiation* derives partly from the new person who emerges after the period of sacrifice and struggle. The initiation *may* be purely metaphorical but there is often a practical side to this, because the person who suffers and sacrifices finds that there are others who have been through the same experience, to whom he can now relate. On an even more down-to-earth level, he may join a club or group as a result of his experiences—this will help him to learn and to grow. He may even develop psychic or spiritual gifts at this time.

On a more mundane level, the Questioner will find himself suspended in some way, waiting for something to happen before he can make necessary changes.

Negative
This card is much the same either way up. However, if reversed, it may indicate that the period of suspension is coming to an end but, more importantly, it warns against the Questioner making *useless* sacrifices or making a martyr of himself.

Death
(Something old has to make way for something new)
Yet another card which is central to the Major Arcana of the Tarot, this one also means change. The Reader must look at the position of this card and any influencing cards in order to assess the actual area of life which is going to change. The idea of the Death card is that the old must die in order to make way for the new—therefore an old situation is going to come to an end so that it can be replaced by something else.

Sometimes this card does actually warn of a death. This is never, in my experience, the death of the Questioner himself, but often someone around him. Be careful when interpreting this card—only suggest actual death if you are absolutely sure that you are right.

Negative
This card is not much different either way up. Changes might be less drastic when the card is reversed, and the death of a person is unlikely. However, the loss of a friend or even of a relationship through some other circumstances is possible.

Temperance
(Getting it all together)
This card shows both a peaceful phase ahead and the ability to cope with everything that is going on around one. There will be harmony, helpfulness and a relaxing and restful time ahead, possibly in the form of a quiet holiday. The Questioner will be able to pull all the diverse parts of his life together and make it work efficiently. Moderation in all things, rest, and a feeling of balance and comfort are on the way.

Negative

The Questioner will be too busy to rest for a while yet; there will be a continuation of pressures and anxieties. He must find some time for himself—he should try to make his life more rounded and less one-sided. Intemperance is a possibility here, but that may be no bad thing once in a while.

The Devil
(The ties which bind)

This ugly looking card upsets those people who are offended by the Tarot because we all know that the Devil is evil. However, Tarot cards are symbolic rather than literal, because they hide their meanings from the uninitiated.

This particular Devil is very much man-made, because the card represents commitment or bondage. The Questioner will soon tie himself to a particular kind of job or a particular person; this may or may not be the right thing for him to do. Alternatively, he may spend time in college, take on a mortgage or some kind of obligation. If he has thought the whole thing through and is happy with his decision, all well and good, but if he is stuck in some kind of difficult situation, then the commitment is not so funny. He may be the victim of his own cowardice. He may fear change or he may not be able to stand up to someone who is oppressing him. He may be tied to his past or persistently behaving in an inappropriate manner. He definitely needs to reassess his life and, if necessary, make some realistic changes.

This card advises the Questioner to look at practical matters or to take a practical view before looking at things from a spiritual viewpoint. Finally, the Devil shows that any forthcoming relationship will be good sexually, whether it is good in other ways or not. It can indicate that sex is at the heart of the Questioner's problems in some way or other. This card may denote a shortage of sex, also obsession, jealousy and fears which in some way are connected with sexual relationships.

Negative

This card shows negative, obsessive feelings, whichever way up it is, but perhaps a period of resentful commitment will come to an end. Sex may not be such an important feature in the Questioner's life in the future, but whether it is or it isn't, spiritual awareness and enlightenment will soon grow and develop.

The Tower
(How are the mighty fallen)

This is a truly nasty card to find in any reading because it shows that the Questioner's life is going to be disrupted in some way soon, and this disruption is likely to come out of the blue. On a practical level, there could be some problem regarding property or premises which either involves the fabric of the property or perhaps the emotions of those who live or work there. If the Questioner has been living in a fool's paradise, this will come to an end. There will be some kind of shock; an awakening and a dawning of truth and reality. Sometimes a Tarot reading over-emphazises a particular aspect of life and if this is the case with this card, the effects which actually manifest themselves later may not turn out to be too upsetting—but there will be a shock nevertheless.

Negative
This card is not very different when it is reversed. There may be an ongoing situation of repression of chronic boredom for the Questioner or the shock which this card represents may already have happened.

The Star
(Faith in the future)
This is a really nice card as it signifies hope for the future, success and an easier life. If the Questioner has had problems they will soon pass; if he has been depressed, he will soon feel better. Things are improving and he has much to hope for. There is a slightly educational feel about this card, therefore any studies will be successful and useful. Even if not studying, the Questioner will soon have the chance to expand his mental horizons. Travel is another possibility, as is pleasant and intelligent company. New ventures will go well, for luck is with the Questioner now.

Negative
This card is much the same either way up, but when reversed, there might be delays in new ventures or studies may prove to be difficult. There will be a slower climb to success and confidence.

The Moon
(Dreams, illusion, lies, self-delusion and overwhelming emotion)
This card frequently shows up when there is an emotionally-charged atmosphere around. The Questioner will not know whether he is on his head or his heels. There could be lies and double-dealing around him. There may be muddles and deceptions which lead to plans failing. The Reader must check the placement of the card to see whether this is at home, work or elsewhere. The Questioner could be deluding himself in some way or he could experience a range of unaccustomed feelings such as desire, anger, fear and sense of loss. His confidence will be undermined and he will feel that he can trust neither those around him nor even his own feelings. Even if everyone is behaving honestly and well, there could still be strange outbursts of hostility and the Questioner's judgement of situations might be poor. On the positive side, this card indicates travel, artistic pursuits and a developing psychic awareness.

Negative

This card is much the same either way up, but when reversed, it suggests that something has not yet been revealed. Things *will* become clearer; the worst could be over.

The Sun

(Happy days are here again)

Joy and happiness are on the way. The Questioner will soon have what he longs for and will be feeling good about himself. If he, or anyone close to him, has been ill, recovery is assured; all areas of life will soon be looking up. It is possible that the summer could be important in some way, particularly if the Questioner is waiting for something to happen. Finally, this card is often associated with children and therefore means good news in connection with them. It may indicate the birth of a child, if appropriate, otherwise the birth of a good creative idea.

Negative

Happiness, success and achievement are on the way but this may be either delayed or of a more modest kind than if the card were upright. There may be problems in connection with children, or the Questioner might decide not to have any more children at this time. Finally, his marriage may be unsuccessful or he may not feel appeciated.

Judgement

(Getting one's just desserts)

This card indicates that a project or a phase in the Questioner's life is coming to an end. This will bring a feeling of completion and a sense of reward for work well done. There may indeed be a reward or an accolade which rounds things off nicely. Another possibility is that something which seemed dead in the past can come alive again in the near future. In a way, these two ideas are linked because it is only when some duty or obligation is lifted that there is time to do the things one has always wanted to do.

On a practical level, this card indicates a good outcome with regard to legal matters but it shows, even here, that something is not quite finished. If a marriage is heading for the rocks, all may not be lost. Loving feelings could just possibly be resurrected and it is at least worth a try even if, in the end, it doesn't work out.

Negative

Finality is definitely in the air—if there is anything due to come to an end, it will do so shortly. Legal matters may have a disappointing outcome for the Questioner.

The World

(The end of the road is here)

The end of a phase is in sight. Situations are coming full circle and things will never be quite the same again. This is not a card of disaster but of natural progression. One could give many examples; one instance might be that of a middle aged woman whose children are leaving her free to do her own thing. There is a feeling of satisfaction, of inner and outer peace and, in amongst all the contentment, the feeling that now is the time to move onwards and upwards and to expand one's horizons in every way.

On a practical level, there can be a move of house or an interesting journey. The World card offers the Questioner the chance to explore the world a little and see what it has to offer.

Negative
The Questioner may prefer to stay in a rut rather than accept change, but this may be a good thing as it suggests continuity as distinct from restlessness. He may be envious of the success of others but, if he makes just one more effort, he will achieve success too. This is an optimistic card whichever way up it falls.

Spreads

There are dozens of Tarot spreads which can be used. Some are good for a general reading while others are ideal for focusing on a particular point. I have demonstrated twelve spreads in my book *Tarot in Action!* and I have used some of them in two different ways to show what can be done. Nevertheless, I shall now demonstrate just one spread in a very simple layout as an example. There are many variations which can be used—I leave it up to you to work out some of your own.

Seven cards strung together—an example spread
1. The Questioner himself   *Page of Cups*
2. The family   *Six of Swords*
3. Personal relationship   *The Hanged Man*
4. Career, aims and aspirations   *Queen of Swords*
5. Money   *Hierophant*
6. Health   *Six of Coins*
7. Travel, sports, holidays, pastimes   *Ten of cups*

All the example cards are in the upright position.

Interpretation
1. **The Questioner** (who, in this case, is female)
   Page of Cups
   The Questioner is or will be studying something new which may or may not lead somewhere worthwhile but is interesting in its own right. She is in a calm state of mind and not particularly interested in changing her relationships or her career at this time. She will soon meet new people and make some new friends.

2. **The Family**

Six of Swords

The family may travel soon. They could all be making minor adjustments to their lives but the outcome looks fairly calm. The Questioner herself may be travelling to visit relatives soon.

3. **Personal relationships**

The Hanged Man

This is the first of only two Major Arcana cards in this reading and is therefore important. There doesn't seem to be much change in her relationship situation as this card indicates suspension. However, she is being warned of sacrifices which she will be making on someone else's behalf which may drain her of energy.

4. **Career**

Queen of Swords

A woman may help the Questioner in her work soon. There may be new ideas to explore and make use of. If this card represents an aspect of the Questioner herself, it shows that she is about to make some cool and calculated decisions shortly with regard to her aims and ambitions. She will have to put these decisions into action quickly and efficiently. This lady works hard and doesn't mind doing so.

5. **Money**

The Hierophant

This is the only other Major Arcana card. In some circumstances this would be a warning to the Questioner to stay on the straight-and-narrow, but in this case the alternative meaning of over-generosity could be more to the point. She must be careful not to allow those who are close to her to take her money and drain her of the results of all her hard work. It seems as if they are only too willing to do so. She (back to the Hanged Man) must make sure that *she* is happy with any sacrifices which she makes on their behalf and not too ready just to buy them off. She will be earning her money by some kind of traditional means, and this is unlikely to be within the black economy, due to the public sense of honesty and duty which is inherent in this card.

6. **Health**

Six of Coins

This placement would be very confusing to a beginner because it looks like a money card in a health position. However the essence of this card is of *spending* or handing out largess. This repeats the message in the earlier cards. The Questioner must conserve energy, time and money or she will become ill. She must spend some cash on a holiday or a break and also on making her life easier and more comfortable. She may have to do this for others around her too, if necessary, but that puts her back on the treadmill of work and energy expenditure again.

7. **Travel, sports, holidays and pastimes**
   Ten of Cups
   This is so obvious that it is laughable. The Questioner needs a break, a holiday, an active hobby and a chance to free herself of chores. She likes doing things with the family and with friends. She should spend a little time eating, drinking and being merry. She needs love and affection and a bit of understanding as well. This card tells her that she should soon be able to have the break she needs and that there will be a spell of happiness ahead for her.

As it happens, this reading was quite clear and definite in its message—that was just the luck of the draw, it doesn't always work out that way. Even this example, however, shows how the Tarot Reader must modify the accepted 'book' descriptions of the cards and pick up the clues which the reading throws out in order to establish the *theme* of the reading and get to the root of the situation which is presenting itself. This kind of reading also demonstrates how to use Tarot for guidance and advice rather than straight fortune-telling, and that is really what the Tarot is all about.

9.

Kabbalistic Astrology

Kabbalistic Astrology is an interesting concept for those who have convoluted minds because it blends the astrology of planets and signs with the Sephiroth (branches) of the Tree of Life. It can be used to interpret a Subject's characteristics and can even be used progressively in order to demonstrate how the personality is going to unfold and adapt through life. I have taken most of the Kabbalistic information for this section from my friend, **Douglas Ashby,** with some help from **Fred Curtis.** I have filled in a few gaps here and there with some ideas from **Rachel Pollack's** book, *The Seventy-Eight Degrees of Wisdom.* Rachel's book is on the subject of Tarot cards but she shows how they can be used in conjuction with the Kabbala in much the same way that I am using astrology in this section.

The Method

In normal astrology, the planets are placed in signs and houses according to their position at the time of the Subject's birth. They are then looked at with regard to their placement, the aspects which they make to one another and their movements around the chart. By contrast, in Kabbalistic astrology, the planets are placed against their appropriate Sephiroth and read accordingly. There are no planetary aspects in the usual sense of the word but the pathways between the Sephiroth can be used as aspects instead. Pathworking, or the connections between the Sephiroth, is a very deep subject which is completely beyond the scope of this book.

The Zodiac, the Planets and the Sephiroth

The signs of the zodiac
Aries   The sign is associated with a pioneering spirit. It denotes energy, assertiveness, spontaneity, self-assertion and generosity. Self-determination and courage are associated

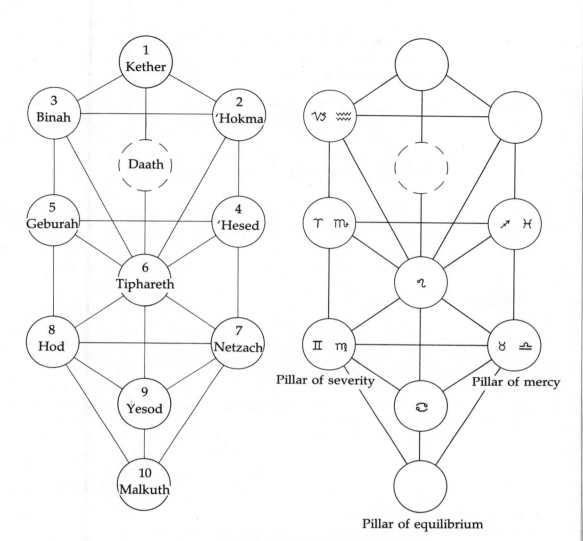

The Tree of Life and its Astrological Significance

with Aries. It rules machinery, engineering, military and para-military organizations. It is connected with a masculine outlook, masculine pursuits and new beginnings.

Taurus Steadfastness, dogged determination and the need to gather valued goods or to sort out one's personal values characterize this sign. It is associated with the land and its products, beauty and beautiful things. Stubborn refusal to change, give up or lose out are Taurean characteristics. Taurus is the sign of conservation.

Gemini Communications of all kinds including education, local travel, sales, telephones and broadcasting are part of this sign. It rules relatives of one's own generation, mental pursuits and the world of logical thought. Gemini is the sign of mental activity.

Cancer   This sign rules the home, one's early experiences and the mother figures. It is associated with security, especially in one's private life, also small shops, collecting of all kinds and business of a local nature, especially insurance. Caring and nurturing are its bywords.

Leo   Children and creativity come under Leo, as do pleasures, holidays and lovers. Entertainment, the stage and the world of sport are Leo characteristics—also tradition, fatherhood, steady growth and achievements. Generous and proud, this sign lends charisma to all it touches.

Virgo   Fussy and analytical, Virgo seeks to put the world in order. Health, nutrition and clothing are ruled by this sign, duties to be done and those which are expected of others. Employers and employment for others, detailed work of all kinds and caring of a practical kind. Virgo cares dutifully and with exactitude.

Libra   Open partnerships and relationships are characteristic of Libra as part of this sign's search for harmony and unity expressed through justice, balance and fairness, also refinement, culture and beauty, a search for perfection and for the 'other half' of anything. Libra is associated with ideas, business and reasonable status in life leading to comfort and companionship.

Scorpio   Commitment and serious intent are signified by Scorpio. Joint finances, other people's money, legacies, taxes, mortgages, alimony and allowances on the one hand, partnerships of a deeply committed nature on the other. Beginnings and endings, birth and death. Getting to the bottom of or inside of anything, therefore surgery, butchery, mining, and sex! Deep matters are ruled by Scorpio.

Sagittarius   Expansion is the keyword here, expansion of one's physical horizons through travel and opportunities for advancement; expansion of one's income and also, if one isn't careful—the waistline. On a deeper level, higher education, philosophical thought, religion and the structure of the law are represented, i.e. expansion of one's mental and spiritual horizons.

Capricorn   Restriction is the keyword here. This sign is associated with structure, which may be in the form of large organizations, governmental structure or personal limitation. Capricorn rules goals and ambitions, public status and position, authority and the organization of masses of people. Achievement, hard work and serious attainment belong to Capricorn.

Aquarius   This sign rules detached relationships and theoretical ideas. It is associated with political and philosophical beliefs, idealism and work for the good of all humanity. Aquarius is associated with teaching and learning, the spread of broad ideas and worthwhile causes. Aquarius rules friendships, groups, clubs and societies, any organization with an altruistic aim. It lends eccentricity and novelty, revolution and chaos to everything it touches.

Pisces   This signifies mysticism and retreat. It is associated with self-sacrifice, sometimes to a higher cause, gentle contemplation, religious fervour and meditative techniques. It rules all which is private, secret and deeply personal, also kindness, care for others and self-sacrifice. It is also associated with places of confinement, self-destruction and even madness or, conversely, extremes of enlightenment.

Quick reference to the planets

The Sun   *Changes for the better*: emphasis of each house as it passes through. Events related to children. Creativity.

The Moon   *Emotions*: the home, property and premises. Parents, especially mother figures. Female matters.

Mercury   *Correspondence*: business, local travel, neighbours and relatives.

Venus   *Affection*: beauty, social life, partnerships with women.

Mars   *Activity*: energy, strength, fast movement. Accidents, partnerships with men.

Jupiter   *Expansion of one's horizons*: legal, educational and financial matters. Opportunity.

Saturn   *Limitations*: lessons of life. Parents. Career and ambitions.

Uranus   *Unexpected events*: tension and change. Novel ideas, education. Hopes and wishes.

Neptune   *Illusions and dreams*: disappointments and inspirations.

Music and art. Mysticism. Charity and caring for others or being cared for.

Pluto
Slow turning points: the law (policemen). Beginnings and endings; birth, death, sex. Committed relationships and partnerships. The public mind. Hidden matters.

The Sephiroth

Kether or Crown
Spiritual impulse both within and surrounding oneself. This may be reached as a result of inward journeys either deliberately chosen or forced upon one by circumstances. It also rules the conception of anything.

'Hokma or Wisdom
Male image, the active male force and one's relationship to it. How things come into being, the process of development. Creative intelligence moving towards a goal of higher development. This kind of intelligence is objective and also carries with it evidence of learning and of skill.

Binah or Understanding
Female image, how one relates to the feminine structuring processes of life. The best kind of understanding comes from experience, it is not really possible to know how someone else feels unless one has suffered in the same way or enjoyed a similar kind of success. This is subjective and receptive in essence.

'Hesed or Mercy
Ideals, the law, religious matters, one's inner will, planning processes and one's compassionate nature. Also worldly gains, work, home, money and friends. How one sees or is affected by worldly gains.

Geburah or Judgement
Active aspirations, ability to act, determination, strength. Ability to destroy the past in order to create the future. Difficulties, loneliness and power used against one or discovered within one's self.

Tiphareth or Beauty
Control, balance, harmony, the heart centre, the centre of being. The active will and things which are definitely coming to fruition. Health matters. This position either opens the gate to creative force or blocks it.

Netzach or Eternity
Emotional nature, feelings, desires, artistic creativity and romance. The requirements of a home and family, the disciplines and slight restrictions of normal everyday life.

Hod or Reverberation
Thoughts, communication, speech and logic. Also the kind of communication which is expressed physically through sexual love.

Yesed or Foundation
Imagination, instincts, habit patterns, food, home environment, sexual needs, dreams, fantasies and desires. The kind of energy which is held in one's unconscious mind.

Malkuth or Kingdom
Environment, external influences, other people, personal and social situations, politics in the general sense. Malkuth rules one's everyday life and normal day-to-day activities.

The Zodiac and the Tree of Life

1. Kether
Doesn't match any zodiac sign.

2. 'Hokma
Doesn't match any zodiac sign.

3. Binah
Capricorn and Aquarius.

4. 'Hesed
Sagittarius and Pisces.

5. Geburah
Aries and Scorpio.

6. Tiphareth
Leo.

7. Netzach
Taurus and Libra.

8. Hod
Gemini and Virgo.

9. Yesed
Cancer.

10. Malkuth
Doesn't match any zodiac sign.

Synthesis
Now we have to work out the birth chart in the usual manner and place the planets on the tree in their appropriate signs. This will show the character of the Subject and the areas of life on which he will need to work in order to improve himself and his circumstances.

A Brief Interpretation for Jeffrey Archer

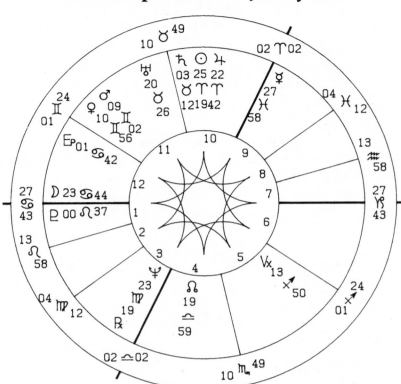

Jeffrey Archer's astrological birthchart

Sun and Jupiter in Geburah
Jeffrey prides himself on being an active man who won't let too much stand in his way. He is honest and honourable but can be unintentionally hurtful or sarcastic. He can cut himself loose from the past in order to create a new future, it is possible that he would earn most of his money (and also sustain losses) overseas. He is liable to losses as a result of power being used against him and he could do with a bit more subtlety in his thinking.

Mercury in 'Hesed
He is generous and compassionate, he has a soft spot for those who are weaker than himself. He will gain from work in the field of communications and would make a good teacher. He thinks a lot of his family and close friends.

Pluto in Tiphareth
This is a generational influence but it does show that Jeffrey can transform himself and his life by being creative and by using his strong will power. He should keep an eye on his health as frustration and unexpressed anger can make him ill.

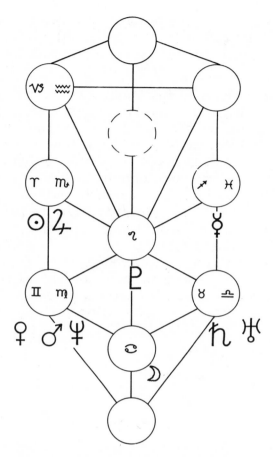

Jeffrey Archer's Kabbalistic birthchart

Mars, Venus and Neptune in Hod

This is the area of communication and logical thought, therefore Mars would show that Jeffrey is admirably suited to working in the field of communication and Venus ensures that he would gain as a result. Neptune shows creativity in communications and the ability to visualize situations and to bring them to life for the enjoyment of others.

Jeffrey would rarely be lost for words. Neptune shows that he can be on the receiving end of lies and strange accusations which would affect his relationships with others. He appears to have very good lines of communication with his wife and they should have a greater than average amount of mutual understanding. He may be a rather authoritarian father to his sons (Son in Geburah).

Saturn, Uranus and the North Node in Netzach

Jeffrey takes his responsibilities to his family very seriously (Saturn) but he can shock them on occasion or land them in a mess (Uranus). He is extremely serious about his writing and approaches his work with a good deal of self-discipline. He is forward looking and rather idealistic being interested in both the problems of youth and old age in the modern world. If, by any chance, he inherited property, there would be some kind of responsibility for him in administering it.

The Moon and Ascendant in Yesed

Jeffrey needs the support of his family around him. He needs a quiet place in which to relax and think. His imagination is vivid, but being an instinctive thinker, he may lack judgement at times. All the signs on this chart show that Jeffrey Archer is strongly sexed and loving by nature but he would prefer to keep his physical love for his wife as he needs to be in a familiar, comfortable situation. Sexual adventures would not appeal to him. His emotions are vulnerable and his feelings deep. There is evidence that he would be a dutiful son to his parents.

The Ascendant in Yesed would suggest that he has a pleasant and rather self-effacing outer manner but this is where traditional astrology has advantages over Kabbalistic astrology. Most of his first house is in Leo (Tiphareth) and therefore he projects himself outwardly into the mainstream of life and uses his charismatic manner to good effect in public life. He may appear arrogant on occasion in order to protect his soft centre.

10.

Runes

Seldiy Bate and Nigel Bourne are well-known and well-respected members of the occult world. They can be seen at psychic festivals all over the country. They hold workshops on a variety of subjects and also write for a number of magazines. As well as their psychic interests, they are both involved in the world of theatre and music. Their first album, *Pagan Easter* on Temple Records, combines magic and music. Their store of knowledge on various aspects of the occult is phenomenal, and I often find myself looking through their comprehensive bookshelf or setting their minds to a problem. They invariably give generously of their time and their knowledge.

This section was contributed mainly by Seldiy, with some amplification here and there by Nigel, during an enlightening evening in their home, over a glass or two of wine. If I reproduced all the information that they gave me, I would have a book which would be well able to stand alone; therefore it is with some slight chagrin that I now pass on to you this somewhat abridged version.

Ritual and Invocation

The best Runes are always those you make for yourself. It is traditional before beginning this to make a dedication to the Norse god Odin who discovered them. The legend tells us that Odin hung himself upside-down from the sacred tree, Yggdrasil (the Hanged man from the Tarot is a similar image). He stayed like this for nine days, during which he reached a stage of enlightenment. He then found the Runes among the roots of the tree. Odin is the Norse equivalent of the Roman god, Mercury, the Greek god, Hermes, and the Egyptian god, Thoth. In other words, he is associated with communication, intellect, logic, travel and healing. However, Odin is particularly associated with divination.

You can burn some incense which is sacred to Odin, such as mastic gum or tiny strips of hazelwood. Make an invocation to Odin, and while speaking this aloud, visualize the god himself. He has only one eye and hides the empty socket under the brim of a large hat which he always wears. He also wears a cloak, carries a blackthorn staff and is accompanied by a raven.

To Odin (to learn the Runes)

  Lord of the Northern Wind, by Sea and Sky,
  By Baldur's burning Sun and Freya's Moon,
  I call upon thee, O Mighty Odin, that I
  May learn the secret of each and every Rune!
  I have worked the Magicks well and poured
  A libation of mead by the trembling blackthorn tree,
  Have listened to the Raven's voice and scored
  My name upon a hazel wand for thee;
  For he that calls the Divine King Odin and proves
  Himself to be worthy of the wisdom will hear
  The eightfold drumming of Sleipnir's flashing hooves
  And know the wisest of the Gods is near.

  A gift demands a gift, Grim Guardian of Death
  Whisper'd secrets on Odin's sacred breath!

(Seldiy Bate, Summer Solstice, 1987)

To Make the Runes

Ideally, these should be made of wood. Hazelwood is traditional, but any type of wood (except yew, the tree of Death) with which you feel compatible will do. If you take a branch from a living tree, don't forget to ask the tree for permission first. Be careful to select a branch which will not damage the tree irrevocably, and place a silver coin somewhere in the tree for payment. Leave the wood for a while to season. Slivers of wood can be used or you can cut the branch into slices like a loaf of bread. You will need to make 25 Runes, but it is a good idea to cut more than this number so that you have some to spare if you make a mistake in the lettering.

 If you practise magic, cut the letters into the Runes with your own personal magical knife, otherwise cut the letters with any good sharp knife or burn them in with a pokerwork needle which you can buy from a craft shop. It is possible to burn the letters in by means of sunlight, concentrated through a lens or even a crystal ball, but this is very difficult to do accurately. If you can cope with the idea, you may place a little blood on at least one of the Runes, therefore either prick your thumb, or in the case of a female Rune reader, use some menstrual blood. You can mark each Rune with a tiny dot at the top to show which way would be upright if you want to use upright and inverted readings. Darken the markings on the Runes with red ink (to represent blood), or a mixture of soot and water, or maybe some homemade red ink made up from 'dragon's blood' (a powdered herb) and alcohol; whisky would be traditional, as it is known in Gaelic as 'The Water of Life', or mead, which is sacred to Odin.

Runes can also be made from slivers of bone or soft stone, such as limestone or slate. Pebbles of equal size can be used and they can look very nice if the design is carefully painted on, and then the whole stone is varnished. Any modelling clay which you can buy in a craft shop can be used. This may be the type you fire, if you are into making pottery, or the kind which hardens by itself such as *Das*. Clay is permissible, because this too is a natural substance. Failing all this, Runes can be bought at any psychic festival or at any shop which specializes in such goods. Buy those which you feel most drawn to.

However you come by your Runes, you will need to consecrate them. They should be washed in natural running water; if this is likely to spoil them, a token dab of stream water is sufficient. You should then waft them through some appropriate incense and make a prayer.

Make yourself a bag to keep them in. This can be leather, felt or silk — ideally something you can wear on a drawstring. Finally, you can make a small Rune wand from a hazel twig or a piece of dowel. This should fit into the Rune bag along with the Runes. You can mark the wand with Runic symbols for your initials, paint and decorate or varnish it.

Casting the Runes

The simplest method is to ask the Enquirer to dip into the Rune bag and pick out whatever number of Runes you need to work with. Alternatively, lay all the Runes out face-downwards, ask the Enquirer first to swirl them around on the table (or Rune cloth, if used) and then to pick out whatever number you require. He should hold his chosen Runes in his hands for a few moments while thinking about his life.

Layouts

A clock shape can be used with each Rune representing one month of the year. The clock shape can also represent the astrological houses (see chapter 5 for the astrological houses). Astrology is not, of course, a Norse divination but many professional Readers find this method convenient because they are usually familiar with it. I guess that a Kabbalistic or numerological layout would work just as well if the Reader were comfortable using it.

A very simple idea would be to use two circles, the inner one being immediate future, the outer one showing more distant events. The

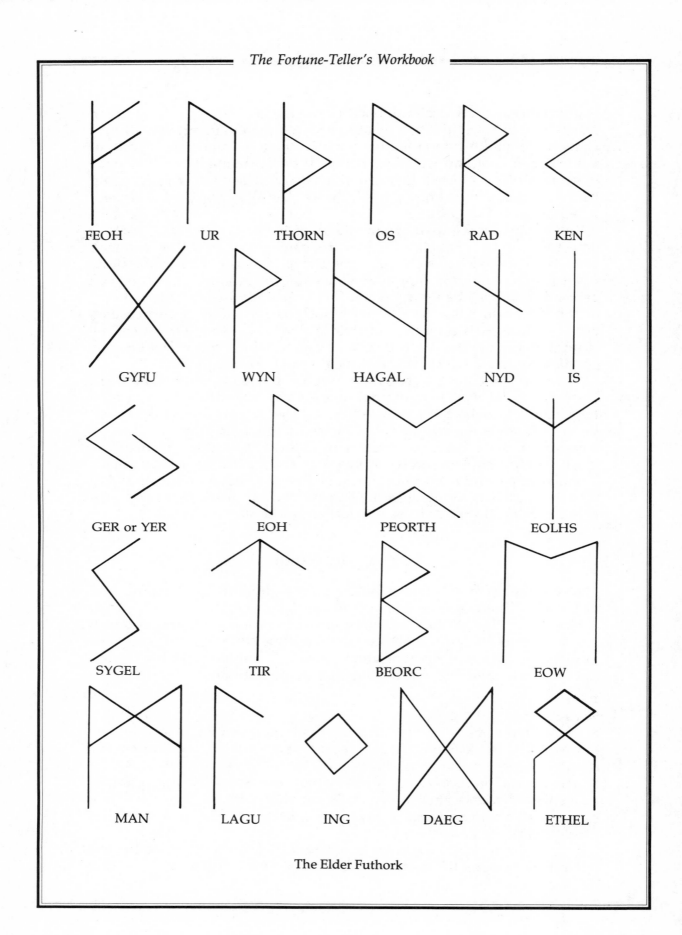

FEOH   UR   THORN   OS   RAD   KEN

GYFU   WYN   HAGAL   NYD   IS

GER or YER   EOH   PEORTH   EOLHS

SYGEL   TIR   BEORC   EOW

MAN   LAGU   ING   DAEG   ETHEL

The Elder Futhork

inner circle would also indicate people and situations which are close to the Enquirer, while the outer one would be the outside environment of work, strangers and distant situations. A square divided into four could show various areas of life such as the family, work, health and relationships. Indeed, a whole roulette table of sections could be worked out. However, a few basic divisions would help, especially when the Enquirer is a stranger and you don't automatically know what is on his mind.

Runes can be used either to give a general reading or to ask a specific question. After Seldiy and Nigel had finished dictating these notes to me, they suggested that I use the Runes myself to answer a question which was bothering them. In this, my first ever Rune reading, the answer came back very clearly and the intense feeling which emanated from the reading backed up what the Runes were saying. A week later, the reading was proved to be correct.

The *Futhork* Alphabet and its Symbolism

There is some variation in alphabets, this one is sometimes called the *futhork* alphabet, after its first six letters.

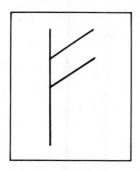

Runic letter   :FEOH
English equivalent :F
Keyword   :Cattle

Cattle represented prosperity or wealth in the ancient world, much as they do in parts of Africa today; so this Rune represents the Enquirer's personal property and funds, his wealth and also status and position; the career (or lack of it!) in terms of material, and often emotional security. Also the fulfilment of love and, if appropriate, pregnancy. Fertility and growth of all kinds.

Inverted meaning
Financial loss, a lack of fulfilment. Sexual frustration, difficulties related to procreation. Female health problems; also problems related to weight gain.

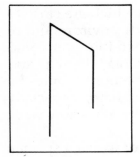

Runic letter   :UR
English equivalent :U or W
Keyword   :Wild ox

The wild ox was considered a symbol of great physical strength. It represents masculinity, the active principle, the physical and material planes. This brings opportunities to better oneself, possibly also a financial improvement, but always with expenditure of energy or strength. The acquiring and controlled use of a physical skill, or the training of such in others.

Inverted
Missed opportunities. Lack of strength; this can be either physical or metaphorical weakness, alternatively perhaps misplaced power or uncontrolled strength.

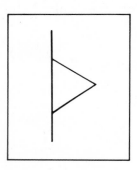

Runic letter   :THORN
English equivalent :TH
Keyword   :A thorn

The thorn protects the plant from predators, therefore this represents protection in all forms; physical, mental or even psychic. This may be protection from attack, physical defences, even the use of an offensive deterrent, if other Runes near it indicate this: also verbal defence and the protection of others. If there are decisions to be taken they will require a certain element of caution and self-protection. The Enquirer must allow matters to run their course and not force anything. Family matters may also be indicated by this Rune.

Inverted
A wrong decision. Aggression used for the wrong reason, a misplaced use of power perhaps; jealousy, an over-defensive attitude. Tension, introversion.

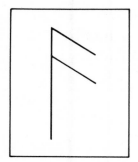

Runic letter	:OS
English equivalent	:A or O
Keyword	:A god

This Rune is sacred to Odin and, therefore, can be used in any invocation to him. Odin is the chief god of magic. It represents authority, superiors, elders and ancestors. Parents and all that can be inherited from them are indicated, as is any kind of father figure or god figure in the Enquirer's life; also the Enquirer's spiritual progress, beliefs and philosophy. Guidance from above.

Inverted
Problems related to parents or authority figures, even government bodies of some kind. An over-dominant attitude and abuse of power. Also blind faith, fanaticism, obsession, mental complexes.

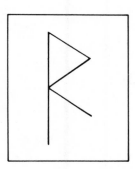

Runic letter	:RAD
English equivalent	:R
Keyword	:A wheel

This represents movement, therefore it could suggest a journey with a purpose. Transport matters and all kinds of physical movement; exploration, not only in reality, but to do with learning and imagination. There could be a movement in the Enquirer's affairs if these have been suspended or neglected for a while. Changes, the turning of events. Progress forward.

Inverted
Difficulties related to travel and transport. Unconstructive changes. Possibly a journey which is necessary, but not liked, such as a visit to the sick or to a person in authority. Immobility, stubbornness and a lack of imagination.

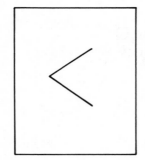

Runic letter   :KEN
English equivalent :K or a hard C
Keyword   :A bonfire

This Rune brings warmth and light into the Enquirer's life. It can suggest mental illumination, a burst of creativity. There will be celebrations, possibly around a bonfire. The Enquirer will be the centre of attention and events will bring social activity. This is especially lucky for a woman, as she will receive love from a man, whilst a male Enquirer would find himself in the position of giving love. This may be the kindling of a relationship. There is a feeling of status and success here, and also an indication of good health and healing.

Inverted
A lack of warmth in the Enquirer's life and also a lack of direction and guidance, a feeling of blindness. There could be the loss of something valuable. There may be health problems, especially heart trouble, or a general lowering of resistance.

Runic letter   :GYFU
English equivalent :G
Keyword   :A gift

This Rune may bring a gift, a contract or an opportunity. It suggests that the Enquirer has some kind of useful talent or gift. It also brings good partnerships and happiness in love, but implies 'give and take' in the relationship. In Runic lore, you never get 'something for nothing', so you must always be prepared to pay in some way for whatever you may receive.

Inverted
There may be a loss or even a swindle now. The Enquirer may find that he lacks the necessary talent for a particular job which he would like to do. This Rune can also suggest a sacrifice and, when reversed, it

betokens a pointless one—martyrdom, exploitation. Also an illness or shortcoming that one has to accept.

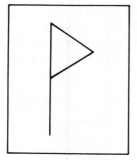

Runic letter	:WYN
English equivalent	:W or U
Keyword	:Joy:

This Rune brings joy and happiness on an emotional level. It is associated with water and therefore suggests a journey over water or a home near water. Alternatively, an important visitor could come from over the water. There could be an artistic or spiritual awakening, gain or luck, particularly in creative or inspirational matters. Sometimes this Rune means a fair-haired man.

Inverted
Over-emotion, martyrdom, depression. The Enquirer is advised to avoid major decisions, as he is too emotionally involved with the problem at the moment. Difficulty in seeing clearly, bad judgement. This Rune suggests the need to wait: three months before making a decision directly related to the emotions, or three days for a decision relating to work. Problems with the digestive system or with the body fluids, or in the case of a woman, problems with the menstrual cycle or hormone balance.

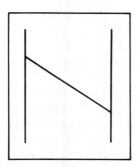

Runic letter	:HAGAL
English equivalent	:H
Keyword	:Hail

This represents a bolt from the blue which may be some kind of natural disaster, or unexpected twist of fate. Havoc, disruption of plans, unforeseen events. Even good events are possible, but they would turn the Enquirer's world upside-down. There may be sickness in the family, also unexpected births. The Enquirer must be prepared for the unexpected. If there is to be destruction, it allows one to rebuild in a better way.

Inverted
Delay, disruptions, accidents, even deserved disaster. This Rune is pretty awful either way up, although one has to see the constructive purpose behind the unexpected and also that the disaster *can* be averted. On occasions, the Rune *could* mean death, but only if other Runes near it emphasize this possibility.

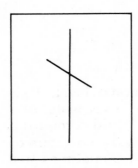

Runic letter	:NYD
English equivalent	:N
Keyword	:Need

Necessity, self-preservation, instinctive requirements. The need to eat, keep a roof over one's head, protect the children, and even save one's own skin. Also other needs, such as the need to be creative, or one's most basic requirements from a job or relationship. The motivating force, the need to function, to achieve, etc. Also a warning to be patient, to exercise restraint.

Inverted
Physical tension, emotional tightness. The kind of cautious, greedy, envious personality which is hard to get along with. Inability to let go, even mental problems, feelings bottled up. Immobility, muscular strain, and stress.

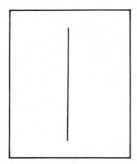

Runic letter	:IS
English equivalent	:I
Keyword	:Ice

An impediment, an obstacle, a feeling that everything is frozen up. Plans may be stopped, money may be immobilized, nothing good can come of the present situation. Leave it: try again another time. Feelings could be frozen, there may be too much detachment for the Enquirer. This is like the ice of winter which always melts in the end, Spring will bring new warmth, but patience is needed.

Inverted

The same—but worse! Fear, coldness, avoidance. There could be a physical impediment such as rheumatism or paralysis, or arthritis, immobility or mental paralysis with no clear or constructive ideas. Also stubbornness, refusal to be moved or to adapt.

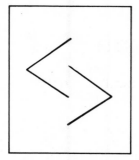

Runic letter	:GER or YER
English equivalent	:Y or soft G
Keyword	:Cycle or harvest

The end of a cycle, the turning of the seasons, the wheel of fortune. There may be a waiting period, a time of expectation and a promise of fulfilment. The Enquirer will reap what has been sown for good or for ill. This time of change is inevitable and should be used constructively. Debts should be paid, new projects started, contracts signed; a change of abode is likely. In other words, now is the time to make a fresh start.

Inverted

This is the same either way up, but there could be missed opportunities through the Enquirer's resistance to change or inability to see the advantages of a situation. A cycle, or indeed a waiting period, of approximately a year is indicated.

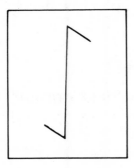

Runic letter	:EOH
English equivalent	:E (as in egg)
Keyword	:Yew bow

The yew bow is flexible enough to adapt itself to a new shape without breaking, therefore this would suggest a kind of recoiling or possibly a stepping out of the way of difficulty. The Enquirer will have to take a flexible approach to life, adapt himself to a new and different situation, or even taken one step backwards in order to move two steps forwards. Pitfalls will be avoided, inconvenient situations will turn out to be advantageous in the end. Using the strength of others against them (as in Judo), manipulation of the power and dominance of others, finding another way round a problem. Lateral thinking.

Inverted
Indecision, vacillation, a retrograde step in one's progress. Withdrawal, even a relapse into mental or physical illness. Deviousness and craftiness. Refusal to face up to problems, escapism.

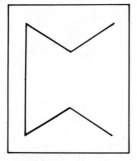

Runic letter	:PEORTH
English equivalent	:P
Keyword	:The secret Rune

Something is not being revealed yet to the Enquirer—he will be given the knowledge or information at the right time. If this is the first Rune to appear in a reading, leave it or try again a few days or even weeks later. This suggests a link with the spirit world, psychism, dreams, visions and trance-like states which may bring forth prophecy. Also, unexpectedly good events, luck, gain; favours, which the Enquirer may have forgotten, being returned. Unexpected benefit.

Inverted
Imaginary fears, disappointment over an expectation. Favours which are *not* returned. Lack of communication, going behind someone's back. This Rune could also indicate subconcious fears, phobias, deeply hidden psychosis.

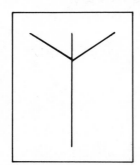

Runic letter	:EOLHS
English equivalent	:E or Y
Keyword	:Hand held upright in greeting: A reed

The reed definition of this Rune has connections with the reed in a musical instrument in that it suggests artistry, poetry and creative talent; self-expression and art for art's sake. Hobbies and cultural interests plus study for pleasure. The greeting definition of the Rune means being part of special group, with special behaviour and vocabulary; something like a Masonic handshake.

Inverted

This indicates people the Enquirer should avoid, such as a group who engage in stupid or illegal activities, or who are a bad influence. Alternatively, a lack of creativity or self-expression or perhaps a lack of opportunity for the Enquirer to express himself in his work or in his life generally.

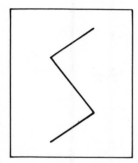

Runic letter	:SYGEL
English equivalent	:S
Keyword	:The Sun

The Sun was viewed as the source of life by the ancient world and to us on this planet, of course, it is just that. This Rune represents the life force, health and healing, also rest and recuperation. Relaxation, activities and interests such as sport, hobbies, holidays and entertainment. On other level, fame, recognition, bringing some creative endeavour or talent out into the light.

Inverted

The same as upright but, if the Enquirer has been overdoing things, this would tell him that he needs and deserves some time off to relax and enjoy himself. The burning-out of energy, muscular strain, overwork.

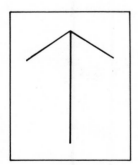

Runic letter	:TIR
English equivalent	:T
Keyword	:Tir the War God

Tir is the Norse god of war (the equivalent of Mars); therefore, this Rune implies activity, energy and heroism. If the Enquirer is male, he will seek romance soon, but if the Enquirer is female there will soon be a new lover or partner. However, any ensuing romance would be pretty high-octane, full of passion and overwhelming feelings. Also anger, aggression, angst and attack.

Inverted
Lack of (or misdirected) energy. For a male Enquirer, a broken love affair or unrequited love, possibly caused by his being too pushy. For a female, possibly falling in love with the wrong person, an obsessive relationship perhaps. Sexual frustration, impotence. Arguments, violence, damage to property. Cuts, burns, bruises, accidents, headaches, allergies.

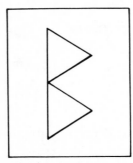

Runic letter   :BEORC
English equivalent :B
Keyword   :Birch tree

The birch is associated with fertility cults, pagan ritual, particularly that which is concerned with the spring and the awakening of the life force. Therefore, this Rune can mean new beginnings, expansion, growth and fertility. The family unit, the community, parties, celebrations, weddings and births. Joy in the family. Also ritual, familiarity, repetition.

Inverted
A plan not coming to fruition, barrenness, delays. Sickness in the family, disconcerting visits, unfamiliar surroundings. Bad news in the community or ill feeling among friends. Fatigue, lack of energy.

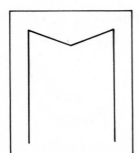

Runic letter   :EOW
English equivalent :E as in egg
Keyword   :Horse

Travel and transport. Movement and methods of transport, e.g. the Enquirer's car, the bus, or even his feet! Animals which may be on a farm, working animals or pets. Change and the methods used to bring it about. Ideas to be put across and the medium used, all forms of movement and communication, progress and how it is achieved.

Inverted
Problems with transport, delays. Sick animals. Failure to get one's message across, or the wrong approach in doing so. Immobility, handicaps.

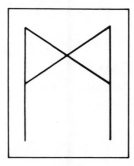

Runic letter	:MAN
English equivalent	:M
Keyword	:Man

A male figure, a man in authority, a professional man. This Rune tells the Enquirer not to go ahead with anything without consulting a professional person. This person may be a doctor, solicitor, accountant, etc. If there are decisions to be taken, the Enquirer should wait a while before taking them.

Inverted
Trouble with those in authority such as the police, judiciary, the boss. Abuse of power or position. An influential person who stands for something different from the Enquirer. An over-strict father figure. Possibly a foreigner or someone from an alien environment. If this is an enemy, look at the adjacent Runes for more information.

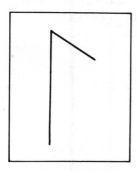

Runic letter	:LAGU
English equivalent	:L
Keyword	:Lake

This is a feminine Rune which is connected with the Moon goddess, the sea, the psychic realms, intuition and the mysteries of childbirth.

Anything which allows change, fluidity and conduction, any kind of medium. Protection and a kind of womb-like safety. A woman in a reading who is capable of giving birth. Fertility, children. The unknown, the universal rather than the personal world of the spirit.

Inverted
Paranoia, inability to cope with the subconscious. Blood, menstrual problems or other cyclic problems. Hormone imbalances. Miscarriage. Escapism, alcoholism, drug dependence. If the Enquirer is over-emotional or too emotionally involved with a problem he should consult someone impartial.

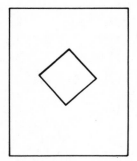

Runic letter	:ING
English equivalent	:NG
Keyword	:The Danes (The family Rune)

Fertility, production, material result. The earth, fruition, children. The result is produced, the project completed. Long term results should be sought. A problem solved. Also, protection, enclosure, security, and staying put in familiar surroundings. Problems will be solved at the end of a cycle if realistic work is put into them. This Rune can mean friends, particularly from abroad, and it is also much associated with magic, divination and women's mysteries. The mother goddess.

Inverted
Non-productiveness, lack of charity or tolerance. Imprisonment, restriction and tension. Also health problems related to tension, stresses and blockages; claustrophobia, infertility.

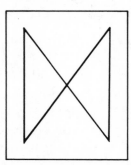

Runic letter	:DAEG
English equivalent	:D
Keyword	:Day

The daytime, warmth and light. Anything which is open, obvious, easily seen. Things which come to light. Face values. Advertisement, image, clarity and recognition. Success in studies, examinations and tests passed, also qualifications. A change for the better, success generally. If this is near the blank Rune, the success will be destined. A short wait because an appropriate date should be set for success.

Inverted
This Rune is usually the same either way up but occasionally it can mean the opposite of day, such as sunset or perhaps the ending of a phase in one's life. Sleep, illness, coma. Things which are hidden, answers which are not immediately obvious.

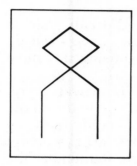

Runic letter	:ETHEL
English equivalent	:E or O
Keyword	:Inheritance

Benefit through property, gifts, help from older relatives. Legacy, heirloom, an actual object which is left to the Enquirer. Documents, wills, legal matters. Matters related to money.

Inverted
Problems with one's house, property or any other physical kind of goods. Theft or loss. Trouble with old people. Physical illness.

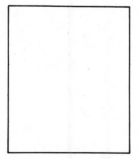

The blank Rune

Keyword   :The Karmic Rune

Karma, of course, is an Indian word but the meaning is clear. Fate, destiny, kismet. Things which are decided for the Enquirer, or known only to the gods. Look at the Runes which are nearby to see what the Fates have in store, or use this in some kind of placement system where the destiny becomes clear by the position of the Rune.

A poem on the Runes

> Ye shall find messages and signs to be read
> Signs most mighty, signs so strong
> Which the soothsayer coloured
> The high gods made
>
> Do ye know how they should be carved?
> Do ye know how they should be read?
> Do ye know how they should be coloured?
> Do ye know how they should be tried?

Words of Warning

Seldiy and Nigel have been working with magical and occult systems for many years and, due to their knowledge of how things *can* go wrong, they wish to warn readers of the pitfalls of abusing this most powerful system of divination.

If you ask a frivolous question, you will get a frivolous answer. If you become big-headed before you have gained the skills, you will find the skill taken away from you. Be prepared to work and to study hard. By all means, practise readings with obliging friends, but always accept some payment, no matter how small or in what form. Remember the words of the god Odin: 'A gift demands a gift'—one does not get anything for nothing.

11.

Witchdoctor's Bones

A few years ago my friends Marian and Michael Atwell went to visit her sister in South Africa. On one of their days out visiting the sights, she found herself in a typical 'tourist trap' shop. 'Okay,' she thought, 'I need to buy presents for friends at home, I'll see what I can find here.' One of her finds turned out to be a small plastic pouch of *genuine witchdoctor's bones*. 'Just the thing for Sasha!' she thought. Marian gave me the bones at her Christmas party and I tipped them out and read the instructions. I guess that the instructions had been translated from a local African language, but the gist of them was quite clear, at least to a practising psychic.

I gave the bones to a young girl to handle and then asked her to throw them down onto a piece of paper which I had marked out as shown in the instructions. The youngsters crowded around the coffee table and, amid much boozy giggling, I started to 'read' the bones. After a moment or two, a change began to come over the crowd because I had apparently hit on something which was actually happening in this young girl's life. She and her family were going on a long-planned visit to relatives in Canada. As the atmosphere deepened, I found myself describing the people who would be around her and the place at which she would be staying. The reading broadened, and I was able to tell her a good deal about her life both then and in the future. The youngsters were entranced and I was amazed. Do the bones work? Too darn right they do!

The Contents of the Magic Pouch

There were two bones which seemed to be from the arms or legs of a small rodent. The instructions said that the larger of these represented a male figure and a smaller a female figure. As there was very little difference in size, I actually drew an 'M' on the back of the larger one. There were four tiny finger bones which were said to represent either children or projects which the Enquirer was engaged upon. In addition to these rather gruesome items there were also four stones. Two of

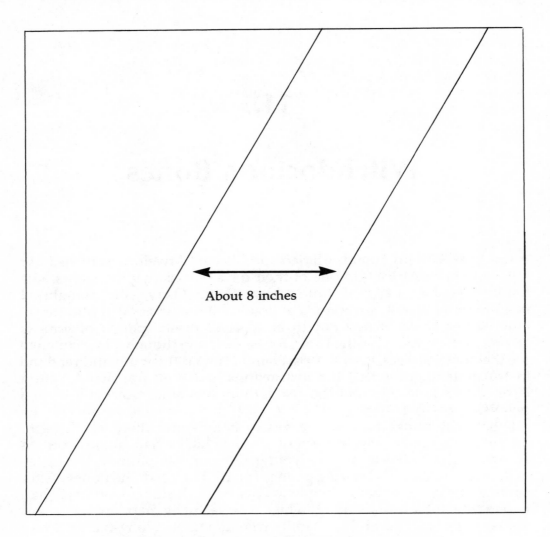

About 8 inches

Two parallel lines drawn on the ground or on paper

these stones were a deep brick red which I recognized as being jasper. These were said to denote evil influences, bad luck, misfortune, illness, etc. The other two stones were the beautiful golden-brown slightly stripy stones known as tiger's eye. These were said to show the good influences which emanated from the Enquirer himself due to his use of common sense and any efforts he made on his own behalf. Finally there were two quite large and rather strange looking seeds representing the 'wisdom of the ancients' which was supposed to protect and guide the Enquirer. This kind of description makes a lot of sense to a psychic as we are well aware of spiritual guidance from the Enquirer's dead relatives or from our own spirit guides.

A few months after I had been given this pouch, my daughter, Helen, spent some time in Zambia and Zimbabwe. She brought me back photographs of real witchdoctors at work, also in a tourist area. The bones and stones which they were using were identical but there was a great pile of them rather than just the few pieces which I had been given. From this, I concluded that a genuine reading would be quite extensive and probably quite accurate if used by a truly psychic Bone-Reader. My conclusion then is that any tools, Tarot, Runes or bones, will do the trick as long as the Reader is familiar and comfortable with them.

The Method

The instruction leaflet (which I subsequently lost) suggested that two parallel lines should be drawn slightly diagonally on the earth with a stick. I substituted a large piece of paper with two lines drawn on it. Any bones, stones or seeds which fell within these lines represented people and situations close to the Enquirer, also current and near future events. Items which fell outside of these lines represented people and situations at a distance from the Enquirer both in terms of time and space. I actually used a method which I developed through psychometry, which was to read the events from the upper left hand corner moving to the right and downwards across the paper. I have since discovered that this is the usual procedure for crystal readings, so I was accidentally working along the right lines (was that so much of an accident, I wonder?)

12.

Palmistry

Introduction

Of all forms of divination, hand-reading is the most familiar to the general public and the most widely misunderstood. Most people expect a palmist to tell them what is happening in their lives and what is going to happen next, so when they go to a palmist for a reading they may be disappointed or just disconcerted. I shall now concentrate upon some of the more common problems.

Psychic and scientific

Firstly, hands can be 'read' in two completely different ways. A 'physic' Hand-Reader may or may not know the meaning of some of the lines on the hand, his main use for the hands is to establish a link between himself and his client and then *tune in* clairvoyantly. He does this in much the same way as he might tune in to a crystal ball or some other kind of physic focus. The 'scientific' Hand-Reader learns the meaning of *all* the features which appear on the hands, often taking many years to learn his craft. He obtains his information by actually *reading* the stories which he sees written in the shapes, lines, mounts, dots and other features on the hand. Of course, many scientific Readers *are* intuitive and even psychic, while many psychics take the trouble to learn at least a little of the meaning of the actual hands which they see. However, in this section of the workbook we are going to concentrate our attention on *scientific* hand-reading. (For a comprehensive guide to this subject, read *The Living Hand* by Sasha Fenton and Malcolm Wright.)

The long and the short term

When a scientific Hand-Reader turns to predictive work, he faces a number of problems. Firstly, there are just too many years on a hand for the smaller events of an Enquirer's life to show up. If every little happening were to be displayed, the hands would have to be the size of a pair of grand pianos! Therefore it is hard for someone working purely through the medium of hand analysis to answer such questions as 'Should I change my job or should I stay where I am?' To be honest, it is the Enquirer's business to choose what he does with his life but he is entitled to expect some objective advice from the Reader. In this case, unless a change of job was to have a truly life-changing effect on the Enquirer, it might not show up at all.

At the other end of the scale, a palmist *can* see the long-term future and, therefore, should be able to give advice and reassurance, but only up to a point. Marks, shapes and lines on a hand *can and do change* considerably during a lifetime, which means that events which look as if they are going to become a fact at some time in the future may never do so! I personally *do* predict a long way ahead for my clients but I always explain that these lines can change and that things may well not work out in the way that they appear at the time of the reading. If I see anything in the far distance which looks bad, I definitely keep this to myself as it would be unforgivable to plant worrying ideas into the mind of my client, especially as the predicted event may never happen. Not only can the events which are shown on a hand change and disappear but the client himself may change his priorities and his outlook over a period of years. Nothing is static in life and our hands will change in response to the changes which we bring about or which occur around us. Can you understand the amount of responsibility that a professional needs to have and the split-second decisions which he needs to make with every reading he does?

Relationships

Another problem is in the fraught area of relationships. This is because the Reader really needs to see both of the sets of hands which are involved, or all three sets of hands if there is a love triangle. This is because it is virtually impossible to gauge the behaviour of other people from one pair of hands. A nightmare question might be 'Am I going to marry the dark haired mechanic or the fair-haired bank manager?' One would need to look at the hands of the mechanic, the bank manager, and probably a few others as well!

Thus hand-reading has its limitations, but it has its virtues too, and these come into their own in the realms of character-reading and also in pinpointing the state of the Enquirer's health and of his mind at the time of the reading. Most scientific Hand-Readers turn to Tarot, Psy-cards or some other form of intuitive skill in order to concentrate upon the day-to-day problems of their clients. It is worth remembering that the same line or mark on different *types* of hand can mean different things.

Predictions

Length of life

I am always surprised to find the number of people who think that a palmist is going to tell them when they are going to die. Any palmist who *does* attempt to hand out a date of death deserves to be shot. There *are* some indications of a long life, but even if these are missing at the time of the reading, one must remember that lines change. Another important point to bear in mind is that relatively young people's hands are still developing and just won't give much information about the latter stages of their lives. However, for what it's worth, here are the indications for length of life.

The major lines
The three major lines of life, head and heart should all be reasonably long and firm in their construction. One short line is no indication of short life but if all the lines seem to fade out or become frayed and wispy, this suggests weakness in health or the loss of the will to live.

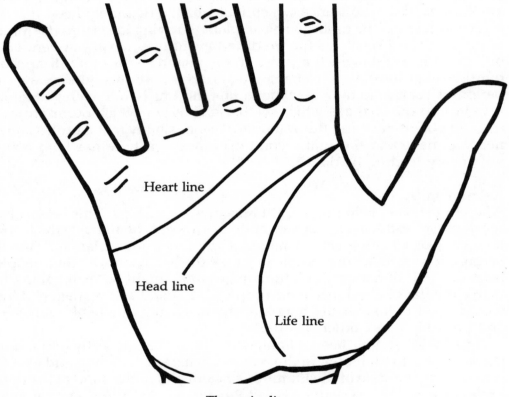

The major lines

Lines at the top of the hand
There should be a number of tiny vertical lines at the northern end of the hand above the heart line, but remember, a young Enquirer may not yet have these lines.

Rascettes
Early palmists used to think that each of the rascettes (bracelets) which appear at the wrists measured thirty years of life, three nice clear rascettes indicating ninety years of life. This does not actually work but

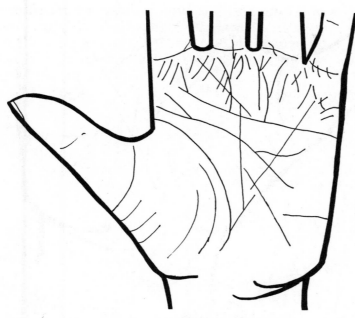

Lines at the top of the hand

nevertheless, clear rascettes are a good indication of strength, resistance to disease, and longevity.

Rascettes

Line of Mars
The line of Mars supports the life line and this is another good indicator

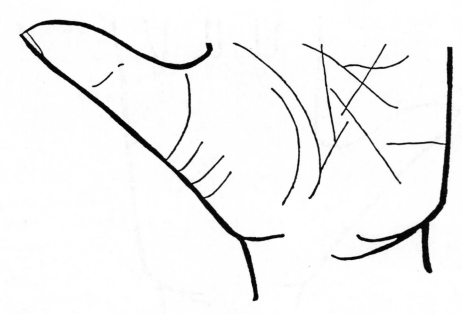

Line of Mars

of resistance to disease and resistance to shock which will help the Enquirer to survive where others might expire.

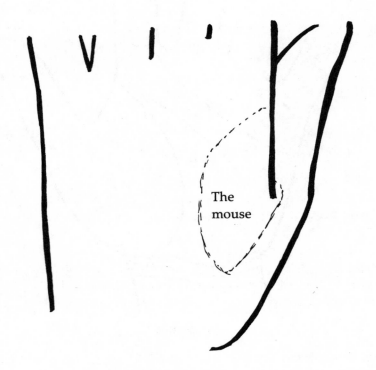

The mouse

The mouse

Health on the hands

It is hardly surprising that our hands should be such a reliable indicator of our state of health: they are after all, a part of our bodies. However, it is far more difficult to assess possible future problems than it is to see problems which are manifesting themselves, just passing away or beginning to developing at the time of the reading. Although I am trying to limit the scope of this book to futuristic divination, I think it would be appropriate to give a brief breakdown of both current and future health problems.

I will only be able to scratch the surface of this subject as there is so much which can be seen with regard to health on the hands.

Colour and texture

Healthy hands should have a good colour (appropriate to the race of the Enquirer) and they should be firm and resilient to touch. Their temperature should be pleasantly warm, bearing in mind the weather conditions etc. It is a good idea to ask the Enquirer to close his thumb into the side of his hand, then turn his hands over so that you can feel the muscle which becomes pushed up when the thumb is closed. This muscle is called the *mouse* and it should be firm to the touch.

Skin colour

If the Enquirer's hands are bluey/grey or mauve around the fingers, he has poor circulation and maybe a weak heart. Yellow hands suggest that something is wrong with the Enquirer's liver, while red ones can show thyroid or blood pressure problems. White hands could result from anaemia or poor circulation, whereas brown patches (apart from those which are associated with old age) could suggest tumours or blockages.

Temperature

Hot, sweaty hands may be due to problems with the thyroid or some other gland, whereas hot dry ones show blood pressure, kidney troubles, or simply the beginning of feverish infection. Cold, dry hands may indicate circulatory problems or, like hot hands, the onset of a feverish illness. Clammy hands show a sluggish liver, whereas cold patches show an uneven heart action.

Soft hands

It is quite natural for elderly people's hands to be soft, the same applies to pregnant ladies and vegetarians. Otherwise this could be an indication of weak health or of a weak, passive or sensual nature.

Finger nails

Fingernails take about six to eight months to grow out so they offer an excellent record of recent events, especially those relating to health.

Longitudinal ridges show problems relating to the bones or the surrounding tendons, liagaments and cartilages. Horizontal dents or ridges show a shock to the system which can be dated from their postion on the nails. For instance, if the horizontal ridge appears halfway up the nail, the event will have occurred about three or four months before the time of the reading. The shock which left its mark on the nail might have been emotional or physical in origin.

Longitudinal ridges   Horizontal dents

Nails which are abnormally white or bluey/mauve would indicate anaemia, circulation problems or heart problems, while yellow ones suggest liverishness. Nails which are 'dished' in shape show either severe nutritional deficiency or some kind of glandular disturbance, while 'watchglass' nails which bulge upwards show severe lung trouble. Moons which are over-large or missing altogether may, in some cases, indicate heart problems, while white spots on the nails suggest some slight deficiency in calcium, magnesium or vitamin C.

The lines

Any disturbance of a line could indicate a health problem but it could show many other things as well. Dots (these look like tiny craters) which appear on the lines definitely do refer to health troubles and these have to be read according to the area of the hand. For instance, dots on the head line would suggest troubles in the head area, which could include headaches, sinus problems, eye troubles, and so on, while dots on the heart line would suggest trouble with the chest area. A very important area of the heart line, as far as health is concerned, is that part which is under the little (Mercury) finger. Dots here, or an island formation, point to potential troubles with the heart and lungs. Problems with the upper part of the digestive system seem to show up towards the other end of the heart line under the middle finger (the Saturn finger).

Dots on the life line show spinal trouble, while any patch of disturbance lower down the life line can point to stomach, kidney or bladder problems (in which case the Enquirer will also have abnormally small nails) and, nearer the bottom of the line, trouble with walking.

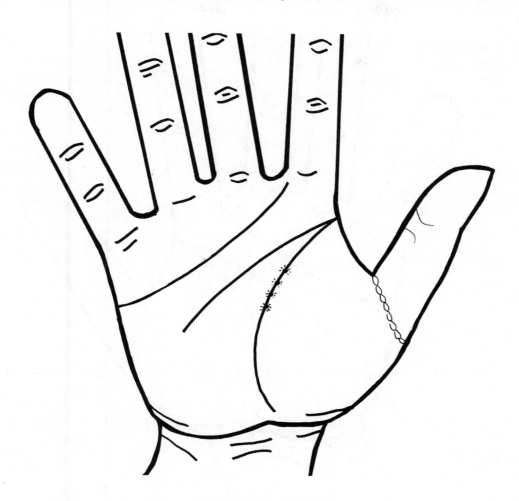

Dots or craters on the life line

Islands or smudgy effects on the heart line sometimes show that the Enquirer's teeth need attention. A garlanded effect under the head line is a classic indication of migraine.

Some reproductive troubles show up in the form of dots and redness in the centre of the heel of the hand, whiles others appear on the percussion in the area of the attachment lines and the child lines. Globules on the thumb edge of the hand or around the attachment/child lines *can* indicate cancer.

The presence of a health line shows that the Enquirer is interested in health and healing. He may work in the medical field, be very health-conscious or he may be the type of person who listens to other people's problems and tries to help them. Some Readers use the health line in order to obtain specific health information; for instance, disturbances at the lower end of the health line would suggest difficulties related to childbirth, while breaks elsewhere in the line can show stomach problems such as appendicitis, colitis and liver problems.

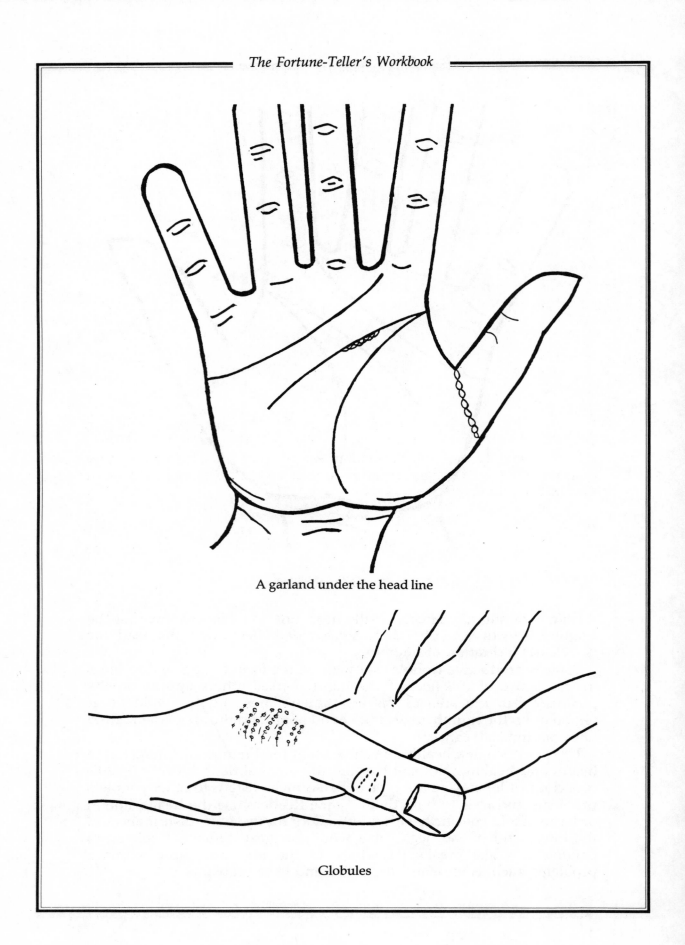

A garland under the head line

Globules

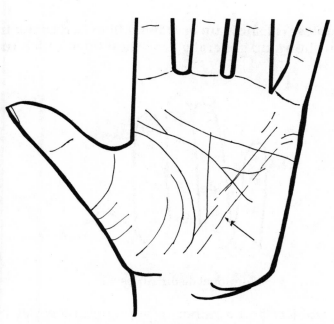

The health line

Diabetes is shown by a peculiar set of very closely packed tiny diagonal lines which appear in the Luna/Neptune area near the bottom end of the fate or life line.

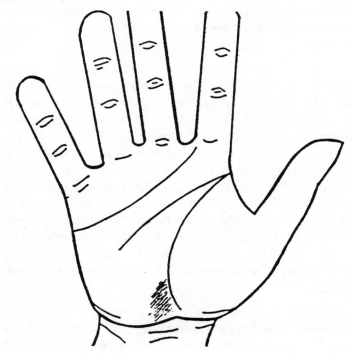

Diabetes

Hormonal troubles will show up as trailing lines across the fingertips, while exhaustion shows up generally as vertical lines which run up and down the fingers.

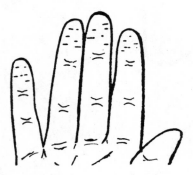

Hormonal disturbances

This is a huge subject and a rather depressing one so let us quickly move on to something more cheerful.

Snakes and ladders

How can we tell if the Enquirer is progressing in his career, standing comfortably in one spot or sliding backwards? There are a number of factors to be looked at here but the two most important would be the condition of the fate line, the head line, and, to some extent, the life line.

The fate line

This is a very confusing line for a beginner to deal with. In the first place, although it is universally known as the *fate line*, it is also sometimes called the line of destiny or even the line of Saturn. Even more confusing is the fact that it varies considerably from one person's hand to another. Some people have a clearly marked fate line while others only have fragments. In some cases the line is straight and well-marked, in others bits of it wander about all over the place. If the fate line is straight and clear, this would be akin to travelling up the motorway on a quiet Sunday afternoon, whereas a messy, fragmented line would be like trying to navigate the Hanger Lane giratory system in the rush-hour. The fate line carries all kinds of information along its length, but is especially interesting in terms of one's career, status and standing in life.

Timing on the fate line

Timing of events in palmistry is notoriously difficult; however a rough estimate can be made as follows: Place a ruler across your Enquirer's hand bisecting the joint at the base of the thumb. This seems to mark the start of independent adult life and will correspond with an age of

The map of the hand

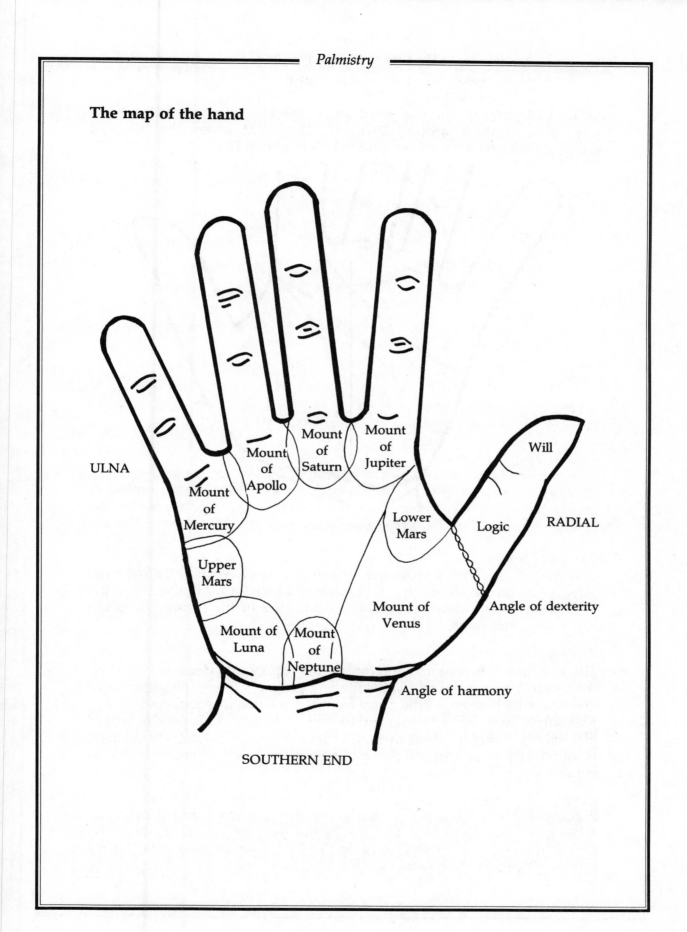

ULNA

Mount of Mercury

Mount of Apollo

Mount of Saturn

Mount of Jupiter

Will

Upper Mars

Lower Mars

Logic

RADIAL

Mount of Luna

Mount of Neptune

Mount of Venus

Angle of dexterity

Angle of harmony

SOUTHERN END

around 23 years or so. The point where the fate line crosses the head line corresponds to around 29 to 32. The point where the fate line crosses the heart line is from around 39 to about 42.

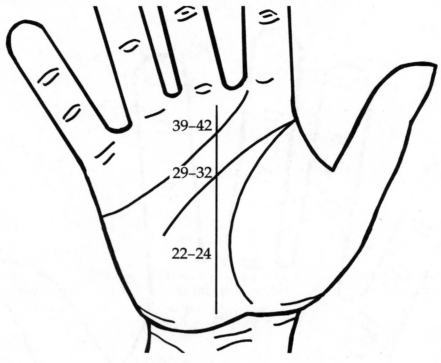

Timing on the fate line

No career at all
The drifter who never manages to soil his hands with work may not have a fate line at all, neither will the well-looked-after housewife type. This could also indicate a person who is sure of his future but is not especially ambitious.

The job-for-life type
The Enquirer who enters a job on leaving school and does more or less the same thing for the rest of his life will probably have a single straight fate line which starts a little apart from the life line and journeys slowly and surely upwards towards the mount of Jupiter. This person would also have a circular whorl formation on his Jupiter finger. He wants a position of power and influence but he is prepared to wait for this to come about.

Chops and changes
Fragmented fate lines show change. If the line stops and a new one takes over, you must look to see whether the new one is closer to the radial (thumb) side of the hand or the ulna (percussion) side. Radial jumps are progressive whereas ulna jumps are regressive. A regressive

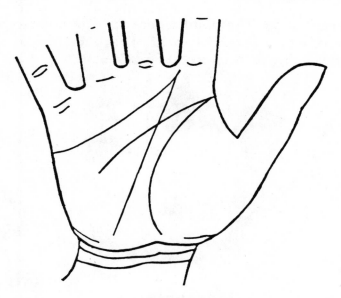

The job-for-life type

jump may occur because the Enquirer is taking time off for study or putting more energy into home and family life at that point.

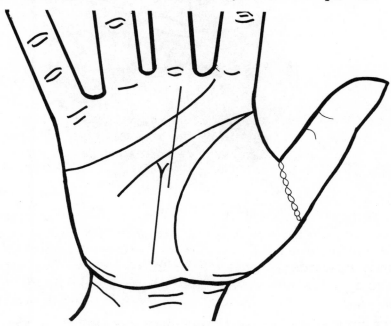

The 'I can't stand this job any longer' type

The 'I can't stand this job a moment longer' phenomenon
This is similar to the fate line which breaks and re-starts soon afterwards, but the bit of line which comes to an end has a characteristic fork at its termination.

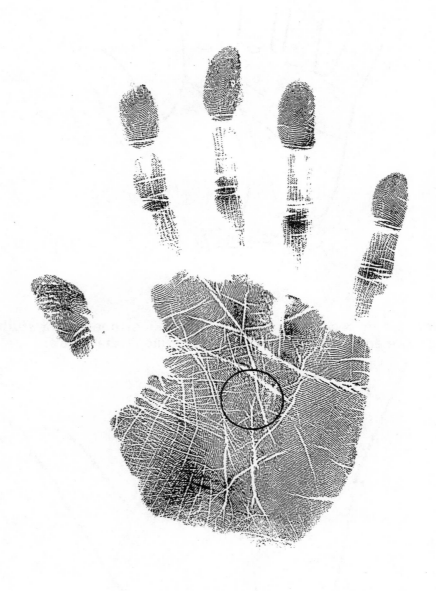

The real thing

The real thing

Just after completing this section, I gave a reading to a client who has the 'I can't stand this job any longer' fork clearly marked on her hand. In this case, the new fate line came in strongly from the *ulna* side of the hand. She told me that she had become dissatisfied with her job at around the same time as it had become convenient to start a family, and she therefore took a rather sudden decision to give up work and pay attention to her home life for a while. She soon returned to work but in another field which gave her scope to enjoy family life as well as her career. Incidentally, the lower end of the life line which reached out into the hand, plus the strong fate line, would mean that in general terms, her career would take precedence over home life.

Problems
Lines which bar the way, islands on the line or a complete fade-out of the line show setbacks in career and finances. Look to see if there is a new section of fate line which takes over from the old one. If so, take note as to whether it is to the radial or the ulna side of the previous one.

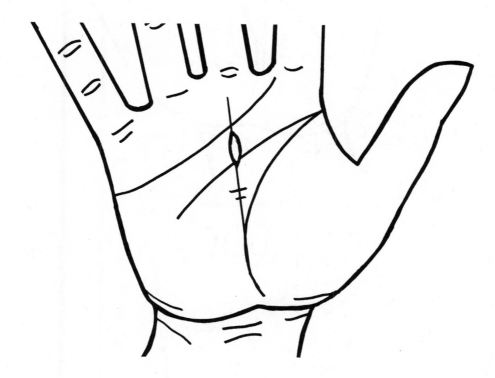

Problems

Self-employment
If the fate line turns into a collection of fragmented pieces, this is an indication of self-employment. The idea is that the Enquirer's efforts can no longer be concentrated on one or two activities but will have to encompass all the skills which running a small business would require. If the Enquirer is not actually at work at the time of the fragmentation, he may be heavily involved in a number of schemes. Women's hands usually show some fragmentation. A line rising from the life line shows self-motivation.

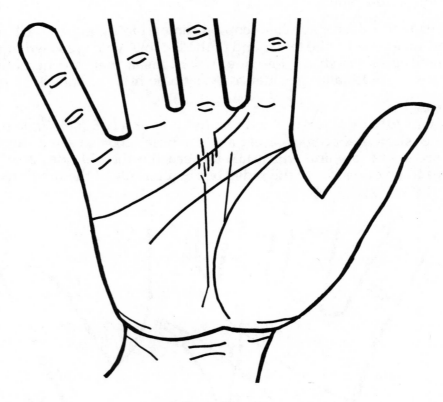

Self-employment

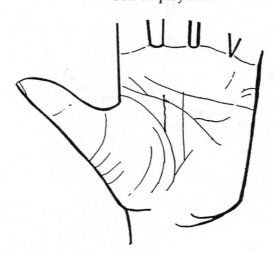

Different approaches to work

Dropping out
Sometimes there is the beginning of a fate line which disappears half-way up the hand. In this case the Enquirer may drop out of the rat-race altogether. The reason for this may be that the Enquirer has to

162

concentrate on family life for a while or, for some other reason, loses interest in work.

Dropping in

This is the reverse of dropping out. Someone whose career begins or 'takes off' later in life has a fate line which starts somewhere in the middle of the hand.

Different approaches to work

Those who start out by working closely with their family have a line which is tied to the life line at the southern end.

Those who are self-motivated may have a fate line which rises from the life line, although it is more usual for this person to have an extra line which rises from the life line.

Attitudes and motives

The end of the fate line can shed some light on an Enquirer's attitude to his career.

If work is seen primarily in terms of earning money and providing the family with security, the fate line travels straight up the hand towards the Saturn mount. Those who put their heart and soul into their career have a line which turns sharply towards Jupiter. Those who want to invest their money (the results of their efforts) into property and land have a fate line which bends at its ending towards the Apollo side of the mount of Saturn. Those who see their job as being particularly enjoyable have a fate line which slews round towards the mount of Apollo. There are even rare people, such as successful journalists and broadcasters, who see their work as a means of communicating with or influencing large groups of people, and these Enquirers will have strong branches, or indeed whole fate lines which turn sharply off towards Mercury.

The head line

The head line shows how we think; therefore by extension it shows the way we approach our jobs, and possibly the kind of work we choose to do. A head line which traces a relatively straight path across the hand would denote a logical, mathematical, and practical kind of mind, whilst a sloping head line shows a more imaginative personality. Branches which rise up from the head line mark those times when extra efforts are being made. It is just this kind of evidence which can help a palmist to spot improvements in the Enquirer's status and career. The start of a successful business venture would also be marked by rising branches. In essence, this shows a generally more businesslike approach to one's job. Lines which droop down show an extra dose of creativity or imagination creeping into the personality. This kind of addition to the head line can mark a time when the Enquirer becomes involved in the management of people, a task which requires both logic and intuition.

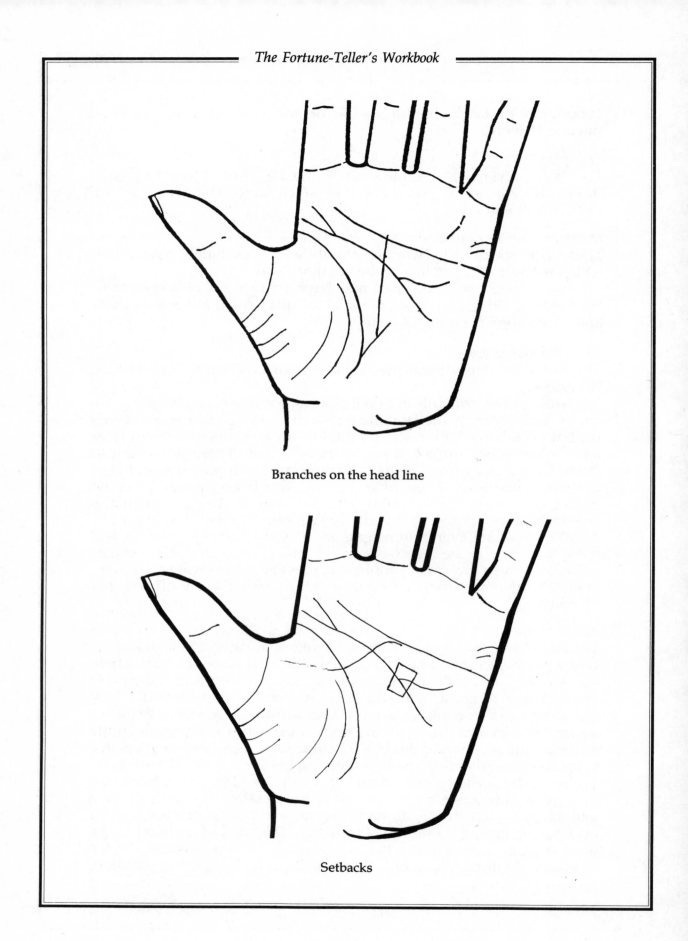

Branches on the head line

Setbacks

Setbacks

Barring lines, islands, and square formations on the head line tell of setbacks. The bars show that someone, or something, is obstructing the Enquirer in some way. Islands show periods of deep unhappiness and a total lack of fulfilment which is going to be, in part at least, in the area of the Enquirer's working life. A square formation which covers the head line shows that the Enquirer is safe from the sack but also rather bored with what he is doing. These squares disappear as soon as changes are made.

The illustration shows a decision line crossing the head line, and a square followed by an upward branch. Both these features would tell of periods of frustration followed by an improvement in circumstances.

The bosses and the workers

The Enquirer whose head line is straight and rather short will be in charge of others, but possibly only in a limited sphere of activity. A long head line which reaches the percussion side of the hand belongs to someone who cannot bear to be removed from the 'hands on' aspect of the job, even if he is technically in management. Long curved head lines are more likely to belong to creative people who work in a freelance manner.

The life line

This can also give a little information about the Enquirer's work. When an Enquirer's working life takes second place to his or her home life, the life line is more likely to cling closely to the mount of Venus. Career-minded people have life lines which reach out into the centre of their hands. If the line stops short and then starts again further into the centre of the hand, the Enquirer may not have started out as a career person but may have had to become career-minded as a result of circumstances. This kind of situation is frequently seen on the hands of a women whose marriage breaks up, as she has to turn her mind to her career rather than continue to spend her life at home with the family.

Desire for a career and family life

The person who wants both a fulfilling home life and an interesting career has a wide split at the lower end of the life line. The chances are that they will put equal energy into both aspects of their life and receive equal rewards as a result.

Travel and work

A person who needs a job which gives him scope to move around the country will have rather splayed out (spatulate) ends to his fingers and also a well-developed area around the mount of Luna.

Overseas travel in connection with work is tricky to spot. The areas of the hand which are associated with travel are the mount of Luna and

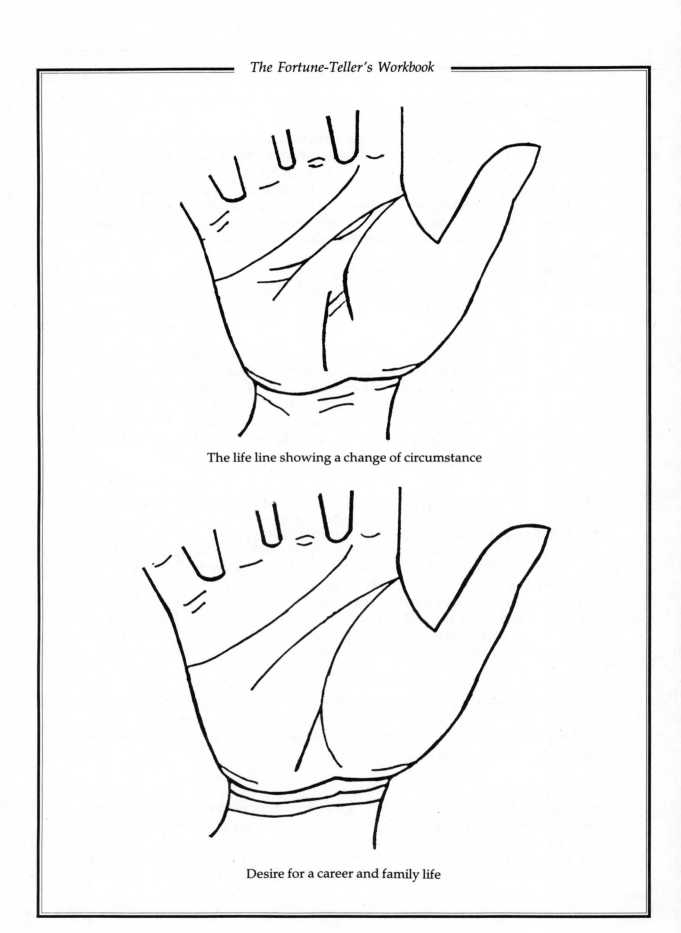

The life line showing a change of circumstance

Desire for a career and family life

upper Mars. Travel lines enter the hand horizontally from the percussion. If this is clear of lines, either the Enquirer will not travel much in his life or he takes trips abroad in his stride and is not particularly affected by them. If the lines are strongly marked, then travel is more important to the Enquirer and if travel lines become attached to any other line, there will be a deeper significance to the journeys. The best indication of travel in connection with work is the presence of travel lines which touch some part of the fate or head lines, turn and trail up the palm for a while.

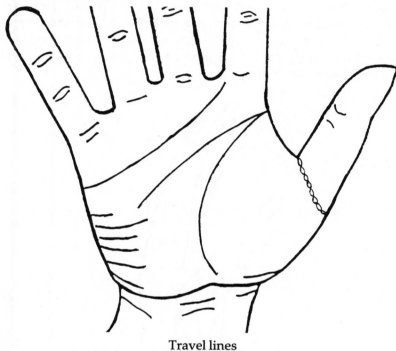

Travel lines

Relationships

Hands do not show documents and wedding rings, therefore when I refer to 'marriage' in this chapter, I am also referring to long-term stable relationships. This would apply just at much to homosexual relationships as to heterosexual relationships; a little common sense and flexibility will be needed here.

How the hands show relationships
It is one thing to work out what an Enquirer wants from life in respect of relationships but it is quite another to work out what he or she is going to get. To do this, one would need to see the hands of all the people involved in an Enquirer's life, and to complicate matters even further

we would need to see them at the times that the events are taking place. If you are dealing with an Enquirer who is a stranger to you, use your judgement and possibly a bit of intuition but don't expect to be right all the time.

I used to worry about this until I stopped to think a bit more deeply about it. After all, astrology—which is a far more detailed form of interpretation—cannot even give a straight answer to the question 'Will I ever be married?' Palmistry usually *can* answer that one and, in the case of a youngish person (under about 35 years of age), it can even give a good idea as to when this will take place, although it cannot reveal the person whom the Enquirer will marry or how, in the long term, it will work out. This is because the lines on the hand change, and a situation which appears to be fairly obvious at the time of the reading can be quite different a few years later.

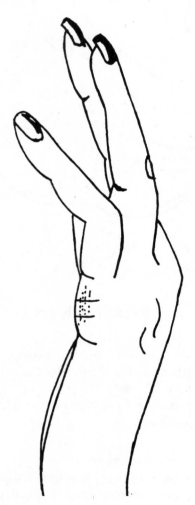

Attachment lines

'Will I ever be married?'

The area of the hand to look at in order to answer this question is on the percussion under the Mercury finger. It is best if you look at both hands, but if there is a difference between the two, take the dominant hand—the one the Enquirer writes with. The little horizontal lines which you will see there used to be called *marriage* lines, but nowadays we call them *attachment* lines.

It is a rare hand which carries no attachment lines at all. The few people with such hands whom I've come across have been either mentally or physically handicapped and therefore unable to relate fully, or the type of person who doesn't want to settle into any kind of permanent relationship. A collection of rather weak lines here shows that the Enquirer is either going to spend a good deal of time searching around for the right person, or is unable to keep anything going for more than a few months at a time.

One strong line shows that the Enquirer wants to be devoted to one person for life, and probably will be; in the event of that relationship ending, he would form another just like it. Two clear strong lines are a much more common feature. This shows an open-minded attitude which will, if the marriage doesn't work out, allow the Enquirer to look for something else. He will question his marriage and will be ready either to rectify matters or, if necessary, to change partners. It is too simplistic to say that one line equals one marriage while two lines equal two marriages, but it often works out that way. If there is one strong line and another weaker one, there will be another person whom the Enquirer loves during the course of his life: this may be before marriage or after it—even during it in some cases!

Other evidence

Stability in relationships can also be seen in the heart line. A clean clear line points to a stable and faithful outlook on marriage. Even if the Enquirer is unfaithful sexually, he will be committed to making the marriage itself last. A choppy, fragmented line shows a less steady course of events, probably due to a less steady disposition. The Enquirer is more likely to demand freedom in marriage if the line is straight and doesn't curve right up to the fingers, but this may be the freedom to travel or pursue a career in addition to having a relationship.

The real thing

This young man's heart line shows a loyal and loving nature. He will want his partner to be someone he can be proud of but he will also be protective and caring towards his family. The evidence for all this is in the gentle curve of the heart line which reaches over towards the idealistic and traditional mount of Jupiter. The small lines which flake down from the heart line show that he can flirt and use charm in his day-to-day life.

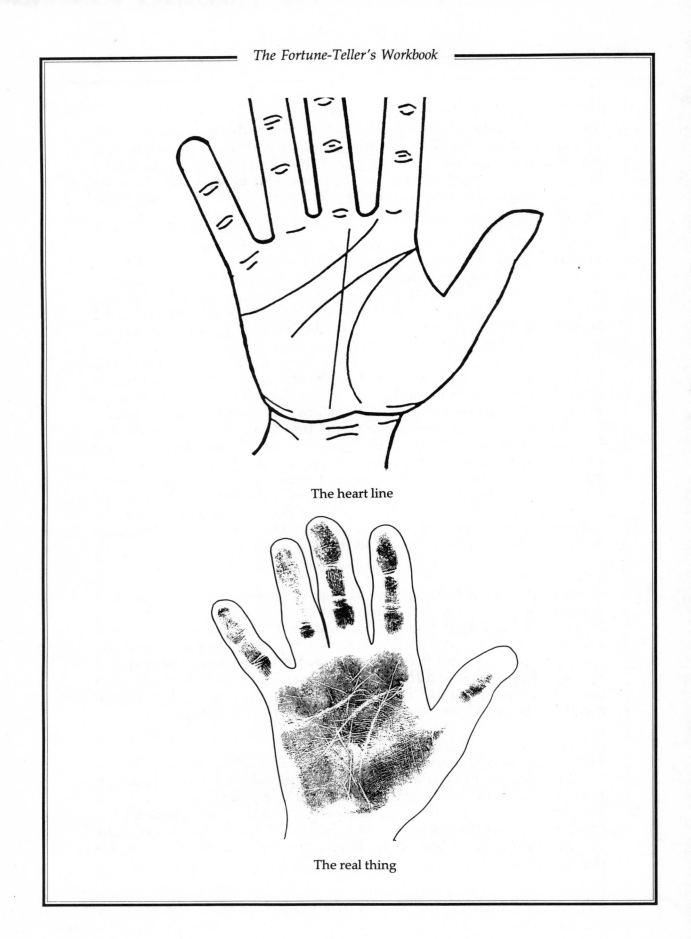

The heart line

The real thing

The course of events

The attachment lines can give some idea of the way a relationship is going. If there are a couple of lines, you may have to ask a few questions to sort out who's who in the Enquirer's life. Remember, the two lines can refer to one marriage and one near miss. Once you know which line you are dealing with, take a look at its appearance.

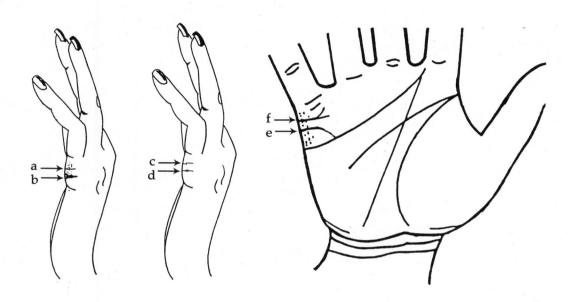

The course of events

If it is clear (a), the relationship is basically sound.

If it is messy (b), there will be problems, but if the line becomes clear again, these problems will be sorted out.

If the line is broken (c), there will be a parting and re-joining. This may be due to circumstances such as work or travel, which keeps the couple apart for a time, but a quarrel and a temporary parting is also possible.

An island (d) shows some worry about the health of the partner, while a fork on the end of the line shows that the Enquirer himself is not happy and may even contemplate divorce. In this case the Enquirer would be the one to end the marriage.

If the line curves or trails downwards (e), this shows that the *partner* could bring the marriage to an end. This is also one possible indication of the death of a partner but this needs careful checking with other features on the hand, so I strongly advise against revealing this to anyone. On the whole, this formation is more likely to suggest that the Enquirer is being put upon by the partner.

A branch which rises upwards (f) shows that the Enquirer's partner will be successful in some enterprise and could do well financially.

Meeting and parting

A line which joins the fate line suggests that someone important is entering the Enquirer's life, and although this *usually* means an emotional attachment, it could also suggest an important working partnership. Sometimes this kind of line shows the birth of a particularly loved child. If there are two such joining lines, then it is worth asking a few questions of your Enquirer. In some cases the first line will show marriage and the second line the birth of the first child. A weak joining line followed by a stronger one suggests an attachment before marriage.

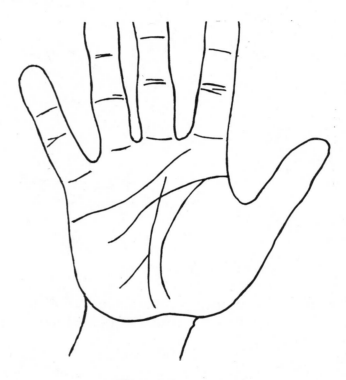

Meeting and parting

Child lines

Children can be most easily seen in the very fine vertical lines which run down the side of the percussion. These lines must cut right through the attachment lines to signify live births. The old adage 'straight lines for boys and curved ones for girls' seems to work quite well in many cases, but don't rely on this absolutely. People who work with children, have a particular love for children, or even treat their pets as children, will have many lines here but the strongest lines which cut right through the attachment lines and almost reach the heart line usually indicate children who are actually born to the Enquirer.

Lines which droop down from the inside of the life line can also

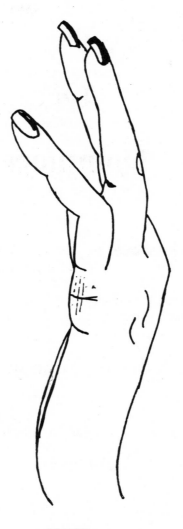

Child lines

represent children but these lines *must be very fine*, otherwise they mean something completely different.

A line which joins or crosses the fate line can suggest the birth of a child and even disturbances on the health line can indicate this, especially if there was a problem attached to the birth.

The relationship aspect of palmistry is not easy even for the professionals but experience will teach you what works and what doesn't.

13.

Dominoes

It is said that dominoes should be consulted only on rare occasions, no more than once a month, and *never* on a Monday or a Friday. Only three or four dominoes should be selected from the complete set, which should first have been moved around face downwards on a table. The meanings can then be found in the following list:

Domino Meanings

Double six
Very lucky combination, happiness in relationships, luck in career or business, and a good omen for anyone wanting a child. Land and property matters are well-starred. Parents will be caring and helpful.

Six/Five
If the Querent is out of work, there will be a job soon. Fair amounts of luck with regard to work and relationships, but this will have to be worked at. Possible trouble involving children.

Six/Four
Early marriage, with children following soon after. A happy life with reasonable security. The Querent will have to be careful of legal matters soon.

Six/Three
Marriage to a reliable type, stability in relationships. Illness in middle age. A journey which is successful, good news regarding vehicles.

Six/Two
Love affairs will go well—marriage could be in the air. The partner will be hard-working and sensible with money. If the Querent is involved in any messy business deals, these will go wrong. Also a useful gift.

Six/One
Two marriages, the second being the happier. Happiness in middle age. Children will travel and do well. A problem solved.

Six/Blank
News of a death, this may be of an animal or a human. Possibility of jealousy and gossip now. Accidents are also possible.

Five/Five
Luck, money, good career, happy marriage. A move of house which is lucky. Improvements in health.

Five/Four
Money worries probably associated with a partner of some kind. Work will bring money and independence.

Five/Three
Luck in money matters. The Querent will never be short of money. Average happiness in relationships. A nice visitor.

Five/Two
Problems in relationships; unrequited love perhaps? A marriage which is made for financial reasons but is lacking in warmth. Could be news of the birth of a child. New enterprises.

Five/One
Parties, social events. A love affair with a charismatic type which will not last. Money problems could be long-term.

Five/Blank
A warning against speculative ventures; also against rushing into marriage. A friend may need the Querent's shoulder to cry on soon.

Four/Four
Parties and social events, sports and young people around. Manual work will go well, but professional people will have difficulties.

Four/Three
Disappointments, especially concerning children. Possible illness. Problems in connection with a vehicle.

Four/Two
Family and domestic upheavals. Unexpected events concerning the home—these could be good or bad. Beware of a flirtatious or philandering type of person.

Four/One

A good marriage with comfort and security but, possibly, no children. The Querent will have to pay off some outstanding bills soon.

Four/Blank

Relationship problems; reconcilliations will be only temporary. The possibility of twins coming into the family! A new outlook or different way of looking at life.

Three/Three

Money will come to the Querent soon. This may be a legacy, a win or a bonus. The love-life could go through a bad patch due to outside interference.

Three/Two

Good domino for the start of any enterprise. A journey will be enjoyable and worthwhile. Dishonesty will be found out; the Querent shouldn't take chances just now.

Three/One

A surprise; good news, but also the possibility of an affair which could get the Querent into hot water.

Three/Blank

Jealousy, broken friendships. Domestic problems due to the weak attitude of the partner or other family members.

Two/Two

All partnerships and relationships will go well. Health should be watched.

Two/One

Loss or failure in business. If the Querent isn't careful, he could lose his home too. A flamboyant but unsettled love life.

Two/Blank

Journeys which have a good outcome. Sales and communication ventures will go well. The Querent will have to beware of thieves. Relationship matters are not good just now.

One/One

Love, money and luck. Happy family life. Parents will be helpful. A decision to be taken soon which will require courage.

One/Blank

A visitor from over the water. Money or resources are in danger of being wasted. Health improves.

Blank/Blank

Loss, theft, disappointment. Trouble is on the way and this could affect the Querent's job, relationships, health, or all three. The Querent should also beware of accidents.

14.

Playing cards

Playing cards actually evolved from the Tarot and are used for divination in much the same manner. Like Tarot, playing cards have four suits which correspond to the ancient elements of earth, air, fire and water.

Element	Tarot	Playing Cards
Earth	Pentacles or Coins	Diamonds
Air	Swords	Spades
Fire	Wands, Rods or Staves	Clubs
Water	Cups	Hearts

There are 52 playing cards in a deck whilst there are 78 cards in a Tarot deck. Each suit of playing cards has an Ace, numbered cards from two to ten, plus the court cards of Jack, Queen and King. The only card in a playing card deck which corresponds in any way to the Major Arcana section of the Tarot deck is the Joker which is similar to the Tarot Fool. The meanings of the cards should, of course, be memorized but a mind-jogging list can be kept nearby while you are in the process of learning the cards.

New Cards

Buy yourself a new deck of cards and keep them solely for fortune-telling. Keep them in a box on a shelf away from other people and don't let anyone else play around with them. Don't use this deck of cards for game playing.

If you care to make a prayer over the cards before using them for the first time, please do so. It is a good idea to bless the cards by asking for guidance to use them well and to encourage the cards to bring comfort, help and good advice to your Querents. If you like incense, a joss stick can be used while you are going through this blessing ritual. Shuffle the cards throughly several times, as this will help them to tune in to your vibrations and also take the newness from them so that they become easier to handle.

Spread Suggestions

There are many layouts which can be used. A good source of information for this would be *Fortune-Telling by Playing Cards* by Nerys Dee (published by the Aquarian Press). Tarot spreads can be adapted for use with playing cards but it may be as well to try this very simple Romany idea to begin with. This was shown to me by Sally, a Romany fortune-teller who uses her cards with a great deal of psychic intuition.

Ask your Querent to shuffle the cards and then spread them out in a line face-downwards on a table. Tell him to choose 15 cards and place them in a rough bunch face upwards on the table. Ask him to spread them out a little. If necessary, you can spread them out a little more, but try to keep them in the same positions so that you can see which cards are touching each other or are adjacent to each other. After giving the reading, go through the whole process again, this time with 21 cards. It is interesting to note which cards turn up in both readings.

Upright and Reversed

As far as I am aware, professional Readers use playing cards only in the upright position. However, if you wish to use reversed meanings, mark each numbered card with a small dot at the top so that you can see which would be the right way up. I tend to use the cards only in the upright position but I *do* take note of any court cards which are reversed as this shows whether the person represented by the card is going to be a helpful influence on the Querent or not. Some Readers use only 32 of the cards, omitting the lower-numbered cards, but I prefer to use the whole pack. The following interpretations are a précis of all the possible meanings of the cards. There are many different kinds of interpretations in use but the following list is probably the most familiar to card readers. If you find other interpretations suit you better, please feel free to use them.

The Meanings of the Cards

NB: Although most cards have a reversed meaning, not all of them do.

The suit of Hearts
Ace
Joy, love, friendship, the start of a romance.
Reversed: Friendship rather than romance, possibly the end of a love affair.

King

Traditionally, a fair-haired man. A kind, loving and affectionate man who will give good advice to the Questioner.
Reversed: Poor judgement. An unreliable and very amorous man.

Queen

Traditionally, a fair-haired woman. A kindly, loving woman who will be good to the Questioner. She is faithful and affectionate.
Reversed: An over-materialistic attitude. A pleasant but lazy and slightly greedy woman.

Jack

Traditionally, a fair-haired young man. Look at the nearby cards in order to judge his intentions.

Ten

Good luck, love, joy. This card improves any bad cards around it and confirms the benefits of any good ones.

Nine

The wish card. Health, wealth, status, esteem. An improvement in circumstances.

Eight

Visits and visitors, journeys for pleasure, meals in good company.
Reversed: Irritating visits or visitors.

Seven

Unfaithful or unreliable person. News.

Six

A generous person, a shoulder to cry on. Shared confidences, unexpected propositions. Good luck.
Reversed: A friend needs the Questioner's help.

Five

Money, but also jealous or unreliable people around.

Four

A journey or change. If applicable, the Questioner will not marry when young.
Reversed: An irritating journey, or an unexpectedly awkward change in circumstances.

Three

The Questioner will have to be cautious; rash statements will upset others.

Two

Success, happiness, luck and prosperity. An engagement, even a marriage.
Reversed: Same but delayed.

The suit of Diamonds

Ace
Engagement or wedding ring. A letter with good news about money.
Reversed: Similar but delayed.

King
Traditionally, a fair-haired man. Obstinate and powerful, but helpful to the Questioner.
Reversed: An angry, obstinate man who will hurt the Questioner or even look for revenge.

Queen
Traditionally, a fair-haired woman. A flirtatious, sophisticated woman who is fond of socializing.
Reversed: Frankly, this woman is a nasty piece of work.

Jack
Traditionally, a fair-haired relative. This person is selfish, dishonest, and only interested in his own requirements and opinions.
Reversed: This person is an absolute beast.

Ten
Money, journeys; possibly help from a married man who lives in the country.
Reversed: Similar but delayed.

Nine
Surprise regarding money; good if the card is upright, poor if reversed.

Eight
A marriage late in life, not necessarily good. Also plans and ideas.
Reversed: Bad late marriage.

Seven
A gift or surprise.
Reversed: Waste, the loss of something valuable.

Six
Problems with marriage, especially second marriages.
Reversed: The Questioner shouldn't even contemplate a second marriage.

Five
Success in business or other enterprises. If applicable, good children.
Reversed: Success but delayed.

Four
Inheritance and/or improvements in finances.
Reversed: Annoyances and irritations.

Three
Legal problems, especially if the Questioner is involved in a divorce. A

bad marriage partner who will make the Questioner unhappy.
Reversed: Divorce, domestic and legal problems.

Two
A love affair which meets with opposition.
Reversed: A disappointing love affair.

The suit of Clubs

Ace
Wealth, success, peace of mind. Happy home life.
Reversed: Same but milder.

King
Traditionally, a dark-haired man. He is honest, helpful, humane and affectionate. A faithful partner who makes everyone around him feel happy.
Reversed: This man may be troubled, tied to some kind of difficult situation, or just plain tricky and dishonest.

Queen
Traditionally, a dark-haired woman. This lady is businesslike, capable, and very attractive to the opposite sex.
Reversed: This lady may be worried or not in a position to help the Questioner; alternatively, she may be calculating and shifty.

Jack
Traditionally, a dark-haired young man. A reliable friend who will help the Questioner.
Reversed: This young man is either not willing or not able to help the Questioner just now.

Ten
Money is coming; this could be a bonus, a win, a legacy or a business idea which takes off quickly.
Reversed: The same but milder or slow to materialize.

Nine
Achievements. If applicable, a new lover.
Reversed: Obstacles and disagreements.

Eight
A greedy, jealous person who is very fond of money.
Reversed: Opposition, arguments.

Seven
Happiness, joy, prosperity; however, the Questioner should be careful with members of the opposite sex as they will cause trouble.
Reversed: The same but weaker.

Six
Business success, especially in partnerships.
Reversed: The same but milder.

Five
An advantageous marriage, helpful friends.
Reversed: Milder; friendship rather than marriage.

Four
Changes for the worse, lies and betrayal.
Reversed: Unreliable people around the Questioner.

Three
Marriage to a wealthy partner.
Reversed: Marriage to a comfortable (rather than rich) partner.

Two
Disappointment, disagreements.

The suit of Spades

Ace
Love affairs, passion, obsession, deceitful friends.
Reversed: Death.

King
Traditionally, a very dark-haired man. An ambitious man, a friend of the great, but this man must be careful that he doesn't lose all that he has.
Reversed: An ambitious, tough, selfish and aggressive man.

Queen
Traditionally, a very dark-haired woman; also traditionally, a widow. An unscrupulous seductive woman.
Reversed: A spiteful, jealous woman.

Jack
Traditionally, a very dark-haired young man. A well-meaning young man who never really gets it together.
Reversed: A layabout.

Ten
Worry, imprisonment of any kind. This will cast a cloud over any cards which are nearby.
Reversed: Same but milder.

Nine
Domestic worries, possibly total loss of money. Calamities, deaths, natural disasters, destruction, war.
Reversed: Still terrible but not quite so devastating.

Eight
Opposition from others, cancelled plans, obstacles.
Reversed: Bad news, opposition, troubles.

Seven
Sorrow, warnings, losses, possibly the death of a friend.
Reversed: Still bad but milder. Tears, sleepless nights.

Six
Improvements, wage increases, rewards.
Reversed: No real recognition for work done.

Five
Good marriage, domestic happiness—but bad-tempered people around the Questioner outside his home environment.
Reversed: Interfering person, anxiety.

Four
Illness, business and money worries.

Three
A marriage with a wealthy partner who is fickle and unreliable.
Reversed: Possibly a hasty decision. A journey, a parting.

Two
Scandal, gossip, betrayal.
Reversed: Possibly death around the Questioner or loss and partings due to interference from others.

Combinations

Playing cards can be read singly or in combinations with other cards. People who are thoroughly familiar with all the combinations make the most skilled card readers. However, there are so many permutations that a beginner would be thoroughly put off. The French tend to go in for combinations in a big way, using this system both for Tarot cards and playing cards. Here are some familiar groupings which are not too hard to cope with:

	Four	Three	Two
Aces	Great success, and a completely new way of life to begin soon. Career, especially well-starred.	Success and help to the Querent. Good news, luck.	Partnerships, possibly marriage. Unusual news.
Kings	Great success, advancement, inheritance.	Success; important business meetings which will benefit the Querent.	Some success; good business partnerships.
Queens	Scandal; also social activity	Back-biting and nasty remarks coming to the Querent. Also invitations.	Some minor gossip; also an interesting meeting with a female friend.
Jacks	Quarrels all round. Also noisy parties.	Some quarrelling.	Argument and discussion. Someone has bad intentions towards the Querent.
Tens	Change of circumstances which is very much for the better.	Money, improvement of circumstances and finances.	Money, a debt repaid.
Nines	Good luck, unexpectedly good events.	Success, most things will go well. Good health, happiness.	Reasonable amount of success. Important documents to be dealt with.
Eights	Problems, troubles, worry. Short trips to see friends.	Family problems, love troubles. It would be best to postpone any decisions until better times come along.	Worry. Desire for love, but disappointment as this will not come yet.
Sevens	Several enemies. Disputes, scandal, conspiracies.	Some people seem to be against the Querent now. Illness.	One active enemy, but the Querent will overcome problems to reach success, achievement.

A Sample Reading Using the Pyramid Layout

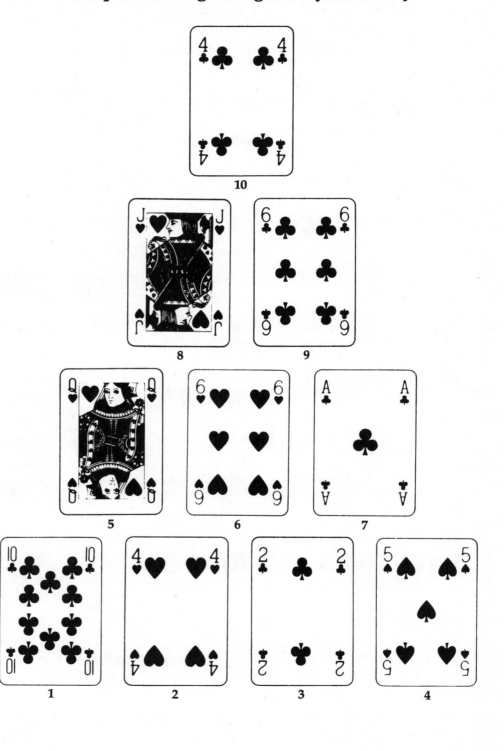

Read from the bottom upwards, using the bottom row as past influences which have a bearing on the present situation; move forward in time as you progress up the pyramid.

This sample reading is for a middle-aged working woman.

1. *Ten of Clubs*
   The Querent has had financial benefits in the past, either through work or by chance.

2. *Four of Hearts*
   She has travelled in the past, possibly in connection with work (the first card seems to point to a career emphasis so far in this reading).

3. *Two of Clubs*
   She has had disappointments and disagreements in the past (connected with work probably).

4. *Five of Spades*
   Although her home life has been all right, she has had to struggle and face opposition in her career or from other outside influences.

5. *Queen of Hearts*
   Help is coming from a fair-haired woman.

6. *Six of Hearts*
   She will find help and kindness from others; a shoulder to cry on; generosity and help.

7. *Ace of Clubs*
   She will do well as this card shows money, happiness and a good home life.

8. *Jack of Hearts*
   A fair-haired young man will become important in some way in her life. He could be connected with the Queen of Hearts—therefore it seems that a family or a group of friends may be kind and helpful to her.

9. *Six of Clubs*
   A successful business partnership to come.

10. *Four of Clubs*
    This final card represents the outcome which shows changes for the worse, lies and betrayal; therefore she should accept help when it is offered, but not lean too heavily on others or expect them to be as decent to her as she would like them to be.

This sample reading would show that this lady is career-minded and has a long way to go yet, but the jealousy of others due to her success will always be a potential pitfall.

15.

Chinese Astrology

Chinese astrology is a huge subject, even more complicated than Western astrology. The only aspect of this which is familiar to Westerners is the 12-year cycle in which each year is associated with an animal in the same way that each of the 12 months in a Western horoscope is arranged into symbols. In this book I have tried, wherever possible, to approach each subject from a purely *predictive* point of view, however with this section I have simply compiled the characteristics of the Chinese year system.

The Chinese New Year, called *Tet*, occurs around the beginning of February. Each year in the 12-year cycle is named after an animal. The choice of animals varies a little from one source to another; I guess this is because the system has been developed over many thousands of years and in places isolated from each other by distance and a lack of communication.

The Year of the Rat

12 February 1888 to 30 January 1889
31 January 1900 to 18 February 1901
18 February 1912 to 5 February 1913
5 February 1924 to 24 January 1925
24 January 1936 to 10 February 1937
10 February 1948 to 28 January 1949
28 January 1960 to 14 February 1961
19 February 1972 to 2 February 1973

These assertive, intelligent people have a great desire to reach the top. They don't give up easily, they keep their goals in sight even if this means riding roughshod over other people or making use of them. They don't set out to hurt or upset others. It's just that they are impatient and can't help considering their own needs to be paramount. Their charm and humour ensures that they are usually forgiven. Rats have good taste, an artistic eye and they often look very good. Their gossipy sociability and confident exterior hides a rather different interior nature. They are afraid to fail or look foolish and they hate being rushed into anything or made to reveal their desires openly. Rats make up their own minds and take their own decisions. When pressed by others, they will tell lies in preference to revealing their plans or allowing their vulnerability to show. They tend to succeed in business, the art world, advertising, sales, politics and journalism.

These creative types cannot abide an uncomfortable or dirty environment, petty mean-spirited people or those who nag. For those of you who seek a generous, amusing and ambitious partner, you need look no further than the nearest Rat. Rats are said to be compatible with Monkeys who are tricky enough to cope with them, or Dragons who are powerful and self-willed enough not to be deceived by their artfulness.

Rats are similar to people who are born under the Western zodiac sign of Libra.

The Year of the Buffalo

31 January 1889 to 20 January 1890
19 February 1901 to 8 February 1902
6 February 1913 to 25 January 1914
25 January 1925 to 12 February 1926
11 February 1937 to 31 February 1938
29 January 1949 to 16 February 1950
15 February 1961 to 4 February 1962
3 February 1973 to 23 January 1974

Buffaloes are comfort lovers who are also materialistic and home-loving. Their steady, trustworthy nature makes them reliable, stoical and practical. They take things in their stride and seldom become irritable, although their slow-burn nature can erupt into a terrible anger. They are generous to those they love and hate to take advantage of anyone. Buffaloes like good food, music and pleasant surroundings although they prefer family life to the high-life. They are pleasant and charming and get on well with the opposite sex and, of course, being sensual they make good lovers.

Buffaloes are money-minded; they fear loss, poverty or discomfort and they can become greedy and over-materialistic as a result. If they can succeed, either in business or in the arts, they will be happy but they do need a *secure* job. They need security in relationships too and therefore make faithful, if rather unimaginative partners. They are physically strong, clever with their hands and, as long as they are secure, appreciated and never rushed, they can be very good to live with and to work with in partnership. They are compatible with the Rat, Cockerel and the Snake.

Buffaloes are similar to people born under the Western zodiac sign of Taurus.

The Year of the Tiger

21 January 1890 to 8 February 1891
9 February 1902 to 28 January 1903
26 January 1914 to 13 February 1915
13 February 1926 to 1 January 1927
1 February 1938 to 18 February 1939
17 February 1950 to 5 February 1951
5 February 1962 to 25 January 1963
24 January 1974 to 10 February 1975

Tigers are fun. Their sparkling personality, humour and charm make them fascinating and they really do enjoy company. Tigers have a strong sense of justice, taking the part of the underdog as they hate to see anyone suffer. Their kind hearts and joyful temperament hide strength and ambition: they aim high and usually get there. They are excellent bosses but far too self-motivated, creative and rebellious to work for anyone else for long. They love to be in charge, using their organizational skills to persuade others to do the dirty work. They can often see original ways around problems but would rather not be bothered by trifling details. They rarely forget those who do them a good deed, but they *never* forget a hurt; once they lose their faith in someone, it can never be reinstated.

Tigers work hard and play hard. Their ambition, coupled with their expensive tastes, ensures that they are high earners. They are great company but temperamental to live with. Their nerves can become frayed and they become overworked and overtired. They do need to be in the centre of things, gathering up the admiration which is their due. Tigers are compatible with Horses, Dragons and Dogs.

Tigers are similar to people born under the Western zodiac sign of Leo.

The Year of the Cat (or Rabbit)

9 February 1891 to 29 January 1892
29 January 1903 to 15 February 1904
14 February 1915 to 3 February 1916
2 February 1927 to 22 January 1928
19 February 1939 to 7 February 1940
6 February 1951 to 26 January 1952
26 January 1963 to 13 February 1964
11 February 1975 to 30 January 1976

Refined and tasteful, these people have an air of exclusivity about them; they hold back from others and prefer not to become involved with or excited by anything that doesn't immediately affect their own well-being. Their company is sought after, as is their advice, which is often sound due to its objectivity. Cats do have feelings, of course, and can become very depressed when hurt; it's just that they find it difficult to wear their hearts on their sleeve. They put a lot into personal relationships and take them very seriously. They can make good working colleagues but there must be mutual respect.

With their pent-up emotions and sensitive nature, they can lash out angrily or become coldly sarcastic in an attempt to cover up their own hurt feelings. Conservative, fascinating and rather difficult to know, Cats are admired or disliked but never ignored. They have a certain sexual charisma resulting from their reserved attitude, fine minds and frequently fascinating looks. However detached and self-assured they appear to be, Cats hide a strong sense of inadequacy, they strive hard to reach their own high standards. Rational, logical and humanitarian, they make wonderful counsellors, doctors, teachers and personnel officers. They can also cope with the complexity of computers, astrology, and philosophic or academic studies. Cats are intuitive and are often attracted to the occult. They are said to be compatible with Goats and Dogs.

Cats are similar to people who are born under the Western zodiac sign of Aquarius.

The Year of the Dragon

10 February 1880 to 29 January 1881
30 January 1892 to 16 February 1893
16 February 1904 to 3 February 1905
4 February 1916 to 22 January 1917
23 January 1928 to 9 February 1929
8 February 1940 to 26 January 1941
27 January 1952 to 13 February 1953
14 February 1964 to 1 February 1965
31 January 1976 to 17 February 1977

This lucky sign promises health, wealth and happiness. These lively people seem to succeed at whatever they do; their inventive, intelligent minds lead them to explore widely and to want to experience all that life has to offer. Their strong will, determination, restless independence and need for freedom make them unpredictable at times. They follow their own path, even if it seems to be illogical. They cannot be made to work in a strictly routine situation because they are far too easily bored. Dragons are quick-tempered and blunt but rarely set out to hurt; it's just that their honesty seems to get the better of them. They are so amusing and genuinely kind that no one can be angry with them for long. In personal relationships they can be unreliable because their hatred of routine and need for exploration can make them unfaithful from time to time, although this is never done in order to hurt a partner.

Dragons have high standards, work hard, and are discriminating and honest. Highly intuitive and interested in philosophical subjects, they may be intellectually drawn to the occult. Good-looking with attractive personalities, they don't really understand jealousy but can be the cause of it in others. Dragons will succeed in any form of work which pushes back horizons and deals with people. Teaching is their speciality, as is salesmanship, politics, advertising and the arts. Dragons are said to be compatible with Monkeys, Rats and Snakes.

Dragons are similar to people who are born under the Western zodiac sign of Sagittarius.

The Year of the Snake

30 January 1881 to 17 February 1882
17 February 1893 to 5 February 1894
4 February 1905 to 24 January 1906
23 January 1917 to 10 February 1918
10 February 1929 to 29 January 1930
27 January 1941 to 14 February 1942
14 February 1953 to 3 February 1954
2 February 1965 to 21 January 1966
18 February 1977 to 7 February 1978

Snakes are reserved people who have a contained kind of power. They are attractive and graceful but not particularly sociable. Snakes are intensely loyal to those they care for, and are totally responsible towards those whom they employ. They remember good deeds but never forget a hurt and they can wait for years to get their own back. Snakes are hard and reliable workers, perfectionists who are often clever with their hands. These people are ambitious, critical of themselves and others, they are tenatious, usually committed to finishing everything that they start. Snakes are secretive and nobody knows how much (or how little) they have. The state of their emotions is even more sacrosanct than the contents of their bank account.

These people have exceptional ability to study and concentrate; they hate small talk or useless socializing; Snakes make good inventors, doctors, scientists, engineers, writers and computer buffs. They are not well-adapted to dealing with people, but may be able to stand any amount of animosity against themselves, because they simply switch off and let others think what they want. The Snake's greatest fear is of becoming dependent or of appearing weak, even to himself. Snakes are compatible with Cockerels.

Snakes are similar to people who are born under the Western zodiac sign of Scorpio.

The Year of the Horse

18 February 1882 to 7 February 1883
6 February 1894 to 25 January 1895
25 January 1906 to 12 February 1907
11 February 1918 to 31 January 1919
30 January 1930 to 17 February 1931
15 February 1942 to 4 February 1943
4 February 1954 to 23 January 1955
22 January 1966 to 8 February 1967
8 February 1978 to 27 January 1979

Horses are attractive, kindly people who make good friends and excellent work-mates. They work hard, take responsibility, and look after their families. Horses are good to look at and make pleasant and intelligent company—therefore they appeal greatly to the opposite sex. Trustworthy and idealistic, they are generous to their friends, although they will not go *too* far to right an injustice on someone else's behalf. They can occasionally be callous and indelicate, without even realizing that they are being hurtful. They have a clear idea of what they need from life and usually make sure that they get it, although they may not be quite so good at seeing that the requirements of others are met, especially if this requires subtlety. At work their organizational abilities and capacity to put in long hours without tiring ensure both success and the respect of others. They make good company directors, teachers, lawyers and farmers. Being patient and good with their hands, they also make good mechanics and builders.

Horses like to think for themselves, they are independent and also restless. They can be impulsive, sometimes cutting their noses off to spite their faces; their tempers, when aroused, can be prodigious. Their sarcastic outbursts and cold sulky behaviour can alienate people although this surprises them because *they* see themselves as being extremely popular. Their health is generally good, and their moderate habits ensure that they generally live long and healthy lives. Horses are said to be compatible with Goats, Dogs and Tigers.

There does not seem to be a close correlation between the sign of the Horse and any particular Western zodiac sign; the nearest is probably a Capricorn/Cancer mixture.

The Year of the Goat

8 February 1883 to 28 January 1884
26 January 1895 to 13 February 1896
13 February 1907 to 1 February 1908
1 February 1919 to 20 January 1920
18 February 1931 to 6 February 1932
5 February 1943 to 25 January 1944
24 January 1955 to 11 February 1956
9 February 1967 to 29 January 1968

Goats are intelligent, studious and slightly reserved. They are pleasant, gentle companions who can both entertain and listen to others. They take an interest in a wide variety of subjects and are inevitably drawn towards the occult. Goats are extremely sensitive to atmosphere; also, being sensitive to the thoughts and feelings of others, they can be hurt by jealousy or spite. Usually found in the world of the arts, music, writing or the caring professions, these people take their work seriously and tend to push themselves to high standards of achievement. They may appear slightly dreamy, unpretentious and light-hearted but they have the ability to think and work on a deep level and when they take on a commitment they try to see it through. They have a natural respect for the dignity of others and a love of children. Being both romantic and vulnerable, Goats don't like to wear their hearts on their sleeves. They may appear casual, even heartless, to a new lover because they hide their feelings in order not to be hurt. Goats are easily embarrassed and would hate to be seen as an embarrassment to anyone else.

Goats need a stable and contented domestic life and they are faithful and loving partners. They enhance the confidence of those they love and appreciate having their own confidence boosted as it tends to fizzle out on them from time to time. Despite periods of depression, Goats are generally happy and are able to provide a comfortable life-style for their families. They can be surprisingly successful in their careers once they have found their niche. Goats are said to be compatible with Boars, Cats, Rabbits and Horses.

They are somewhat similar to people who are born under the Western zodiac sign of Pisces.

The Year of the Monkey

29 January 1884 to 14 February 1885
14 February 1896 to 1 February 1897
2 February 1908 to 21 January 1909
21 January 1920 to 7 February 1921
7 February 1932 to 25 January 1933
26 January 1944 to 12 February 1945
12 February 1956 to 30 January 1957
30 January 1968 to 16 February 1969

Monkeys are great company. They are intelligent, humorous and exciting. They like to live in the fast lane, with plenty of change, challenge and a stream of new faces around them. They do not cope well with routine, time-tables or necessary chores; they are easily bored. They learn quickly and are intuitive to the point of clairvoyance, but being quick on the uptake themselves they can be impatient with those who are slower to catch on. Monkeys read quickly and absorb ideas fast but many Monkeys prefer to gain their information from the television or on the grapevine. Their sarcasm can be hurtful and they make formidable verbal adversaries. They are surprisingly hard workers, but they have to set their *own* goals; they never seem to work for the approval of others and, for this reason, are probably best suited to self-employment. They frequently put other people's backs up and are then able to walk away from difficult situations while allowing other slower types to carry the can for them. They have an air of arrogance and may look down on others who are not as bright as they are. Monkeys make good journalists, advertisers and drivers.

They are surprisingly successful in relationships because they really do need to love and be loved but they haven't much patience with a sickly partner. Monkeys of both sexes need a motherly partner who allows them enough rope to get away with some of their tricks while keeping a weather eye on them. They can become strangely downhearted. Monkeys are good with children, especially their own. They are said to be compatible with Dragons, and Rats.

Monkeys are similar to people who are born under the Western zodiac sign of Gemini.

The Year of the Cockerel

15 February 1885 to 7 January 1886
2 February 1897 to 21 January 1898
22 January 1909 to 9 February 1910
8 February 1921 to 6 February 1922
26 January 1933 to 13 February 1934
13 February 1945 to 1 February 1946
31 January 1957 to 18 February 1958
17 February 1969 to 5 February 1970

These outgoing, glamorous people make friends easily and enjoy being in the middle of things. They work hard, often in an inventive and original manner but they can never hide their light under a bushel. Cockerels have little time for dull-witted people or those who don't catch on to an idea quickly. They have broad minds and are often well read. Cockerels can be opinionated, even boastful at times but they never sulk or bear grudges. They can take offence quickly and give it even more quickly but they soon forget and return to their normal cheerful natures. Although flirtatious, they are usually faithful once they settle down and will care for their family in a responsible manner.

Cockerels have such lively minds that they love any kind of novelty. They can achieve a great deal through study and work and hate to be kept from reaching the top of the tree. They are honest and open, courageous and outwardly confident, even if this confidence is sometimes more apparent than real. Cockerels are original, difficult to live with but basically honest and decent. They are said to be compatible with Snakes, Buffaloes and Dragons.

Cockerels are similar to people born under the Western zodiac sign of Aries.

The Year of the Dog

8 January 1886 to 23 January 1887
22 January 1898 to 9 February 1899
10 February 1910 to 29 January 1911
7 February 1922 to 14 February 1923
14 February 1934 to 3 February 1935
2 February 1946 to 21 January 1947
19 February 1958 to 7 February 1959
6 February 1970 to 26 January 1971

These clever, versatile people are good workers who can cope with details. They are sometimes workaholics but they don't usually rise too highly up the promotion ladder. Dogs are intelligent, pleasant and very quick-minded but they like to work at their own reasonable pace without being hassled by company politics. These creative people are friendly, charming and pleasant and they excel in the arts where their discriminating eye and attention to detail can take them far. They can be critical of both themselves and of others and at times be somewhat hurtful. Dogs are a little reserved and they hate displays of emotion and are easily embarrassed. They can be sarcastic when using their defence mechanisms.

Dogs are good-looking and are also good listeners, which ensures their popularity with the opposite sex. They are faithful in marriage and make reliable partners. They can be hard to live with because they take life seriously and their nerves can get them down from time to time. Dogs can also use their quick minds and tongues to lash out in a particularly sarcastic manner on occasion. On the whole though they will put up with a lot and try to do what they see as their duty. They need a nice home with a few good quality material possessions around them. They like to look good and also to eat well-prepared, sensible foods. Dogs are said to be compatible with Cats, Horses and Tigers.

Dogs are similar to people born under the Western zodiac sign of Virgo.

The Year of the Boar

24 January 1887 to 11 February 1888
10 February 1899 to 30 January 1900
30 January 1911 to 17 February 1912
15 February 1923 to 4 February 1924
4 February 1935 to 23 January 1936
22 January 1947 to 9 February 1948
8 February 1959 to 27 January 1960
27 January 1971 to 18 February 1972

Boars have an outwardly gentle and retiring attitude which belies their quick minds and stubborn determination. They may appear easily taken in but this is not so. Boars are honest, reasonable, hard-working, kindly and sincere. They hate trickery and dishonesty and cannot understand advantage takers. They think and read deeply, have a philosophical turn of mind and an enjoyment of art, music and culture. Boars can do very well in a position of reasonable responsibility but may not be ambitious enough to aim for the top. They are dutiful, intelligent and capable and they don't make unneccessary waves as they prefer to keep their opinions to themselves. Although generous to their loved ones, they can be stingy to themselves and love to get the full use out of anything.

Boars need a change of scene from time to time, and as they also value their freedom, they don't like to be questioned as to their intentions or their whereabouts. They are intensely loyal to their family and their small circle of friends, they make devoted and faithful partners and very loving parents. Their resilience allows them to bounce back from illness or problems so that they can continue their steady and fairly unambitious progress through life. Boars make good administrators but may have some difficulty in dealing with people due to their own shyness and reserve. They are said to be compatible with Cats and Dogs.

Boars are similar to those people who are born under the Western zodiac sign of Capricorn.

16.

Pendling and Dowsing

Divining Rods and Pendulums

Divining rods and pendulums are normally used to locate things. They can also be used predictively for giving a straightforward *yes* or *no* answer to a question. Rods can be used to find underground sources of water, drain pipes, sources of specific minerals and lost objects; a pendulum can be used to identify an illness or spot a dietary deficiency. Rods or pendulums can be held over a map or sketch of a specific place in order to find the position of something or someone.

Preparation and Ritual

Before using a new pendulum or set of dowsing rods, hold them in your hands and ask your spiritual guides to help you use them in a caring and truthful manner. Imagine yourself calling down a shaft of white light, mentally allow this to settle around your feet and then wind it up around your body in a clockwise direction (clockwise winding is said to be more effective).

Once you have prepared your rods or pendulum, you will have to establish which kind of movement will be your *yes* and which will be your *no*. If using dowsing rods, hold them out in front of you at a comfortable distance from your body and think *yes*. If the rods cross, this will be your *yes*; if they part, then parted rods will be *yes* for you. If you are using the pendulum, wind the string or chain around your little finger, and allow the chain to run across the fingers and down over your index finger. Think *yes*. The pendulum may move from side-to-side or it may move backwards and forwards or in a circle. The movement will be in direct response to your brain patterns and nerve endings—the pendulum and you yourself are merely channels for your guides to use. The pendulum does not have any life of its own except for the receptive energy with which it was charged when you went through the preparation ritual. After doing this, go through the same exercise again, this time thinking *no*: this will give you your *no* movement.

You can now form a question in your mind but remember that you must put this in such a manner as to receive a straight *yes* or *no* answer. Dowsing cannot cope with ambiguity. If you are seeking an ailment, write down a list and think of each, one at a time and wait for a reaction. Another method is to make a list and then hold the pendulum over each illness in turn. Allergies can be dowsed for in the same way. There is actually quite a lot more to this than I have mentioned; for instance, you would need a pendulum with a long string because certain ailments require the string to be a specific length so that you can dowse for them successfully. The same goes for substances; for instance, one length would be required to dowse for a lost gold ring while a different one would be required if the ring was silver.

Ley Lines

These are lines of energy which criss-cross the surface of the earth. Churches and ancient religious sites tend to be built along these strange lines. Some Ley lines are positive and others are negative; some are large, like main railway lines others are smaller and weaker like branch lines. Living or working on a negative line will make the averagely phychic person feel ill and miserable, so if you feel like this for no real reason, it may be worth dowsing for a negative line and then moving your sitting, sleeping or working position away to one side of the line.

To find a positive line, think of a positive line and ask the rods or pendulum to find it. A *yes* reaction will show that you have found one. The same procedure can be used to find a negative line.

17.

Dreams

Scientists tell us that we dream every time we sleep. Sleep deepens and lightens in a fairly fixed 90-minute pattern with dreaming taking place during the lighter phases. Dreaming is the mind's way of sifting all the impressions with which it has been bombarded during the day, keeping those which are relevant and rejecting those which are not. If a natural pattern of dreaming is essential to mental health, then it is obvious that any drug which interferes with this could cause some kind of side-effect.

It used to be said that eating cheese directly before going to bed caused bad dreams! Certainly too much food or alcohol can give one a bad night. Pain, of course, or a high temperature will bring bad dreams, therefore it is always wise to look for a logical and obvious reason for remembering a dream before looking for some kind of special significance. Every now and then, a dream will seem to stay with us and haunt us for weeks afterwards. This kind of dream probably *does* have a special meaning and even more so if the dream recurs.

Many dream messages tell us something about our state of mind. They try to bring to our attention things which are at the back of our minds but which for a number of reasons we do not wish to acknowledge consciously. I can remember a client telling me that shortly before her marriage, she dreamed several times that she was locked away in a prison. The meaning here is fairly obvious. Either she feared the responsibilities of marriage, or she felt deep down inside of herself that her forthcoming marriage was going to be a mistake. Years afterwards she remembered these dreams and felt that is was a mixture of both. As it happened, she coped very well with the responsibilities of marriage and motherhood but the relationship did turn out to be difficult and, although the difficulties were eventually overcome, the seeds of doubt were obviously there in her mind from the beginning.

I occasionally have dreams in which I go to look for my car and it isn't where I left it, or I get to it and it begins to roll slowly down the road away from me. Another typical dream of mine is to arrive at an airport with the family, all set to go off on holiday, only to find that I have left one of the suitcases behind. I realize that these dreams reflect my over-busy lifestyle and feelings of not always being able to cope. Incidentally, I *always* forget something when I am travelling (with or without the family) and could quite easily leave half the luggage behind! Perhaps this *is* a predictive dream—I hope not!

Occult Significance

Of course, there are dreams which have a specific occult significance. These might warn the Subject of some forthcoming problem or predict a particular event. I have a friend who has, on occasion, dreamed of impending disasters of one kind or another only to find the next day that these actually happened either at the time of the dream or a day or so afterwards.

There might be some kind of symbolism hidden in a particular dream which a psychic who specializes in dreams would be able to unravel. A simple example would be of a broken wedding ring or two wedding rings which would suggest losing one partner and then finding another.

The following is a list taken from *Everybody's Book of Fate and Fortune* compiled by Edward Lyndoe and originally published by Odhams Press, but now out of print.

Health
The Chinese believed that certain kinds of dream indicated particular health problems. They felt that dreams of terror indicated heart problems and dreams of bloodshed pointed to trouble with the lungs, while dreams of difficulty such as hacking one's way through the jungle showed liver trouble. Sharp pain dreams meant kidney disorders, while dreams of some kind of repetitious action, such as swinging to and fro, showed anaemia.

Examples of dream meanings
The following short list shows some traditional dream interpretations. This is purely divinatory and doesn't take any kind of deep pychological meanings into account. Although this kind of divination is only meant as a bit of fun, I have found it to work quite well. I recently had a vivid dream in which I found myself looking down at my own funeral! This shook me a bit, but when I looked up the meaning in a couple of books and also asked a couple of psychic friends about it, the answer from all quarters came back that this dream signified a fresh start. This makes sense as *death* in most divinations means transformation; the end of a phase and the beginning of another.

Dream Interpretation List

Dreams about babies

Baby
Good luck for the Dreamer and his family.

Birth
Good fortune for the Dreamer.

Cradle
Hopes and wishes to be fulfilled.

Pregnancy
Good news on the way.

Dreams about marriage

Bells
Good news.

Bouquet
Slight disappointment.

Horseshoe
A pleasant journey.

Wedding
Joy and happiness ahead.

Dreams of death

Burial
The Dreamer will soon be married.

Cemetery
The Dreamer will hear of a death.

Death
Turning point, transformation, good fortune and happiness.

Gallows
Prosperity.

Shipwreck
Hesitation and disappointments.

Tomb
A long happy life foretold.

Dreams about men

Doctor
Illness on the way.

Friend
Good luck and happiness.

Horseman
Plans fulfilled.

Lawyer
A warning of legal or financial difficulties.

Old man
Happiness for the family.

Policeman
Peace and safety.

Postman
Long awaited news.

Sailor
Difficulty or delays in plans.

Dreams about women

Actress
Deception from those you trust.

Empress
Pride could cause a fall.

Nun
Peace of mind.

Witch
Difficulties in the near future.

Dreams of friends

Drowning friend
Someone will render the Dreamer a service.

Friend's house
Good luck in work and other plans.

Friend in difficulty
Either a friend will need help, or you will need help from your own friends.

Dreams about children

Children playing
Happiness is on the way.

Crying child
A wish will be fulfilled.

Dancing child
Difficulties ahead.

Death of a child
A welcome visitor.

Sleeping child
Good luck coming.

Dreams about animals, birds, insects and fish

Ants
Hard work ahead but the results will be worthwhile.

Bat
Danger threatens.

Bear
Disagreements with friends.

Bees
Prosperity and progress.

Cat
Beware of treachery.

Cock
Success and joy soon.

Cow
Prosperity.

Crab
A parting.

Dog
Malicious gossip about you.

Donkey
Trouble in store.

Dove
Happiness in love.

Duck
A stranger will bring bad news.

Eagle
Success.

Elephant
Plans will succeed.

Fish
Unexpected news.

Fox
Plans succeed beyond your wildest expectations.

Goose
Someone you love will let you down badly.

Hedgehog
Business difficulties and complications.

Hen
Celebrations and parties.

Horse
Black: Disappointments in store.
Brown: Stagnation and delays.
Grey: Restlessness and uncertainty.
White: Financial progress.

Lambs
Wishes will come true.

Lion
You will take the lead in an important enterprise.

Parrot
A trusted friend will quarrel with you.

Peacock
Wealth coming through the family.

Rabbit
You will soon make a good and useful friend.

Rat
A supposed friend is working against you. Women dreamers should beware of meeting a 'rat'.

Snake
You will be the victim of gossip. This is also sexual, possibly the end of a period of frustration is in sight.

Spider
Danger of being involved in a quarrel.

Swallow
Domestic circumstances will change a little; could go either way.

Swan
Financial progress and happiness.

Tiger
Hidden danger threatens.

Toad
Hidden danger causing worry.

Vulture
Illness in the family.

Wolf
Business losses and worries.

Worms
A number of small worries.

Dream about conditions

Applause
A friend will tick the Dreamer off.

Attack
Rashness will cause difficulties.

Battle
Health worries.

Climbing
Success coming slowly.

Competition
Improvement in circumstances which make it easier to attain ambitions.

Crime
Success in plans.

Dancing
Pleasure and parties.

Dispute
Caution will be needed for a while.

Drowning
Difficulty will make planning useless.

Exile
Loss of something or someone valuable.

Falling
Confusing time ahead.

Finding money
Loss.

Flying
Advancement in circumstances. Also the desire to escape. This could also be a psychic experience—astral travel.

Following one's own funeral
Turning point, transformation. Great and lasting success.

Gambling
Success at last.

Honours
The Dreamer's reputation will suffer as a result of slander.

Imprisonment
Hold-ups and problems which are hard to sort out just now.

Kidnapping
Success in plans.

Legacy
Financial loss.

Murder
Successful outcome in plans.

Nakedness
Financial losses.

Poverty
Change for the better.

Presents
Loss which wipes out previous gains.

Reading
Pleasure coming from a new source.

Screaming
Bad news coming.

Shopping
Unexpected benefit coming.

Singing
Success in endeavours.

Suicide
Upheaval and major changes.

Swimming
Improvements after a bad patch.

Travel
Friends will let the Dreamer down.

Undressing
Lack of foresight will cause problems.

Visiting
A grave injustice is on the way.

Wealth
Disillusionment.

Weeping
Good news is on the way.

Wrestling
The Dreamer will win through.

Writing
Danger of offending a friend.

Dreams about money

Finding money
Difficulties are on the way.

Losing money
Plans will succeed beyond the Dreamer's wildest hopes.

Counting money
Gains coming.

Spending money
Losses on the way.

Dreams about health

Amputation
Slights and injustices.

Asthma
Difficulties ahead.

Burns
Success coming and an end to troubles.

Loss of a tooth
Loss of a friend or relative.

Problems with feet.
Prosperity.

Problems with hands
Parting from a good friend.

Ulcer
Temporary difficulty.

General dream list

Aeroplane
Ambition to be fulfilled.

Ambulance
Illness in the family.

Anvil
Hard work ahead.

Axe
Help from a friend.

Bag
Full: Prosperity.
Empty: hard times ahead.

Ball
Great moves forward.

Bank
Money problems.

Banner
Achievement, honours and fame.

Barrel
Full: Improvement in circumstances.
Empty: Money worries.

Basket
A welcome invitation.

Bath
Happiness to come.

Beans
Danger to the family.

Bed
Rest.
Unmade: Take care not to get into trouble.

Bell
Good news, joy.

Bicycle
Success.

Blood
An accident.

Boat
News, a successful journey.

Bottle
Wishes coming true.

Bread
Good luck.

Bridge
Troubles will soon pass.

Butterfly
Muddles and fluctuations.

Buttons
Peace and joy in the family.

Cage
Breaking up of the family circle.

Candle
Lighted: A birth in the family.
Extinguished: A death in the Dreamer's circle.

Castle
Unexpected pleasurable event.

Cave
Problems ahead.

Chain
Difficulties.

Chariot
Efforts will meet praise.

Cheese
Financial gain.

Church
Peace after a period of trouble.

Clock
Important business which will require the Dreamer's attention.

Clouds
Quarrels with friends.

Coal
The Dreamer will impress his superiors.

Coffee
Disappointments.

Cottage
Health and happiness.

Crown
Honours.

Cross
The Dreamer will be proved to be right.

Crossroads
Important decision.

Dance
Unexpected pleasures.

Dice
Beware of gambles, there could be losses.

Dungeon
Danger for those around the Dreamer.

Earthquake
Someone close is running a risk.

Eggs
Up-turn in finances, good health.

Eyes
A lover is on the way.

Factory
The Dreamer's efforts will be rewarded.

Fan
Things are looking up.

Field
Prosperity and good fortune.

Fingers
Litigation concerning money.

Fire
Unexpected happy event.

Fireplace
Someone is going away.

Flag
Change in life will bring success.

Flowers
A trip or a move to the country.

Fountain
A busy time ahead.

Garden
Temporary financial difficulties.

Glass
Full: The Dreamer will soon hear from a loved one.
Empty: Temporary difficulties.
Broken: Wishes will come true. A wedding is possible.

Globe
A worthwhile journey.

Gloves
Negotiations.

Gun
Some disappointment; limited success.

Hammer
Recklessness will cause problems.

Hand
The Dreamer will be surrounded by flatterers.

Harp
Things are looking up.

Hat
Disappointment.

Honey
Increase in income.

House
Striking success.

Ice
The Dreamer should beware of becoming trapped.

Iron
Risky ventures.

Island
Loneliness.

Jewels
Upturn in finances.

Key
The Dreamer will fail in an important interview.

Kitchen
Money will improve.

Knife
Danger around the Dreamer or in his circle.

Knot
Complications in business affairs.

Ladder
Patience will bring success.

Lamp
Lit: Good for business affairs.
Extinguished: Concealment of something important from the Dreamer.

Leaves
Changes in the family.

Light
Money, honour, enlightenment.

Lighthouse
Good advice is on the way.

Linen (dirty)
Arguments in the family.

Lock
Likelihood of theft.

Map
Long journey.

Meat
Raw: Prosperity.
Cooked: Disappointment.

Medals
Problems due to over-confidence.

Mirror
Flattery from the opposite sex.

Mistletoe
Good relationships to come.

Milk
Tranquility.
Spilt: Plans will not work out.

Moon
Difficulties and disappointments.

Mountain
Improvement in affairs.

Mushrooms
Success and well-being.

Music
Things are looking up.

Nails
Hard work and difficulties.
Finger nails: Quarrels and financial difficulties.

Necklace
Happiness and fun.

Needles
Gossip.

Nest
Unexpected sum of money coming.

Net
Financial improvement, also raise in status.

Nuts
Problems solved soon.

Oak tree
Parting from a friend.

Oil
Troubled relationships smoothed over.

Opals
Happiness in love.

Oranges
Happiness and pleasure.

Palace
Sorrow for a friend.

Palm tree
Dearest wish coming true.

Paper
Clean: Your status will rise.
Used: The Dreamer will suffer an injustice.

Pin
Loss of face.

Pipe
An argument will be lost.

Pit
Severe problems.

Plough
Respect for good work done.

Pond
Stagnation in affairs.

Prison
Mental and physical exertion will be required.

Purse
Full: Slight loss.
Empty: Unexpected gain.

Quagmire
Many small problems.

Race
The Dreamer will soon be ahead of others.

Railway station
A journey.

Rain
The Dreamer will be put upon by others.

Rainbow
A brighter future.

Razor
A quarrel brings unhappiness.

Road
Work will bring rewards.

Rocks
Temporary difficulties.

Rose
Social success.

Salt
An advancement in affairs.

Sand
Hopes will come to nothing.

Scissors
A quarrel and the loss of a friend.

Sea
Calm: Happiness.
Stormy: Anger.

Shooting star
Success in every way.

Silver
Miserliness will cause the Dreamer harm.

Sky
Wishes will be shortly fulfilled.
Night sky: Temporary difficulties.
Stormy sky: Great change in the Dreamer's way of life.

Smoke
A bad business transaction incurring losses.

Spectacles
Self-esteem will take a knock.

Stairs
Improvement and change in circumstances.

Stick
Journey causing difficulties.

Stockings
Financial gain, but if holed, losses for a time.

Sugar
The Dreamer will have to be careful whom he trusts.

Sun
Success rewards efforts.

Sword
Success in assured.

Table
Improvement in health.

Telegram
Unexpected news, should be all right.

Tent
Unaccustomed activities.

Thorn
The Dreamer will bring unhappiness to a friend.

Thunder
Danger to someone in the Dreamer's circle.

Throne
Changes in lifestyle.

Tower
Ambitions realized.

Trees
Ambitions realized.
Felled or fallen: A parting from a loved one.

Treasure
Hopes will fail.

Trumpet
Temporary difficulties.

Tunnel
The Dreamer will need every effort to pull through. This could involve the death of someone close to the Dreamer.

Umbrella
Open: Friends will help.
Closed: Prosperity in business.

Violin
Love affairs will go well.

Volcano
Great upheavals and physical efforts to be made.

Wall
Caution will be needed.

Water
Clear: Well-being and material prosperity.
Muddy: Danger from disputes.
Hot: Unexpected danger.

Weathercock
Vacillation and indecision.

Wheat
Material increase.

Wheel
Change for the better.

Wind
Change for the better

Window
Open: Problems solved.
Closed: Unexpected danger, but the Dreamer should be safe.

Wine
Social events and happiness.

Yacht
Change in fortunes; improvement in status.

18.

Tea Leaves

Preparation

Use a teacup rather than a mug. The rather shallow type of cup with a plain interior is the best, as patterns and fluting will interfere with the reading. Ask the Enquirer to swirl the tea round in the cup in an *anti-clockwise* direction three times using his left hand. Then ask him to place the cup upside down onto the saucer. Either you or the Enquirer should now turn the cup three times in an *anti-clockwise* direction, once again using the left hand.

After this turn the cup over, keeping the handle towards you, tilt it to a convenient angle and take a good long look inside.

Location of events

The handle represents the Enquirer, therefore, any leaves in that area suggest events concerning him or occurring in his home. The opposite side of the cup refers to strangers and events away from the home.

Symbols which point towards the handle are approaching the Enquirer and symbols which point away from the handle suggest people or situations which are leaving the Enquirer. The bottom of the cup shows sorrows, the top shows joys.

Timing of events

The rim of the cup is the near future, half-way down shows events within a few months, while the area close to the bottom shows the distant future. If there are any numbers visible, these can help with timing of events. For instance, an anchor (which would signify a journey) accompanied by a number three would tell of a journey to come in three month's time.

How the events feel

The happiest part of the cup is near the rim, the saddest is at the bottom.

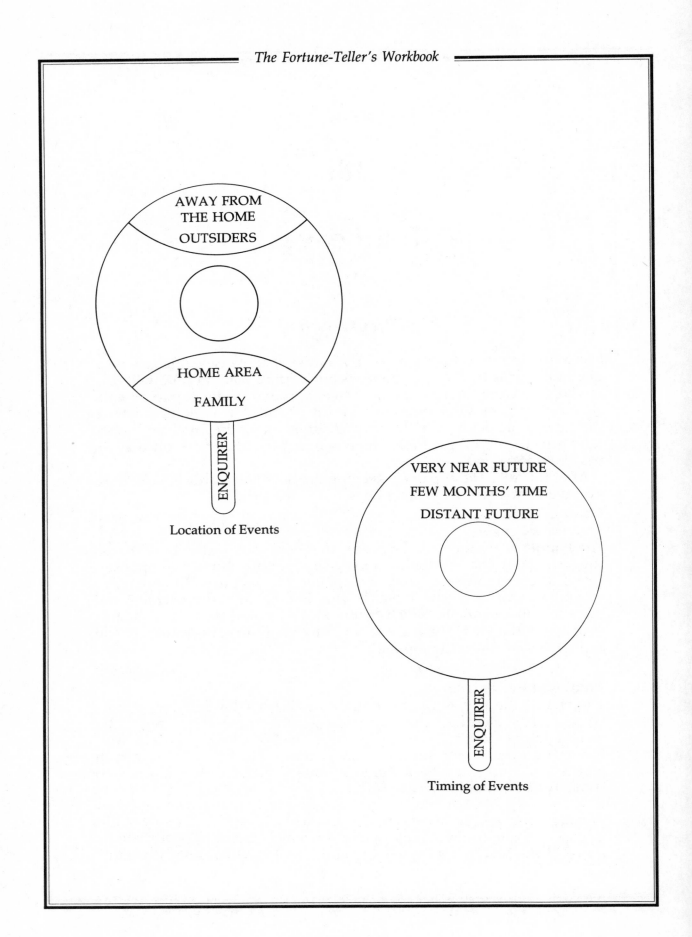

AWAY FROM
THE HOME

OUTSIDERS

HOME AREA

FAMILY

ENQUIRER

Location of Events

VERY NEAR FUTURE

FEW MONTHS' TIME

DISTANT FUTURE

ENQUIRER

Timing of Events

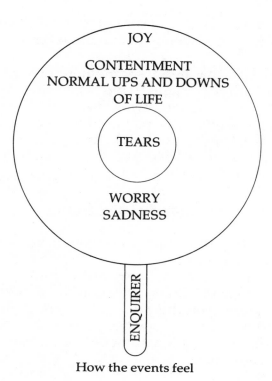

How the events feel

Some Useful Tips

My friend, Denise Russell, supplied this information which had been given to her by her grandmother who used to read tea leaves.

A full cup of tea

1 If two spoons are accidentally put into one saucer, there will be news of twins.

2 If a spoon is accidentally placed upside-down in a saucer, there will be news of a close relative becoming ill.

3 A single leaf floating on a full cup of tea means that the Enquirer will be coming into money.

4 A single leaf stuck at the side of a full cup of tea shows news of a stranger entering the Enquirer's life. (This may be advance news of a romance.)

When the tea has been drunk

1 If, after the tea has been drunk and the swirling and twirling ritual has been done, the leaves are in a rounded pile against the side of the cup opposite to the handle, there is trouble coming. This trouble is *not* of the Enquirer's own doing and it will come without warning.

2   If the leaves are rounded up on the handle side, there will also be trouble, but this time it will be of the Enquirer's own doing.

Denise also mentioned that her grandmother always told her that only intuitive people *asked* for a reading, and when they did so they would hear good news and good of themselves, whereas if a Reader felt impelled to offer a reading to someone, there would always be bad or sad news. I have found this notion to be true of other kinds of readings as well. If I feel *compelled* to give someone a reading, there is always some kind of warning to come out of it.

Further Tea Leaf Lore

My mother-in-law used to say that if two people poured out of the same pot, one of them would have baby on the way by the end of the year. The old joke was that the 'baby' would turn out to be ginger twins!

Letters of the alphabet signify the names of people who will be important to the Enquirer in the future. A symbol which is found close to the letter will give a clue as how the person will affect the Enquirer. For instance, the letter 'A' accompanied by a monkey might indicate a gossipy person, whose name begins with 'A' whom the Enquirer must be wary of. The position of the letter and accompanying symbol will give a clue as to where this person might be found. For instance, if they are near the handle this will happen around the Enquirer's home, but if away from the handle it will be away from the home.

Stalks represent people, often strangers. A long firm stalk represents a man while a shorter thinner one suggests a woman. If a straight stalk is found, the stranger will be reliable, while a bendy one indicates a fickle friend or someone who is not in a position to help the Enquirer much. Slanted stalks show unreliable or untrustworthy people. The colour of the stalk could give a clue to the colouring of the person.

If your Enquirer wants to know when he or she is likely to get married, you can try this ruse. Take a clean dry teaspoon and balance it on the edge of the cup. Pour a little tea into the bowl of the spoon, one drop at a time, until the spoon falls into the cup; the number of drops show the number of years the Enquirer will have to wait. Rings show marriage. If a ring is near the rim the marriage will be happy and this also shows that marriage is probably not far off for the Enquirer. Broken rings or rings at the bottom of the cup show broken marriages or unhappiness in marriage. A double ring could indicate two marriages or just one which the Enquirer rushes into and then regrets later. A bell is also a sign of a wedding.

Lucky signs are horseshoes, circles and rings, flowers, trees, animals and crowns; also the number seven. Triangles are usually lucky but if they are found at the bottom of the cup or with the apex pointing downwards, there would be spell of bad luck ahead or something which has been all right so far could begin to become difficult. A triangle which points upwards denotes a win or a legacy to come. Another interpretation is a fortunate meeting connected with money.

Squares represent protection and restriction. If a dangerous symbol such as an arrow appears facing towards the handle (therefore towards the Enquirer), this shows that a letter containing bad news will be on the way, but if there is a square around the arrow, the Enquirer will be protected from the worst. A square can show a restricting situation for the Enquirer such as a commitment to an unsatisfactory or boring job. Crosses of all kinds mean sadness and problems to be faced.

Dots always symbolize money. If the dots are close to another symbol, read them together. Mountains show efforts which will have to be made while clouds show illusion and muddled problems. Lines represent journeys; clear straight lines show good journeys while broken or wavering ones suggest problems *en route*. (If you would like a fuller explanation of tea leaf lore; plus a wider tea leaf 'dictionary'; please read my *Fortune-Telling by Tea Leaves*.)

Tea Leaf Symbols

Acorn
The start of something which is destined to grow into maturity and success; also a long life and good fortune. If it is in the middle area of the cup it indicates an improvement in health; other positions indicate that the Enquirer's finances are soon going to improve.

Aeroplane
A sudden journey for the Enquirer or someone close to him. If the aeroplane is ascending, things are on the up and up; if it is descending there will be unexpected trouble ahead. If the plane is travelling towards the Enquirer, there could be a visitor from overseas.

Alligator
Treachery, rivals, secret enemies all lying in wait.

Anchor
A hopeful sign. Near the rim of the cup: success in career plus true love; a wish will come true soon. Half-way down: a journey which is successful. If there are dots around the anchor, this will be very lucky indeed. If at the bottom of the cup, the Enquirer will have help from friends and will overcome any difficulties. Only if the symbol is partially covered would it indicate continued troubles.

Angel

Good news. Love, happiness and peace. There could be spiritual help on the way. Any new project, especially the birth of a child, will be accompanied by good luck. If it is near the handle of the cup, the home area will be particularly happy.

Anvil

Concentration and hard work which will result in success. Also strength, stability and practicality.

Arch

A happy marriage. A fresh start and unexpected benefits. A lover proposes. Temporary states become permanent.

Apple

A time of achievement, happiness and success. Hopes and wishes will be fulfilled in connection with either work or relationships. At the bottom of the cup, over-indulgence or temptation.

Arrow

Bad news. If it points towards the handle, bad news is coming to the Enquirer; if it points away, the Enquirer could be the carrier of bad news to someone else. Dots show that the trouble is financial.

Axe

Difficulties. However, also a time to wield power and to clear away the dead wood. Sometimes a 'battle-axe' type woman will enter the Enquirer's life.

Baby

A baby may be born into the Enquirer's family soon, especially if the symbol is near the handle. It could also mean the birth of a new idea or a new project. If this symbol is at the bottom of the cup, the indications are that a plan, or indeed even a pregnancy, could miscarry.

Bag

If closed, the Enquirer will be caught in a trap. If open, he will manage to escape.

Ball

Ups and downs in life, but the Enquirer will be able to bounce back from problems. There could be some great stride forward occurring soon.

Ball and chain

Commitments; obligations which are onerous if at the bottom of the cup. A knotted chain suggests entanglements; a broken chain shows that the Enquirer will soon be free of a particular burden.

Balloon

Success in life.
(a) If near the rim this will be while the Enquirer is still young.
(b) If half-way up the cup, the Enquirer will be successful in middle age.
(c) If near the bottom, the success will come in old age.

Barrel

Changing financial circumstances. A broken or empty barrel suggest financial hardship or a set-back in plans. A complete barrel shows good fortune and good times ahead.

Basket

The birth of a child, social success, happiness and good fortune in and around the home. Usually a good omen, but an empty basket or one obscured by other symbols could indicate domestic problems to come.
(a) If near the rim, money and luck soon.
(b) Near the handle, a baby coming.
(c) Flowers lying in the basket, happiness and fun.
(d) Dots around the basket, money coming soon.

Bat

Three interpretations here:
(a) False friends.
(b) A gift, good wishes and a long life.
(c) More than one bat, great good luck.

Bed

(a) A neat bed denotes a tidy mind, rest and peace.
(b) A rumpled bed speaks of sleepness nights and worry.
(c) Any kind of bed tells of sexual activities to come.

Bee or swarm of bees

Social and financial success plus social gatherings.
(a) Near the handle, family gatherings and celebrations in or around the home. Visitors bringing gifts and interesting news.

(b) A small business to be launched.
(c) A bee approaching the handle, a welcome guest.
(d) A swarm of bees away from the handle suggests business meetings, conferences, seminars, etc., all of which should have a good outcome.
(e) Money, success and honour are on the way; the Enquirer could soon be addressing an audience.
(f) A bee at the bottom of the cup means that the Enquirer will be worrying about family commitments and finances.

Beehive

Much activity at work, success and wealth from business.

Bell

Important news is on the way; a bell attached to a rope is definitely good news, sometimes of a wedding.
(a) Near the rim, promotion soon.
(b) Half-way up, good news generally.
(c) Near the bottom, sad news.
(d) A handbell means a public announcement which will benefit the Enquirer.
(e) Two bells indicates great happiness and celebrations. A romance or a wedding are one the way, and any forthcoming marriage will be very successful.

Bird

Good news, good luck coming. If the wings are extended, this is a very good omen.
(a) Birds flying means travel, also good ideas which can be translated into money.
(b) Surrounded by a circle or a square, a bird indicates a proposal.
(c) Standing birds, plans held up.
(d) Birds in a group indicate talks, discussions, maybe a business meeting.
(e) In a cage, obstacles, restrictions. The Enquirer may be living with a difficult person or in a restrictive situation. If the door of the cage is open, the situation will soon change.
(f) Bird holding a branch, making up after an argument, a compromise solution.

Bird's nest

Security, stability, affection and good family life.

(a) Eggs in the nest, children or a nest-egg to come.
(b) Broken nest, a broken home.

Boat

(a) Protection from danger, a safe refuge to come.
(b) A journey which teaches the Enquirer something.
(c) A capsized or broken boat suggests danger, unreliable people and upsetting circumstances.

Book

(a) If the book is closed, studies and research or a new skill to be learned.
(b) Closed book, a secret.
(c) If the book is open, help and success in legal matters.
(d) Open book, success in the future.
(e) Open book, an open person who does not present the Enquirer with unpleasant surprises.
(f) Marriage to a writer if a stalk is near the book.
(g) Book and pen, the Enquirer will write for his living.

Boomerang

Gossip, there may be false friends around. If the Enquirer gossips, this could come back on him. Alternatively, an unprincipled course of action which has been taken in the past could also rebound.

Boot

(a) Changing situations, moves are afoot. If the boot is near the handle, the changes will be in the home area; if away from the handle, the changes will be in the Enquirer's public or social life.
(b) Loss of a job, getting the boot, being booted out.

Boots (a pair)

(a) Protection from pain or loss.
(b) Business which involves local travel, sales, contacts, deliveries, etc. will be successful.

Bottle

(a) The Enquirer must take care of his health now.
(b) There may be a connection with people who work with bottles soon, for instance, a chemist, publican, milkman, etc.
(c) This can also indicate parties and celebrations, or even a tendency to 'hit the bottle'.

Bouquet of Flowers

Celebrations, joy, success and prosperity. Parties and social activities soon, possibly a wedding.

(a) If the Enquirer is to be married, this is a good omen for the future.

(b) All new ventures will be successful now. If there are other good omens present, the Enquirer's dreams will come true.

Box

(a) Open, a romantic problem will soon sort itself out.

(b) Closed, something which has been lost will soon come to light.

Broom

Time to clear out old problems and make a clean sweep, a fresh start. This can be a sign of a forthcoming marriage or other commitment. (This idea is derived from magical rites of both Europe and Africa).

Bull

(a) Important contact with a Taurean person.

(b) Strength and power which the Enquirer could put to good purpose.

(c) There could be arguments and bad feelings soon. The direction the bull is facing will show whether the anger is coming to or from the Enquirer.

Butterfly

Fickle lover, a short-lived affair. If surrounded by dots, the Enquirer will waste money as well as time.

Cake

Celebrations, hospitality; the Enquirer could give a party or have a family celebration soon.

Candle

(a) Help from others, also inspiration given to others.

(b) Zeal for knowledge, enlightenment.

(c) A moth near a flame, a disastrous attraction (probably sexual).

(d) A guttering candle shows that someone near the Enquirer is becoming weaker in health or less important to him.

Candelabrum
Sudden illumination, solution to problems.

Cannon
(a) Good luck, help from powerful friends.
(b) News from someone in the forces.
(c) Promotion, especially if there is a star nearby.

Cap
Discretion will be needed; the Enquirer must be careful as to whom he trusts. Not a time for new or speculative ventures.

Car
Local travel, changing circumstances. May also be a sex symbol!

Castle
(a) A strong person or one in a position of authority who influences the Enquirer.
(b) Security and safety; a good home life.
(c) A ruined castle represents ruined hopes and dreams.

Cat
If the cat is pouncing, there will be treachery, false friends. If seated, contentment and good luck.

Chain
(a) The Enquirer is being advised to put his energies into his work.
(b) A partnership, a commitment to others.
(c) Broken chain, a disappointment.

Chair
(a) A visitor, also a time to rest.
(b) With dots around, financial improvement.

Chimney
(a) If smoke rises straight up; things will go well.
(b) Smoke sideways, restrictions, boredom.
(c) No smoke, hidden danger.

Christmas tree
(a) Good luck around Christmas time.

Church
Help, safety, unexpected benefits. A legacy perhaps.

Circle or ring
(a) Successful event coming, often a sign of an impending marriage.
(b) Circle with dots, a baby — three dots, a boy.
(c) Two circles, either a hasty marriage which brings regrets or two marriages.
(d) The completion of a project or the end of a phase.

Clergyman
(a) Blessing, end of an argument.
(b) Religious ceremony to come. With a circle, a wedding.
(c) Baby or child on the way, christening.
(d) If at the bottom of the cup, a funeral.

Clock
(a) Improvement in health, work and money if symbol is near the rim.
(b) Bottom of the cup, a death.
(c) Time to get on with things.
(d) The Enquirer could meet someone influential and important soon.

Clouds
Trouble on the way, doubts, unsolved problems.

Coach and horses
Better way of life with a rise in status. Influential friends, a more up-market home and life-style.

Cock

(a) New beginnings, good news, an achievement, but it may go to the Enquirer's head.

(b) Failure of plans if near the bottom of the cup. The Enquirer shouldn't be too quick to crow about himself.

Coffin

A bad omen, sad news, regret, loss, a forced decision to bring something to an end. Someone may go out of the Enquirer's life, but this could be a relief.

Column

(a) Promotion, success, but a warning here against arrogance.

(b) Help from friends.

(c) Broken column, failure in business, relationships or health.

(d) An unfaithful friend.

Comet

Unexpected events, unexpected visitors.

Cornucopia

The horn of plenty is a symbol of abundance, joy and fruition of plans. Good food and an easy life for a while.

Cot

A baby coming.

Crescent

(a) New Moon, new interest in life, success in financial affairs.

(b) Journey over water.

(c) Success for or through women.

(d) Changes coming at the time of the new Moon.

(e) A wedding.

(f) Old Moon, delays—patience will be needed.

(g) Moon with star, exceptionally lucky.

Cricket bat

The Enquirer could take up a sport soon or he could be a good sport over something.

Cross

Troubles, suffering, worry and loss, also sacrifice. Illness around the Enquirer; sad news soon if near the rim.

Crown

(a) Honours and success, efforts will be rewarded.
(b) With stars, luck out of the blue.

Cup

Success and fulfilment, especially in creative and emotional matters.

Dagger

(a) A jealous person will make trouble.
(b) Warning against haste, trouble on the way.

Deer

(a) Good omen for studying and taking examinations.
(b) A quarrel.

Devil

(a) Commitment to a course of action or a person.
(b) Passion, lust, a hectice love affair.

Dice

Warning not to gamble if clouds, dagger or other bad omens are nearby; otherwise some speculation should be all right.

Dog

A faithful friend. If the dog is running and happy, there will be happy meetings; if sad or near the bottom of the cup, a friend will need help.

Donkey

The Enquirer will have to be patient and prepared to make a few sacrifices, especially if this symbol is near the bottom of the cup.

(a) If near the rim of the cup, good luck, even an inheritance.

(b) Otherwise peace and happiness.

Dot

A single dot increases the importance of any symbol near it; otherwise dots mean money.

Dove

Peace, love and happiness. A good omen all around, but probably most lucky in the domestic arena.

Dragon

Unforseen problems, major clashes and upheavals which will need to be dealt with rather than avoided.

Drum

(a) Rows and arguments; if near the bottom of the cup there could be rumours and scandal attached to the Enquirer.

(b) A successful career involving the general public. The Enquirer could reach a position of power and influence.

Duck

Money coming, luck in speculation, and any work connected with travel and foreigners.

Eagle

(a) A move of house.

(b) A time to grasp opportunities and make the most of them. The Enquirer should use his knowledge, skills and wit and make a concerted effort to reach the top. In short, he should 'grasp the nettle' as quickly as possible.

Easel

A good omen for anyone engaged in creative work. Dots around the easel will bring money.

Egg
A symbol of fertility and abundance. A good omen for any kind of new start or the birth of an idea or project. Can also indicate the birth of a child.

Elephant
A symbol of strength, wisdom and a slow climb to success. Any venture will go well now; an excellent time to start a new business or a new relationship.

Envelope
Good news is on the way. A letter or number on the envelope may give a clue to when and from whom.

Eye
(a) Take care, watch out for slippery unreliable people.
(b) Protection from problems or the overcoming of problems as result of vigilance.
(c) Knowledge, intelligence and comprehension. A time when the Enquirer's eyes may be opened.

Face
(a) This could indicate changes for the worst.
(b) If the face looks like someone the Enquirer knows, he will be dealing with that person soon.
(c) If a face is smiling, the omen is good; if it is scowling or looks crafty, this warns of difficult people.

Fan
A warning not to talk too freely. Could also mean that a flirtation is on the way.

Figurehead
(a) This could refer to the president or some other head of an organization.
(b) Sailing into calmer waters.

Fish
(a) One of the very best omens. It indicates luck in anything the Enquirer is doing or wants to do.
(b) Travel or a move of house is a possibility, or just a lucky encounter with a foreigner.

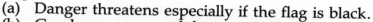

Flag

(a) Danger threatens especially if the flag is black.
(b) Good news or good fortune (if backed up by other good omens).
(c) Death of a king or ruler of some kind, especially if the flag is at half mast.
(d) Time to put on a good front and be courageous.

Foot

Good news but not immediately.

Fork

(a) False friends, beware of flattery.
(b) New interests if the fork is pointing upwards, old problems reappearing if it is pointing downwards.
(c) This can also point to a choice of pathways to follow.

Fork in the road

Two possible pathways forward.

Fountain

Joy, satisfaction and happiness. There is a sexual side to this as it indicates the forces of life.

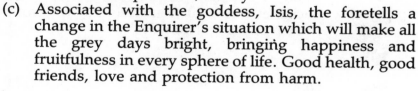

Frog

(a) A move of house or premises.
(b) Avoid self-importance, vanity.
(c) Associated with the goddess, Isis, the foretells a change in the Enquirer's situation which will make all the grey days bright, bringing happiness and fruitfulness in every sphere of life. Good health, good friends, love and protection from harm.

Gallows

Bad luck coming; the Enquirer's judgement may not be all that good, but neither may the judgement of those who want to hurt him.

Garland

(a) Achievement, honours, also happiness in relationships.
(b) At the bottom of the cup, a wreath, a funeral.

Gate

An unexpected opportunity, a chance in a lifetime.

Gauntlet

A challenge.

Grapes

(a) Grapes are associated with the Roman god Bacchus or the Greek god Dionysus and therefore talk of wine and revelry; but these gods can be deceptive and dangerous so the Enquirer is warned not to allow his situation (or his wine) to go to his head.
(b) A sick person will be better soon.
(c) Pleasant romantic involvements.
(d) Visit to a hospital to see a sick friend.

Grasshopper

(a) Keep on the right track as jumping around could cause problems.
(b) A friend who has been away will return.

Greyhound

Symbolic of speed, a time to forge ahead and make a success of things and take a few chances. Also a good time to gamble.

Guitar

Social events which include music. Romance, even a chance of being serenaded!

Gun

Quarrels, violence, war, even death by violence. If the gun is in the home area, that is where the danger will be. Otherwise mugging and assault are a possibility. If the gun is at the bottom of the cup, there is a real danger of death by violence or as a result of war.

Hammer
Work to be done, not all of it pleasant but it will have to be tackled. May also indicate a need to be ruthless.

Hand

(a) Look and see where the hand is pointing as it may show where a situation is likely to develop, e.g. near the handle, in the home.
(b) If the hand is open, a good friend.
(c) If the fingers are closed but the thumb is showing, protection and safety.
(d) Thumbs up, go ahead now.
(e) Thumbs down, wait.
(f) A fist shows quarrels, resentment and enemies around.
(g) Clasped hands, friendship, an agreement.
(h) A clenched fist at the bottom of the cup shows that the Enquirer will have to keep his feelings and emotions under tight control.

Handmirror

Prophetic dreams, enlightenment.

Hat

A man's hat is supposed to be unlucky while a woman's is a fortunate sign. May be the sign of a visitor or of a social event which will require wearing a hat, such as a wedding or christening. If the hat is bent or broken, plans could fall through; if at the bottom of the cup, there could be a rival or enemy coming into the Enquirer's life.

Handcuffs

Problems, possibly being in a situation which is not of the Enquirer's choosing.

Hawthorn

(a) Could mean problems in the home if symbol is in the handle area.
(b) Away from the handle, lucky, especially for romance.
(c) Prosperity to the Enquirer and his nearest and dearest.

Heart

This has always been a symbol of love.
(a) Hearts with arrows through them, a passionate romance.
(b) Other marks with this bring extra happiness, e.g.

dots—money, circle—a wedding; a heart with small leaves nearby, marriage to a wealthy partner; two hearts close together plus small leaves, a lover's tiff.

(c) If at the bottom of the cup, there may be health problems, especially heart trouble, for someone close to the Enquirer.

Helmet

(a) This could mean that the Enquirer is going to have to fight for his rights soon.

(b) This could also mean a passionate love affair is on the way.

Horse

(a) A galloping horse means that good news is on the way.

(b) A rider on a horse brings good news from far away.

(c) A horse's head indicates a faithful lover to come. If surrounded by dots, he or she will be wealthy.

(d) Clouds around the horse's head, delays in a romance, but this should be all right in the end.

Horse and cart

A move of house or business premises. If the cart is loaded, the move is good; if the cart is empty, the move could be due to a loss.

Horseshoe

Good luck, good health, money coming.

Hourglass

Decision time is here.

House

(a) If near the handle, there could be domestic strife or problems.

(b) If near the rim, a move to a better home or business premises is possible.

(c) A change for the better. For lovers a wish will come true.

(d) On the side of the cup, a temporary move or a holiday.

(e) Obscured and at the bottom of the cup, care will be needed in business and personal life.

Initials
These refer to people who influence the Enquirer's life.

Insect
Minor worries, soon to be overcome.

Iron
Problems can be ironed out soon, others will co-operate.

Island
A place to retreat to, an enjoyable holiday.

Jester
(a) Parties and fun.
(b) An amusing friend.
(c) A fresh start.
(d) A warning not to make a fool of oneself.

Jug
(a) Near the rim, good health.
(b) Near the bottom, extravagance causing losses.
(c) Other positions in the cup, power, prosperity and a position of importance.

Juggler
This could herald a new job or a new opportunity at work. The Enquirer will get a chance to use his skills and talents successfully. There is a warning here not to be taken in by others.

Kettle
(a) Near the handle, comfort and contentment at home.
(b) if accompanied by clouds or unpleasant omens, there will be discord in the home.
(c) Bottom of the cup, domestic problems or ill health.

Key
(a) A move of house or premises is a possibility.
(b) If double or near the bottom of the cup, a robbery is possible.
(c) This can indicate that a passionate love affair is on the way.

(d) Crossed keys, a position of authority and honour, possibly in public life. Also success in romance.

(e) A bunch of keys indicates health, wealth and happiness in love.

Keyhole
This is sexual—it stands for the female in a relationship. Usually a lucky omen with regard to love and sex, but if at the bottom of the cup, there could be loneliness and frustration.

Kite
A wish will be granted. The Enquirer is being encouraged to go ahead with schemes but also to keep a realistic attitude and not to aim too high.

Knife
An unlucky sign showing quarrels and separations.
(a) Near the handle, there will be a broken home.
(b) Away from the handle, a stab in the back coming from outside one's home, possibly at work.
(c) Bottom of the cup, legal matters going wrong.
(d) A knife anywhere can indicate surgery, injections or dental treatment.
(e) Crossed knives, violence; broken knife, impotence, helplessness.

Knight in armour
A strong personality will help the Enquirer overcome his problems. If the Enquirer is female, this could herald a new lover.

Ladder
(a) Spiritual enlightment, prophetic dreams—like Jacob's ladder.
(b) Advancement, promotion, a time to take one's career a stage higher.
(c) Missing rungs, setbacks but not failure.
(d) At the bottom of the cup, financial misfortune.

Ladle

Working partnerships will go well.

Lamb

If near the handle or facing it, plenty of food and drink in the home. Otherwise, no particular shortage of the necessities of life.

Lamp

(a) Financial success.
(b) Near the rim, a celebration soon.
(c) Near the handle, a discovery in the home.
(d) Otherwise, finding things out or finding things which have been lost.
(e) At the bottom, a celebration will be postponed.
(f) Two lamps show that the Enquirer will be married twice.

Lemon

Something turns sour, others may become jealous or bear the Enquirer grudges.

Lines

A good time to progress but the position of the lines, and any other signs around them, should be taken into account. Wavy lines mean uneven progress forward.

Log

(a) Lighted, warmth and companionship. May have something to do with Christmas celebrations.
(b) Unlit, wasted opportunities.

Luggage

A journey, large items of luggage or lots of it may indicate emigration which will be lucky for the Enquirer.

Man

(a) If facing towards the handle, a visitor. If the man is distinct, he will be dark haired; if not, he will be pale in colouring.
(b) With an arm stretched out, he will bring gifts.
(c) If facing away from the home, this man could be leaving.
(d) Carrying bags, a hard-working man.

Maple leaf

(a) Could indicate a visit to Canada or a pleasant event in the autumn.
(b) Don't waste money or opportunities now.

Maypole

A sign of fertility which could mean pregnancy or a better time at work. Also an indication that the spring will bring a change for the better.

Mermaid

(a) Temptation of some kind—offers may not be all they seem to be.
(b) A seductive person who doesn't mean what they say.
(c) Someone around the Enquirer could be seduced or lured away.
(d) Someone who is nice to the Enquirer's face but nasty behind his back.

Monk

Religious and spiritual matters will become important to the Enquirer. A time for retreat; contemplation, inward journeys and rest.

Monkey

A flattering person who wishes to harm the Enquirer. Gossip may cause trouble.

Moon

(a) A love affair.
(b) If obscured by other leaves, depression and emotional muddle.
(c) If in the first quarter, new projects.
(d) If in the last quarter, the Enquirer's luck is running out.
(e) Surrounded by dots, a relationship or marriage based on money.

Mountains

(a) Obstacles.
(b) If the peaks are clear, the Enquirer will be ambitious and also able to clear away any obstacles.
(c) With dots, hard work brings financial rewards.

Mouse

(a) Timidity could result in missed opportunities.
(b) Poverty.
(c) A theft, especially if the mouse is at the bottom of the cup.

Mushroom

(a) Business setbacks.
(b) Expansion of one's horizons.
(c) A home in the country.
(d) Expansion of awareness and sensitivity, beginning of enlightenment, development of psychic power.
(e) Illusion, delusion, confusion; drug-induced ailments are possible.

Necklace

Love ties will be important. These are successful if the necklace is complete, but there will be break-up if the necklace is broken.

Nurse

Illness on the way.

Oak tree

Sign of strength and courage and of building something which will last. Health, wealth and happiness in marriage are foretold.

Octopus

Entanglement, a messy situation is on the way.

Onion

The Enquirer must be careful that a secret does not get out or that confidential information is not leaked.

Ostrich

(a) Travel.
(b) No point in burying one's head in the sand.

Owl
Gossip, scandal and allegations against the Enquirer.

Palm tree
Success, honour and respect for the Enquirer and family, especially children.

Parachute
A lucky escape from harm.

Parcel
A surprise, possibly a gift.

Parrot
(a)   A journey.
(b)   Scandal and gossip—don't pass gossip on.

Peacock
(a)   With spread tail, buying land or premises.
(b)   If clear, a good marriage; also health, wealth and happiness.
(c)   Success in one's career, a comfortable life.
(d)   Success, fame and fortune for one's children.
(e)   If at the bottom of the cup, disappointment from children, one's plans will not work out, and a loss of dignity.
(f)   At the bottom of the cup, illness.

Pear
A comfortable life with plenty of money.

Phoenix
Recovery, re-birth. This might apply to an aspect of the Enquirer or some kind of situation which he is in.

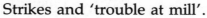

Pickaxe

Strikes and 'trouble at mill'.

Pipe
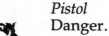
(a) A problem will be solved.
(b) A man will be kind, helpful, even loving.

Pistol

Danger.

Plough
The start of a project which will require patience, but this will be rewarded.

Policeman

Help from those in a position of authority. If the Enquirer has not been entirely honest in his dealings, this is a warning that he may be found out. Illegal acts will definitely not work out well for the Enquirer in the future.

Poppy
(a) Bottom of the cup, loss, sadness.
(b) Half-way up, a struggle of some kind. This could be a struggle against illness or even the need for an operation if knives etc. are found nearby.
(c) Near the rim, a recovery from loss or illness or the illness of someone else.
(d) There will be a reason to remember those who have suffered as a result of war.

Purse
(a) Enough money coming in for comfort.
(b) At the bottom of the cup, expenses, losses or theft.
(c) With dots, a profitable venture.

Pyramid
This is a spiritual symbol of increased awareness. Otherwise it talks of achievements which have to be worked at.

Question mark

Hesitancy; caution will be required.

Rainbow

Future happiness and prosperity. Look to see where the end of the rainbow falls; if in the home area, that's where the Enquirer's luck will come from, otherwise he may be luckier outside the home.

Rake

(a) The Enquirer will have to work hard and attend to details.
(b) Any outstanding business will have to be cleared up soon.
(c) Sport or hobbies should go well.
(d) Near the bottom, old grievances could be raked up.

Rat

Treachery, deceit and loss. Friends could turn out to be absolute rats. In the case of a woman, she may become involved with the type of man who could be described as a 'rat'.

Raven

Bad news. If at the bottom of the cup, someone may fall ill. Otherwise, losses and sadness.

Razor

Accidents, quarrels, danger, partings.

Ring

(a) Complete, a wedding or a happy and successful marriage.
(b) If near the middle of the cup, a proposal.
(c) A happy and prosperous life.

Road

Two parallel lines, which look like a road, show that the Enquirer's situation is about to change. If the lines are straight, the way forward will be easy; if they are wavy, there will be difficulties but the goal can still be reached. If there is a fork in the road, choices will have to be made, A bend would suggest unexpected changes in the Enquirer's life.

Robin

(a) Oddly enough, the robin is a symbol of death, therefore there could a death around the Enquirer. In all forms of divination 'death' is often symbolic of change, the idea being that the Enquirer's circumstances are going to change radically and possibly his outlook on life will be completely changed as a result of a particular experience.

(b) Another interpretation of a robin is that there will be luck during the winter.

Rocket

Happy events to come, possibly marriage for one of the Enquirer's children. The Enquirer himself could fall in love, in this case with a considerable amount of passion.

Roof

The Enquirer will soon be married and possibly also buying a new home.

Rose

(a) A sign of great success, especially in creative enterprises; also popularity for the Enquirer.

(b) A fortunate sign for love and marriage.

(c) The name, Rose, could begin to mean something to the Enquirer.

(d) If at the bottom of the cup, there may be delays and setbacks in plans, but they will still work out well.

Ruined buildings

Shattered hopes, but also a time to pick oneself up and begin again.

Runner

Messages coming. If the accompanying symbols are fortunate, the news will be good. If the runner is obscured or at the bottom of the cup, the news will be sad.

Saddle

Changes, journeys. The Enquirer should take advantage of new opportunities.

Scaffold

The Enquirer must keep within the law and avoid sticky situations now.

Scales

A lawsuit is likely. If the scales are balanced, all will be well; if they are uneven, there will be losses. Alternatively, someone could do the Enquirer an injustice.

Sceptre

Honours and rewards will come. The Enquirer will reach a position of authority.

Scissors

A separation, quarrels and misunderstandings. Look at the area of the cup to see how this affects the Enquirer.

Seagull

Stormy times ahead.

See-saw

Ups and downs in fortunes, but the result should work out all right.

Shell

(a) Good news, luck and money are on the way. This is fortunate for relationships too.
(b) If the Enquirer is fighting against an injustice or is involved in legal matters, there will be a good outcome.
(c) A sign of rebirth, also of spiritual awareness and a change of consciousness.

Ship

A journey will be lucky especially if it is connected with business. Also good news from abroad.

Shirt

A generally good sign, but if the shirt is obscured the Enquirer will lose out by speculation.

Sickle

Death or sorrow around the Enquirer.

Signpost

Look and see where this is pointing and interpret the symbols which you find there because these will be especially important for the Enquirer. This pattern may give some advice or direction to the Enquirer.

Skeleton

(a) Losses of some kind can be expected soon; these may be financial, or there may be spell of ill health for the Enquirer.
(b) Loss of a friend.
(c) A skeleton will emerge rather embarrassingly from the cupboard.

Skull and crossbones

This smacks of piracy on the high seas, therefore it warns the Enquirer to be on guard against a confidence trick or even a potential hijack!

Soldier

(a) A powerful friend who will come to the aid of the Enquirer.
(b) Hostility. People against the Enquirer.

Spade

Hard work but successful results.

Sparrow

(a) If the Enquirer is short of money, this shows that the situation will soon improve.
(b) Oddly enough this sign, like the robin, can warn of a

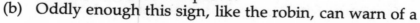

death on the way. The death will be a strange one; the usual interpretation is that an important person will be murdered by a nonentity which causes a mystery —a typical situation of this kind would be the death of President Kennedy.

Square

Restrictions and hardships, but also protection from real loss or harm.

Stag

A vigorous young man. If the Enquirer is female, there will be a strong young lover on the way.

Stairs

(a) A rise in status both in work and private matters.
(b) The Enquirer will experience some kind of spiritual enlightenment, possibly prophetic dreams or a glimpse of heaven.

Star

(a) Six-pointed, good fortune.
(b) A five-pointed star has magical connections which might involve the Enquirer in an increase of spiritual awareness or actual dealings with earth magic.
(c) Small stars near the handle suggest talented children.
(d) Large numbers of stars suggest problems, loss and grief for the Enquirer, but finances will be all right.
(e) A single star near the bottom of the cup is an advance warning to the Enquirer to change direction as his present situation is deteriorating.

Sticks

These represent people. The shape and colouring of the sticks will suggest what they look like. For instance, a long dark stick would be a tall dark man, while a pale, short, fat stick would be a woman who is 'fair, fat and forty'.
(a) Crossed sticks suggest arguments and partings.
(b) Leaves clustered round the sticks mean bad news.
(c) Dots or very small leaves nearby show that the person represented by the stick will bring the Enquirer the opportunity to obtain money.
(d) A ring nearby indicates a marriage.

Suitcase
Travel or a visitor from over water.

Sun
(a) Happiness, success, influence and power.
(b) A child could become important to the Enquirer.
(c) A new enterprise will flourish.
(d) The summer will be important and lucky.
(e) A Leo person will be important to the Enquirer.
(f) If obscured, vanity and pride will bring a fall.

Swallow
(a) This brings a change for the better in every way: in the Enquirer's love life, home, career, health, finances, everything.
(b) Near the handle, protection to home and family.
(c) An unexpected journey to a hot place which will be very pleasant. If this is a business trip then it will be very successful.

Swan
(a) Progress and a contented life.
(b) An unexpected and unusual lover.
(c) An improvement in finances.
(d) At the bottom of the cup, death or separation from a long-term companion.

Sword
(a) This is a Tarot symbol which suggests that the Enquirer will have to take swift action in order to set something on the right path. It may indicate sudden journeys or immediate attention being given to a health matter.
(b) Otherwise this indicates quarrels and separations, divorce, loss, ill-health and even a death around the Enquirer. Swords represent the end of a phase which will shortly clear the way for a new beginning.
(c) Crossed swords, strategic action will be needed.
(d) A broken sword, defeat.

Table

(a) A business conference or a family 'council' to be held.
(b) A celebration; if near the handle, this will be in the Enquirer's home.
(c) A nice new friendship.
(c) If dots are nearby, a discussion with an accountant or bank manager.

Telephone

The Enquirer will either make or receive an important call; look around to see whether this will be good or bad.

Torch

(a) Idealism and the desire for change.
(b) If at the bottom of the cup or broken, a parting or broken love affair.

Tower

If the Tower is in one piece, the Enquirer is building something which will last. More often than not, the tower is not complete, which means that there will be a failure in plans requiring a change in direction.

Train

A fortunate journey.

Tree

(a) Recovery from illness.
(b) An ambition or wish fulfilled.

Triangle

Unusual talent; an unexpected opportunity to be creative.

Trumpet

An announcement.

Turkey

(a) This symbol is connected with Christmas in Great Britain and Thanksgiving in the USA, therefore it means celebrations and family get-togethers.

(b) In the American theatre, a 'turkey' is a flop, therefore this can mean a failure in a project. However, the turkey would have to be at the bottom of the cup for this interpretation.

Umbrella

The Enquirer will need help and even a roof over his head. If the umbrella is open, he will get it; if closed, he will not. If the umbrella is inside out, the Enquirer himself will be responsible for his difficulties.

Unicorn

A secret relationship or marriage.

Van

(a) A move of house; note where the van is situated.

(b) A parcel arriving.

(c) Business travel or deliveries.

Vase

A friend will need help and advice from the Enquirer. A time to make an effort to make others happy and gain Karmic rewards as a result.

Violin

(a) In increase in popularity.

(b) Success may go to the Enquirer's head.

(c) Music and entertainments.

(d) An independent and very individual type of person.

Volcano

(a) Passion and emotions may harm the Enquirer's career.

(b) Explosive bouts of temper will cause trouble.

Vulture

This is a really nasty omen as it indicates loss and theft, jealousy and spite.

Wagon
(a) A wedding.
(b) Breaking new ground and succeeding at it.
(c) If the wagon is empty and near the bottom of the cup, the Enquirer is better off shelving plans for the time being and keeping to familiar methods.

Wall
A time to build for the future, but there will be obstacles to be overcome.

Wasp
(a) Problems in love relationships.
(b) Spiteful remarks. Possibly justified criticism which is painful to the Enquirer.

Weathercock
Indecision, possibly an unreliable lover or partner.

Web
(a) Don't ignore sincere advice.
(b) Intrigue. Being caught up in situation not of one's own choosing.

Whale
(a) Success in a large project which involves many new ideas.
(b) A maternal woman who might find herself being taken advantage of.
(c) The Enquirer's mother-in-law could come to stay for a while.

Wheel
(a) Progress and changes for the better. Earned success, rewards for past efforts.
(b) Travel will be important.
(c) If at the bottom of the cup, delays in proposed moves or impulsive action which could be harmful.

Whip

(a) The Enquirer should not be too domineering, but he will have the upper hand.

(b) The Enquirer might develop a taste for sexual deviation.

Windmill

A tricky venture which will probably work out well, but it will require a lot of hard work.

Wolf

(a) Jealousy from those in the Enquirer's neighbourhood. He must be careful not to be swindled.

(b) Can be a lucky sign if the Enquirer has sick or teething infants because this shows that they will soon be feeling much better.

Woman

This has to be read in combination with other symbols around. If the symbol is clear and uncluttered, there will be harmony and happy times to come. If clouded or surrounded by other bad omens, there could be trouble for a woman in the Enquirer's life or jealousy and bad behaviour coming to the Enquirer from a woman around him.

Wreath

News of a death if at the bottom of the cup; otherwise a fairly good sign (*see also* garland).

Yacht

The sign of an easier lifestyle, possibly due to retirement. The Enquirer's financial position will be much better and life will become quite pleasant.

Yew tree

(a) This can indicate a death or the loss of a partner, also the ending of a relationship.

(b) Achievements are possible later in life, possibly something special that the Enquirer has not had the time to work at.

(c) With dots nearby, a legacy.

Zebra

(a) Overseas adventures and possibly a wandering lifestyle.

(b) The Enquirer will have an affair which will be very enjoyable so long as nobody finds out.

19.

Superstitions

I suppose it would be natural to imagine that professional psychics are terribly superstitious, but in my experience this is not especially so. I have heard psychics and non-psychics sigh 'seven years' bad luck' when breaking a mirror, and many will keep a 'lucky' talisman in the same way that non-psychics will take a mascot along with them when they want to win something or pass an examination, but on the whole, the psychic world is *not* a particularly superstitious one.

I grew up in a highly superstitious family. In our extended household, we had Jewish, Russian, Polish and French superstitions together with those attached to the tailoring trade. I spent many childhood and teenage years in show business which, of course, is ridden with superstitions due to the insecure nature of the job. I always seemed to be transgressing some unknown 'law', always unwittingly doing something wrong; as a result, I have tried to avoid pushing these useless fears and phobias onto my own children. I *do* turn over the odd piece of silver when seeing a new moon and, of course, I hate breaking mirrors. Daft isn't it? We all do it although we know that these silly beliefs cannot possibly be reponsible for our happiness or otherwise.

Here are a few superstitions which I have collected during a quick round-up of family and friends:

Luck bringers
- Spit on a coin when you find one in the street and the chances are you will be able to win or earn a good many more.

- See a pin and pick it up, all the day you'll have good luck.

- Turn over a silver coin and make a wish when you see a new Moon, but don't do this through glass.

- It is lucky to break a glass but unlucky to break a mirror.

- A new baby brings its own luck.

- A new baby means a new home.

Bad omens
- Passing on the stairs means that a quarrel will follow.

- Two people wiping their hands on the same cloth will quarrel.

- Crossing knives on a table brings bad luck.

- Putting keys on a table 'locks the table'; this means that starvation will surely follow (an ever-present threat in nineteenth-century Russia).

- Opening an umbrella indoors is unlucky.

- Walking under a ladder will bring misfortune.

- Salt is a protection against the Devil, therefore if it is spilt a little should be thrown over the left shoulder into the Devil's eyes.

- Bad things happen in threes.

- If you hear of a death, you will soon hear of two more.

- It is unlucky to put shoes on a table. This is because they used to be placed on a dead person's coffin.

- Friday the thirteenth is considered evil because there were 13 at the Last Supper. Also tradition has it that the original Good Friday was on the 13th of the month.

- My dad's old grandmother used to say that a howling dog meant a death in the family, but my friend Rose reckons a single magpie is always an omen of this.

The tailoring trade
- If you buy a tape measure, you buy seven years' service in the trade.

- Lose the end of a piece of cotton on the reel and you lose a friend.

- Never whistle in the workshop, you whistle the work away (work was needed to keep everyone in employment in the sweatshop days —perhaps it still is).

- If the iron falls off the board, you will get the sack.

The stage
- It is unlucky to whistle in the dressing room. If anyone does so, they must leave the room turn around three times and wait to be asked back in.

- In the Variety theatre, it was considered to be bad form and possibly even bad luck to watch an act on the first night of a run.

- *The* Scottish play is notoriously unlucky and no one recites any of it for fun. The last few words of the play are not even read out during rehearsal. The bad luck comes from the fact that the witches' chanted curses are *genuine spells* with a strong power to destroy.

Pregnancy

The following ideas are Jewish in origin:

- A pregnant woman should not look at anything ugly as this will affect the baby; monkeys are supposed to be especially unlucky, probably because they look human (all very well in a monkey but not what one wants in a cherished baby!)

- A fall during pregnancy may cause a birthmark on the baby. (Don't worry—it won't really!)

Odds and ends

- My solicitor started his business on a Tuesday as his mother told him it was unlucky to start on a Monday.

- Astrologers will never start anything on a *void of course Moon*. This is when the Moon will make no aspects to any other planet before leaving one sign of the zodiac and entering another.

- Black cats are lucky to some, unlucky to others, especially when they cross one's path. Black cats, of course, are supposed to be the familiars of witches.

Conclusion

Chicken's Entrails

I hope that this book will prove to be both an enlightening and an entertaining 'read'. Most of it is quite serious but there had to be a few light moments. Amateur psychics do tend to take the whole business very seriously, being careful to keep their Tarot cards wrapped in silk, never letting the uninitiated touch whatever artifacts they use for their readings and even going the whole hog by dressing in a way that makes a statement about their 'specialness'. Some even become sanctimoniously vegetarian in an attempt to join the clan. The professionals do whatever seems natural to them. A good many *are* vegetarian, either because they feel that all life is sacred or because they follow the Hindu ideas of reincarnation. Most of us take the tools of our job fairly seriously and don't want them messed around with by sceptics, lost under the sofa or chewed by the dog, but we don't worry unduly when another psychic takes our cards or Runes to try them out.

Some Readers specialize in the learned skills such as astrology, numerology, etc. and are respected for their learning, while others are gifted psychometrists, tea leaf readers or clairvoyants, being equally respected for their learning and their gifts. Whether we come into this kind of work alone or whether we come from a family of professionals, and whatever way we choose to work, it doesn't really matter. The professional 'in joke' is that a good psychic knows something about all these skills and can even, if necessary, read from the entrails of a chicken!

It is not the way the reading is done which counts but the psychic's ability to tune in sympathetically to his client and, with God's help, give the help, guidance and understanding which is needed.

Further interest

THE LIVING HAND

Sasha Fenton and Malcolm Wright

Sasha Fenton and Malcolm Wright are both practising palmists with over 45 years of hand reading experience between them. They bring to this book much that is new and revolutionary in palmistry, yet in all cases the ideas have been thoroughly researched and backed up by numerous readings.

The combination of Malcolm's stunning illustrations and Sasha's ability to express complex ideas in a clear, easy style make this book ideal for anyone wishing to learn hand analysis or to update their technique.

Contents include

- truly lifelike illustrations bringing depth, vision and precise accuracy
- new concepts, such as energy rhythms and sibling lines
- an accurate method of timing events on the hand
- numerous practical examples and case histories

TAROT IN ACTION !

Sasha Fenton

More and more people are becoming interested in learning to read Tarot cards, but many find themselves not only using just one or two spreads, but also having difficulty in interpreting the cards in conjunction, rather than individually. Sasha Fenton solves both these problems, providing detailed descriptions of a selection of spreads, from the simple to the complex, and giving word-for-word accounts of real-life readings using each spread.

Sasha Fenton has been an astrologer, palmist and Tarot Reader for more than ten years and, in this entertaining and instructive book, she shares both her common-sense approach and the wealth of knowledge which she has acquired over the years.

Written for beginners and experienced Readers alike, and beautifully illustrated with the cards from the *Prediction Tarot Deck, Tarot in Action!* will give encouragement to novices and inspiration to experts.

FORTUNE-TELLING BY TEA LEAVES

Sasha Fenton

It is thought that tasseography (reading tea leaves) began in ancient China. They used to read the inside of their handleless teacups and the pattern formed by the tea leaves came to have a divinatory significance.

Sasha Fenton, author of the best-selling *Fortune-Telling by Tarot Cards*, has written this long-awaited practical guide for anyone who wants to dip into the future. Fully illustrated, the book covers everything you need to know, from the symbolism of the tea leaves and the significance of the different parts of the cup, to how (in the age of the tea-bag) to brew a proper cup of tea!

Contents include

- a brief history of tea leaf divination
- making intuitive/interpretive readings
- cup preparation rituals
- an A-Z of all tea leaf shapes
- actual readings with explanations

PREDICTION TAROT GIFT SET

Sasha Fenton and Bernard Stringer

The ideal gift set, for Tarot enthusiasts and beginners alike, contains:

Fortune-Telling by Tarot Cards, the best-selling primer by Sasha Fenton, a professional Tarot reader for over ten years. The book provides a straightforward yet comprehensive guide to the art of reading and interpreting Tarot cards.

The Prediction Tarot Deck, a hauntingly beautiful set of 78 full-colour Tarot cards conceived by Bernard Stringer and painted by Peter Richardson. The simplicity of design makes it an ideal deck to use for fortune-telling.

Together they make a unique package which will enable anyone to embark upon a voyage of discovery into the world of the Tarot.